Stakeholders Matter

The dominant shareholder-value model has led to mismanagement, market failure and a boost to regulation, as spectacularly demonstrated by the events surrounding the recent financial crisis. *Stakeholders Matter* challenges the basic assumptions of this model, in particular traditional economic views on the theory of the firm and dominant theories of strategic management, and develops a new understanding of value creation away from pure self-interest toward mutuality. This new "stakeholder paradigm" is based on a network view, whereby mutuality enhances benefits and reduces risks for the firm and its stakeholders. The understanding of mutual value creation is operationalized according to the license to operate, to innovate and to compete. The book develops a vision for a strategy in society in which, rather than the *invisible* hand of the market, it is the *visible* hands of the firm and the stakeholders that lead to an overall increase in the welfare of society.

SYBILLE SACHS is Professor and Head of the Institute for Strategic Management: Stakeholder View at the University of Applied Sciences Zurich (HWZ). In addition, she is an affiliate professor of the University of Zurich, where she established the module for Business and Society in 2000 and adjunct professor at the University of Southern Queensland in Australia. She has published numerous articles and books in the fields of strategic management and stakeholder management and is co-author of the book *Redefining the Corporation* (2002).

EDWIN RÜHLI is Professor Emeritus for Business Administration at the University of Zurich. He is also Senior Advisor at the Institute for Strategic Management: Stakeholder View of the University of Applied Sciences in Zurich. He is the author of the groundbreaking German management book *Unternehmungsführung I–III* and has published more than 150 peer-reviewed publications in the fields of international management, corporate governance, strategic management and stakeholder management.

Business, Value Creation, and Society

Series editors

R. Edward Freeman, *University of Virginia*
Stuart L. Hart, *Cornell University and University of North Carolina*
David Wheeler, *University of Plymouth*

The purpose of this innovative series is to examine, from an international standpoint, the interaction of business and capitalism with society. In the twenty-first century it is more important than ever that business and capitalism come to be seen as social institutions that have a great impact on the welfare of human society around the world. Issues such as globalization, environmentalism, information technology, the triumph of liberalism, corporate governance and business ethics all have the potential to have major effects on our current models of the corporation and the methods by which value is created, distributed and sustained among all stakeholders – customers, suppliers, employees, communities, and financiers.

Published titles:

Fort   *Business, Integrity and Peace*
Gomez and Korine   *Entrepreneurs and Democracy*
Crane, Matten, and Moon   *Corporations and Citizenship*
Painter-Morland   *Business Ethics as Practice*
Yaziji and Doh   *NGOs and Corporations*
Rivera   *Business and Public Policy*

Forthcoming titles:

Maak and Pless   *Responsible Leadership*
Mansell   *Capitalism and Corporate Responsibility*
Hemingway   *Corporate Social Entrepreneurship*

Stakeholders Matter

A New Paradigm for Strategy in Society

SYBILLE SACHS
and
EDWIN RÜHLI

CAMBRIDGE
UNIVERSITY PRESS

CAMBRIDGE UNIVERSITY PRESS
Cambridge, New York, Melbourne, Madrid, Cape Town,
Singapore, São Paulo, Delhi, Mexico City

Cambridge University Press
The Edinburgh Building, Cambridge CB2 8RU, UK

Published in the United States of America by Cambridge University Press, New York

www.cambridge.org
Information on this title: www.cambridge.org/9781107624634

First published 2011
First paperback edition 2013

A catalogue record for this publication is available from the British Library

Library of Congress Cataloguing in Publication Data
Sachs, Sybille.
   Stakeholders matter : a new paradigm for strategy in society / Sybille Sachs,
   Edwin Rühli.
      p.   cm. – (Business, value creation, and society)
   Includes bibliographical references and index.
   ISBN 978-0-521-19639-0
   1. Strategic planning.   2. Customer relations.   I. Rühli, Edwin. II. Title.
   HD30.28.S2217   2011
   658.4′012–dc23
   2011020616

ISBN 978-0-521-19639-0 Hardback
ISBN 978-1-107-62463-4 Paperback

To Alexandra Sachs, for whom the paradigm shift matters

Contents

Figures

All figures and tables in this book are our own illustrations, except where stated otherwise.

Tables

Foreword

Stakeholders Matter: A New Paradigm for Strategy in Society is an important book. It ushers in a new wave of scholarship in management theory. The new era that is upon us obliges us tell a new story about business, as an institution that is firmly set in society, rather than apart from it. The authors take globalization, mega-change due to information technology, and the emergence of new and innovative business models as normal to this new era. The old way of thinking about business as a purely economic and instrumental tool for the benefit of financiers is no longer useful. The new narrative of business must be told in stakeholder terms to allow for the diversity of business forms that we are seeing in the twenty-first century.

When the authors claim that a new paradigm has emerged for strategic management, they are being too modest. Their proposals do no less than rewrite the contract between business and society. First of all, they broaden the notion of business as the engine of economic activity by focusing on value creation for stakeholders rather than economic value for shareholders. Business in the twenty-first century must be seen as an institution which creates value for customers, suppliers, employees, communities, financiers and society. Second, one of their key arguments is that this new narrative about business, indeed the new social contract, contains three licenses: (1) license to operate; (2) license to innovate; and (3) license to compete. The combination lays out a new agenda for thinking about the purpose of the firm, its strategic vision and its business model for value creation.

Equally as important as the substance of their argument, is the process of research on which this book is based. It comes from a multi-year, multi-company, multi-disciplinary perspective which the authors have developed over the past decade. It shows us a different way to conceptualize research that is at once intellectually rigorous, based on an analysis of good practice, and speaks to academics and thoughtful practitioners. Business research in the twenty-first century needs to reflect the massive changes that the institution itself has undergone. We cannot afford only narrow disciplinary studies that stand closer to scientism than to improving and interpreting business practice. As the authors demonstrate, there is no trade-off between rigor and relevance. Good research must be both conceptually rigorous and practically relevant. *Stakeholders Matter* is such a work.

It is an honor to publish this book in the series on Business, Value Creation, and Society. The purpose of this series is to stimulate new thinking about value creation and trade, and its role in the world of the twenty-first century. Our old models and ideas simply are not appropriate today. We need new scholarship that builds on these past understandings, yet offers the alternative of a world of hope, freedom and human flourishing. Professors Sachs and Rühli have produced just such a volume.

R. Edward Freeman
University Professor
Academic Director, Business Roundtable
Institute for Corporate Ethics
The Darden School
University of Virginia
Charlottesville, Virginia USA

Acknowledgments

We are especially grateful to have experienced "mutual value creation" with, and hopefully also for, different "stakeholders" in our "network" in the course of writing the book.

First of all, we want to thank Isabelle Kern, who supported us from the beginning to the end of the book. Also we want to thank Ruth Schmitt who, as a co-leader of joint research projects, contributed many ideas to our understanding of the stakeholder paradigm. The work could not have been written without the support of our research team: Manuel Heer Dawson, Andrea Gäumann, Claude Meier, Marc Moser, Irene Perrin and Thomas Schneider (in alphabetical order). With them mutual value creation took place in its purest form, which we profoundly appreciate. The research team members represent a broad range of scientific disciplines: information technology, economy, political science, sociology and psychology. This diversity greatly enriched our ideas and insights.

We want to thank Christine Luisi for making our English more readable. In refining the language, she had the opportunity to challenge the logic of our argumentation, which was of unique value.

We are grateful for the outstanding support from R. Edward Freeman, the general editor of the series "Business, Value Creation, and Society." He has been a formative influence from the beginning of our research. He stimulated us to integrate strategy and stakeholder theory, and to emphasize the humanistic aspect of value creation. We had the advantages of a great reviewer team with Joseph Mahoney, James Post and Grant Savage. From their different perspectives, they challenged and advised us with valuable comments and encouragement. We also received excellent support from Paula Parish, our editor at Cambridge University Press. She was a true "benefit provider."

We thank all of our interview partners in the different case studies for providing us with insights on how mutual value creation takes place in real life situations and not just in theory.

Furthermore, we would like to include an even broader "cast of stakeholders" in our thanks: Simone de Colle, Sabine Döbeli, Hans Groth, Ulrich Gut, Jeffery Harrison, Gilbert Lenssen, Guido Mattanza, Bruce Millett, Bidham Parmar, Lee Preston, Nigel Roome, Thomas Streiff, Jean-Paul Thommen, Sandra Waddock, Christoph Weber, Patricia Werhane, Duane Windsor and Donna Wood (in alphabetical order). We had the privilege to meet and discuss with them, and to learn from their publications.

As we have based our ideas on a wide range of literature, we are grateful for the innumerable impulses and the richness of the ideas we received from all of the authors.

We are grateful to the University of Applied Sciences HWZ for supporting our research and providing us with the necessary work conditions.

1 | Challenges for a new paradigm in strategic management

The future of business in society: social and economic changes

During the last decades, both business and the society have undergone enormous changes. A few key examples may illustrate this: technological and scientific progress, changes in social structures and mindsets, globalization, development of new players in the world economy such as Brazil, China and India, and the downturn of Communism. This has opened new horizons for firms but also for customers, suppliers, citizens, and for many other kinds of stakeholder groups.

However, there have also been fundamental challenges and negative effects caused by these changes that also impact the firm and its stakeholders. The rising defaults on subprime mortgages in the United States illustrate such a fundamental challenge, as these defaults triggered a global crisis in the financial system. As a result, leading investment banks collapsed and the US government carried out massive bail-outs. Similar observations can be made for Europe and Asia. Even national economies have encountered serious difficulties. Greece and Ireland, for example, have had to be bailed out by the European Union and the International Monetary Fund (IMF).

For economic theory, these incidents turn out to be empirical tests in the worst sense, as Barbera claimed shortly after investment banks collapsed worldwide: "But for the majority of economists, those who use theory to try to make sense of the world, shouldn't we all agree that the new classical framework failed in spectacular fashion last year?"[1] Not only was the economy greatly affected but also the whole of society, as Stiglitz emphasized: "The financial sector has imposed huge externalities on the rest of society. America's financial industry polluted the world with toxic mortgages."[2] Due to the global crisis in the financial system the confidence in corporations has waned and led to a crisis which has had a strong impact on society as a whole. All

1

these developments have become an economic and a social challenge at the same time.[3]

In the interplay between business and society today, areas of conflict need to be overcome and the focus needs to be shifted away from the one-sided dominance of the economic sector, as Reich emphasizes: "Something I call supercapitalism was born. In this transformation, we in our capacities as consumers and investors have done significantly better. In our capacities as citizens seeking the common good, however, we have lost ground."[4] Already a decade earlier Habermas blamed the dominance of the economic sector, when he recognized a structural transformation that "restricts the latitude of national governments, their remaining options no longer allowing them to 'cushion' undesirable social and political consequences of transnational economic transactions."[5] The roles of the nation state and of the economy are challenged, as market mechanisms have gained weight excessively in relation to other social and political processes. Giddens concludes, "A good society can be defined as one in which there is an effective balance between a competitive marketplace, a robust third sector or civil society and the democratic state."[6]

The dominance of the economic sector has been questioned by a wide range of people. This can be illustrated by a worldwide BBC poll in twenty-seven countries, including over 29,000 people. It showed that people are highly dissatisfied with free-market capitalism; only 11 percent said that the free market was working well, and the majority thought that the capitalist system was in need of regulation and reform.[7]

The economic and social changes also impact individual firms and their stakeholders. They are confronted with new expectations and growing complexities and dynamics in the context in which they operate, and this leads to new or changing and more demanding stakeholder interactions. Until recently, most corporations concentrated on one or very few stakeholders who are directly related to the firm's value creation process. Freeman *et al.* describe the concentration on one stakeholder by using different narratives of capitalism: "These narratives do not simply ignore other stakeholders. Rather, each narrative presumes that by focusing on the interests and rights of their dominant group, all other stakeholders will benefit."[8] But more and more firms realize that this narrow business model no longer fulfills the expectations of their strategically relevant stakeholders, including shareholders. The need to shift to a new paradigm in strategic management is evident and has to be understood in the larger context of economic and social development.

Requirements for a new paradigm in strategic management

Historic nature of paradigms

The challenge of change is not only prevalent in reality but also in the sciences, and can be the kick-off for a paradigm shift. At any given period of time, scientific ideas are closely related to the dominant worldview. Worldview is defined by Habermas as the basic construct with which we interpret the world.[9] Science is a social construct, as it is conceived by human beings. Like other social realities, it is subject to different systems of interpretation, and therefore different scientific worldviews have existed over time (see also the Appendix in this volume). Since the seminal work of Kuhn's *Structure of Scientific Revolutions*, there is a general understanding that there are no timeless and universal concepts of science or scientific methods that would satisfy all claims.[10] Insights such as new scientific findings evolve, or conditions undergo extreme transformations when findings or changes cause anomalies in previous scientific explanations.

To understand such changes in scientific ideas, Kuhn uses the term "paradigm": "On the one hand, it stands for the entire constellation of beliefs, values, techniques, and so on shared by the members of a given community. On the other, it denotes one sort of element in that constellation, the concrete puzzle-solutions which, employed as models of examples, can replace explicit rules as a basis for the solution of the remaining puzzles of normal science."[11] This definition makes evident that each theory has underlying core values. Even though economic theory claims to be objective and not to rely on values, it is grounded in specific values.[12] Putnam calls such values epistemic.[13] The epistemic values of a researcher impact why he selects a specific theory and which basic assumptions he presupposes. Putnam concludes with a historic overview of how researchers approach science: "Many who refer to values as purely 'subjective' and science as purely 'objective' continue to close their eyes to this same fact."[14] In this realm he refers to Sen's book *On Ethics and Economics*,[15] in which

Sen reflects on the basic assumption of self-interest of actors: "The idea that only self-interested values are rational is even harder to defend."[16]

Origin of the economic paradigm

In the natural sciences in the last century, the confirmation and refutation of hypotheses were the ideal methodology, and objectivity was consequently in the foreground.[17] It has also shaped the current understanding of the economic paradigm, which we will discuss in more detail in Chapter 2.

The understanding of the economic paradigm is originally rooted in the period of the Enlightenment. Adam Smith developed his famous concept of the invisible hand based on the liberal ideas of utilitarianism. It makes the assumption that the actions of individuals based on self-interest and market coordination lead to an increase in total welfare: "And he is in this, as in many other cases, led by an invisible hand to promote an end which was no part of his intention."[18] Adam Smith makes the moral assumption that human beings – and not the government – know best what makes them happy and under which circumstances. His theory is based on his observations of the political and economic developments in the eighteenth century.

In the course of development, the understanding of the economic paradigm with the basic assumptions of individual self-interest and the hypothesis of market efficiency still impacts the strategic management of firms today,[19] the theory of the firm[20] and also shapes our current understanding of capitalism.[21]

Post-Enlightenment Capitalism

Until recently the underlying basic assumptions of the economic paradigm were accepted by many scholars and were seldom criticized with any effective results by powerful social movements. But this acceptance started to be questioned as stakeholders manifested dissatisfaction with economic developments (e.g. negative effects of globalization). Striking incidents of corporate scandal took place in 2003 (e.g. Enron) and later in 2008 in the financial crisis. The oil spill in the Gulf of Mexico caused by a drilling rig explosion in 2010 and the Fukushima disaster in Japan are further examples.

Since then discussions about a new understanding of strategic management, the theory of the firm and the capitalist system have taken place regularly, even at such prestigious events as the Academy of Management's annual meeting (see Chapter 2, p. 34) and at the conference of the European Academy for Business in Society (EABIS).[22] In this context the responsibility of business schools is also being questioned, as most of them do not critically reflect on the dominance of the traditional economic paradigm.[23]

Shortly after the wake-up calls mentioned above, scientists in the economic field began to discuss what the future of capitalism could or should be. Nobel Prize winner Stiglitz, for instance, claims that wrong basic assumptions are one of the main reasons for the financial crisis: "Conservative ideology, along with unrealistic economic models of perfect information, perfect competition, and perfect markets, fostered lax regulation, and campaign contribution helped the political process along."[24] In addition to these unrealistic models he questions the basic assumptions of self-interest of the actors: "Our rules and referees were shaped by special interests; ironically, it is not even clear whether those rules and referees served those special interests well. It is clear that they did not serve the national interests well."[25] He is quite clear about the boom of regulations taking place at the moment, and states that they are just of a cosmetic nature and not the solution for the real problems. Nobel Prize winner Phelps also questions the term "free market" and calls for more innovation in business: "Capitalism is not the 'free market' or laissez faire – a system of zero government 'plus the constable' ... If we still have our humanist values we will try to restructure these sectors to make capitalism work well again – to guard better against reckless disregard of uncertainty in the financial sector while reviving innovativeness in business. We will not close the door on systems that gave growing numbers rewarding lives."[26] There seems to be a growing agreement that traditional capitalism based on abstract models and basic assumptions such as self-interest and efficient market hypothesis is not the solution.[27]

Mainstream thinking in strategic management, in the theory of the firm as well as in the understanding of capitalism, is challenged to move ahead to a modern way of thinking. Vidal calls this "Post-Enlightenment Capitalism": "If a Post-Enlightenment Capitalism emerges in response, it will require markets that function for the general interest as much as they do for the private interest, and government, firms and civil society working on a scale of effectiveness the likes of which history has never before witnessed."[28]

Multi-paradigm concepts to reflect reality

To contribute to these diverse expectations, multi-paradigm concepts are being explored.[29] In this stream of thinking, scholars are trying to bring together aspects of different paradigms at a meta-level for a better grasp of reality. But if we are drawing on the bases and the assumptions of different paradigms we are confronted with incommensurability. Scherer and Dowling emphasize, "In modern times the problem of incommensurability has been recognized by all sciences especially since the term was introduced by Thomas Kuhn (1962, 1970) as a catchword for the assertion that one cannot reach a meta-level point of reference to decide objectively between competing theories from different paradigms."[30]

But Gioia and Pitre offer a solution to handle the issues of incommensurability: "The multiple-perspectives view implies a kind of meta *triangulation* not across methods *within a* single theory or paradigm, as is currently in vogue, but *across* theories and paradigms."[31] The authors emphasize that the methodological assumptions of subjective and objective are not clearly distinct notions but actually a continuum. To capture these blurred boundaries they label the parts of such continuums as "transition zones." Our contribution to the stakeholder paradigm builds on Gioia and Pitre's concept (see Chapter 5, p. 80).

Our contribution to the stakeholder paradigm

In our research we are motivated by the challenges mentioned above. We aim to contribute to the upcoming stakeholder paradigm for value creation based on a multiple-perspectives view.[32] In today's society, human beings are understood to combine their interest and purposes in different organizational forms from informal groups to highly professionalized organizations. Giddens deals with the origin and the development of such organizations in the course of history.[33] Every society has to address the issue of integration. In a simple, small society, social integration is made by face-to-face communication. In developed and increasingly large societies this kind of social integration is not possible anymore due to the complexity. Therefore, different kinds of organizations (e.g. firms, legal authorities, NGOs, specific stakeholder interest groups, etc.) are needed for mediation in large societies.[34] These different organizations are connected with each other through various interactions. Together they make up the whole of a society. Such organizations can develop the capability to be part of mutual value creation processes (see Chapter 4, p. 58). A vision for a strategy to achieve mutual value creation in society is required, and our aim is to contribute to it. This is the focus of this book.

Our theoretical and empirical journey of the last nine years has shown us that the Stakeholder View of Strategy, as described in the book *Redefining the Corporation*, to which we also contributed, was a development in the right direction.[35] But with respect to the changes and the challenges mentioned above it did not always go far enough. What we have experienced, primarily since 2002 when the book was published, is that if we want to advance the stakeholder paradigm, we not only have to consider stakeholders as potential risk or benefit providers for a given firm, but we have to think of the firm and the stakeholder interlinked in a network with each of them contributing to value creation. Stakeholders generally have to deal with issues that are similar to those of the corporations, or are involved in the development and use of innovative products or services. This fact emerged very impressively during our empirical investigations, where we talked with managers and stakeholders in semi-structured interviews in order to understand their perceptions of value creation. Managers increasingly acknowledge that stakeholder relations are a key element in their value creation process, and that it is not possible for the firm to fully control the complexly evolving stakeholder networks. Stakeholders not only provide potential benefits and risks to the firm, but very often they are highly qualified and experienced in the field they are active in. Others are impacted involuntarily by value creation processes. We also learned during the interviews with representatives of the firms and stakeholders that they are exploring new forms of interactions with each other when they engage in value creation.

We therefore have new material from our case research to present: as an example, pharmaceutical corporations, healthcare insurers and patient organizations have different and sometimes opposing perspectives on what is useful for advancing the health of patients. In the past, the corporations and their stakeholders fought among themselves and lost sight of their common purpose of enhancing healthcare. Each of them tried to control the other's reaction to specific issues and thereby missed opportunities to advance healthcare for their patients. In the setting of our action research, they have started to realize that despite their different approaches, they also have similarities and common views. Building on these similarities has helped them to overcome the "old" management paradigm of controlling the other stakeholders, and has enhanced their ability to find new and innovative solutions together.[36]

Path toward a new stakeholder paradigm

As discussed thus far, firms and their stakeholders are confronted not only with purely economic change but also with the growing complexities and dynamics of the social context in which they operate, as well as with more and increasingly differentiated expectations. The existing theories under the umbrella of the dominant economic paradigm are not sufficiently developed to tackle the economic and social changes as discussed above.

On the basis of these considerations, we propose a stakeholder paradigm for value creation that embraces how corporations and stakeholders can work together in networks, to create innovative products and service or innovative solutions for common issues. This suggests a new understanding about what stakeholders are, and the corporation's role in its stakeholder network.

In order to develop our understanding of a stakeholder paradigm (see Figure 1.1 for an overview), we will begin in Chapter 2 to analyze and compare according to specific criteria the basic assumptions of the economic theory of the firm and the dominant theories of strategic management. In this way, we can recognize the important strength of these approaches, and can also work out where they fall short.[37] These approaches are contributing elements to our understanding of the stakeholder paradigm. In Chapter 3 we discuss those elements of the stakeholder theory, on which we build our own understanding of the stakeholder paradigm. Chapter 4 looks at approaches already discussed in the literature of a stakeholder paradigm in strategic management. Applying the same criteria in Chapter 2, the basic assumptions of the two approaches, the stakeholder theory of the firm and

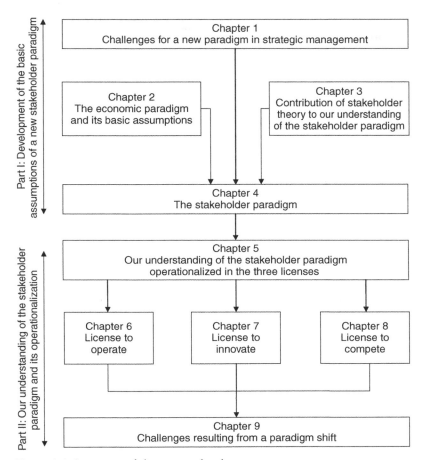

Figure 1.1 Structure of the current book

Stakeholder Capitalism, will be analyzed. Here the contributions to our understanding of the stakeholder paradigm will be identified, as will the further developments that we perceive as necessary.

The heart of the book is Chapter 5, in which we present our understanding of the stakeholder paradigm. Also, the differences in the basic assumptions from the economic paradigm will be pointed out. The operationalization of the stakeholder paradigm as we understand it will be developed by the three licenses: to operate, to innovate and to compete. These licenses are not exclusively the legal authorization for corporate activity, but rather a comprehensive entitlement for a mutual value creation process between firm and the stakeholders. The operationalization is supported by our empirical case research. In Chapters 6 to 8 we discuss how, in the perspective of the three licenses, the firms and the stakeholders engage in value creation with greater benefits and fewer risks for themselves and for each other. The basic assumption is that value creation based on mutuality in a network view is more valuable than satisfying pure self-interest in an unrelenting struggle for more individual profit. In the concluding Chapter 9, we address the question of how such a paradigm shift could come about, and what the resulting economic, cultural and legal/structural impacts might be.

This book seeks to stimulate a new approach to the understanding of value creation. In so doing, it places human beings and their quality of life at the center of the consideration. The paradigm change we propose is not a revolution, since it should build on, maintain and increase previous approaches to value creation. Rather, it is a fundamental evolution, in which the mutuality of value creation in networks is the primary concept.

PART I

Development of the basic assumptions of a new stakeholder paradigm

2 | The economic paradigm and its basic assumptions

As developed in Chapter 1, a major part of traditional theory building in the field of strategic management is rooted in the economic paradigm. Every theory is based on assumptions that allow but also limit the insights it provides;[1] therefore it is important to be aware of these basic assumptions. In the following sections, we discuss the assumptions underpinning the modern theory of the firm and those of strategy theory, so as to emphasize the differences from the upcoming stakeholder paradigm which will be the content of Chapter 4.

The economic paradigm of the theory of the firm

The neoclassical model of economic theory is anchored in the basic assumptions of "homo economicus" as self-interested and rational actor.[2] In general the theory of the firm shares this understanding. However, this concept has been increasingly questioned as anomalies have been observed in decisions, which contradict the assumption of decision-makers acting completely rationally.[3] Simon's early articles established a basis for this development,[4] by distinguishing two basic perspectives: "perfect rationality" and "bounded rationality."[5] Bounded rationality was based on the limited informational and cognitive capacity of the decision-makers on the one hand, and environmental uncertainties on the other. Thus, not optimization but satisfaction is important when making decisions.

In the following section, the questions posed in Figure 2.1 will be used to describe the assumptions that underpin the theory of the firm. In fact these questions are commonly used as criteria for analyzing the underlying assumption of modern firm, organization and strategy theories.[6]

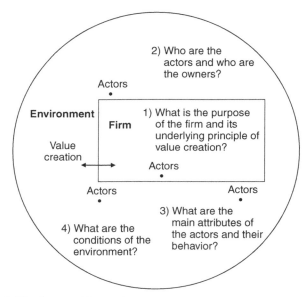

Figure 2.1 The firm and its environment

What is the purpose of the firm and its underlying principle of value creation?

Most probably the theory of the firm was first discussed by Knight in 1921, but Coase is seen as the father of the modern theory with his seminal article "The Nature of the Firm" in 1937.[7] In this view, the firm as the unit of analysis is seen as an economic entity whose purpose is to optimize cost and benefit. Since then different streams of research have been established for the theory of the firm, such as the principal agent theory,[8] the transaction cost theory[9] and the property rights theory[10] to explain why firms exist and how firms perform successfully.[11] Freeman *et al.* emphasize four concepts of business in this realm: business as markets and maximizing shareholder value represented by Friedman, business as agency proposed by Jensen, business as competitive strategy introduced by Porter, and business as transaction–cost economizing by Williamson.[12]

The purpose quite generally of the firm in these approaches is to allocate resources to activities that increase its economic success. Friedman emphasizes this thinking in the following quotation: "In such an economy (a free economy), there is one and only one social responsibility of business – to use its resources and engage in activities designed to increase its profits so long as it stays within the rules of the game, which is to say, engages in open and free competition, without deception or fraud."[13] Jensen focuses on the maximization of a firm's value that is also expressed in purely financial terms.[14] Managers must aim at increasing the firm's value in the long run. Jensen claims that firms are not able to maximize more than one value dimension, and therefore should concentrate on maximization of the market value as this is also beneficial for social welfare. This understanding of a firm's purpose reflects the underlying assumption of homo economicus, as making rational decisions based on his own and his firm's best interest. This is supposedly in harmony with the aim of society to maximize social welfare.

Who are the actors and who are the owners?

The modern theory of the firm is often called shareholder focused for two main reasons: first with respect to the principal agent theory, which focuses on the principal as shareholder.[15] And, second, with respect to property rights theory, as the owners are very often the shareholders as sole residual claimants.[16] Based on their property rights, the owners are also legitimated in controlling the firm. All other stakeholders are modeled in a nexus of (complete or incomplete) contracts.[17] Therefore, capital investors are of key importance as they enable a process of value creation by investing financially in the firm.

What are the main attributes of actors and their behavior?

All the different streams in the modern theory of the firm are still based on the assumption of rationally behaving individuals;[18] however, they have also examined important limits of rationality. The amplification of the concept of "homo economicus" means the gradual broadening of the behavioral foundation. Therefore opening the neoclassical black box leads to the challenging task of building models that take the new insights on individual behavior into account, while at the same time preserving the overall uniformity of the former neoclassical model.[19] Furthermore, the aggregation of individual behavior is not always the optimal solution for society as a whole.[20] Modern economic models need to take into account that the aggregation of individual behavior might not reflect important cause and effect relationships, and that they therefore have to consider the different conditions under which firms act.

With regard to bounded rationality introduced by Simon,[21] Foss[22] maintains that not many theories of the firm actually include it. The reason is that bounded rationality is difficult to model as it describes behavior as a "decision process response."[23] He also explains that economists are not interested in modeling bounded rationality, because they believe that this is not necessary for explaining why incomplete contracts exist.[24] They regard it as self-explanatory. Depending on the theoretical approach, the boundaries of the actors' rationality are considered differently (see also Table 2.1).

What are the conditions of the environment?

In economic theories, the environment of the firm is primarily seen as consisting of markets. Firms are embedded in these markets. Market forces, structures and equilibrium are therefore the center of interest and are considered as efficient coordination mechanisms. This is called the "efficient market hypothesis."[25] Coase raised the question of why firms exist at all and why transactions are not handled exclusively via the market.[26] He found his answer in connection with transaction costs. He submits that in some cases the transaction costs are lower in the hierarchy of the firm than in the market. Therefore it is more efficient to produce goods and services within the firm rather than to buy them from the market. This means that competition in the market is not always the most efficient coordination principle. This also explains the boundaries of the firm.

Final remarks

In the paragraphs above, we mention some similarities of the different approaches of the modern theory of the firm with respect to the underlying assumptions.

Table 2.1 summarizes these common assumptions, along with some differences among the three main theoretical approaches, namely property rights theory, transaction cost theory and principal agent theory. We are thankful for Joseph Mahoney's valuable specifications.

Table 2.1 *Main theories of the firm*[a]

Common assumptions	Theories of the firm		
	Property rights theory	Transaction cost theory	Principal agent theory
Purpose of the firm and value creation			
• Firm as an economic institution • Value creation for capital investors	• Efficient handling of residual claims and property rights regarding the value creation of the firm	• Efficient transfer of property rights and the related transaction costs in corporate value creation	• Efficient design of the firm's management structure in corporate value creation
Main actors and owners			
• Owner (shareholder) primacy (sole residual claimants) • Nexus of (complete or incomplete) contracts • Property rights based on capital investment	• Individual actors with right of use (property rights), residual control rights and disposition rights (residual claims)	• Individual actors to whom property rights are transferred	• Contractual agreement between principal and agent
Main attributes of actors and their behavior			
• Individual profit maximization/ opportunism (aggregation of individual actors) • Bounded rationality • Self-interest	• Bounded rationality (through information processing capacity)	• Bounded rationality (through information processing capacity)	• Bounded rationality (information asymmetries)
Environmental conditions			
• Hierarchy (firm) • Competition (market)	• Team production • Leverage effect	• Uncertainty/ complexity • Specificity	• Adverse selection • Moral hazard • Hold up

Summarizing the economic paradigm, we can conclude that the ability to characterize the firm as a profit-generating institution integrated in markets in abstract models is still salient. As one of the main advantages of these kinds of models, Hart sees that "theory lends itself to an elegant and mathematical formalization."[27] The extension of "homo economicus" does not question the tradition of economic models as being cause-and-effect related and measurable.

Still it would be narrow-minded to blame the modern theory of the firm for being a mere caricature of a firm, as Hart claims for the former neoclassical model.[28] Rather we can conclude that these kinds of models are able to show, on the one hand, fundamental cause–effect relationships with respect to economic problems of firms; and on the other hand, that important parts of these relationships are measurable. The main purpose of theorizing about the firm as models of limited economic cause-and-effect relationships is to increase economic rationality by illustrating why and how firms are more profitable. We will discuss the limitation of these models in more detail in the last paragraph of this chapter (see pp. 32–34) and turn now to strategy theory, in which the main premise of economic theory since the 1980s is to be found.

The strategy theory: general remarks

Strategy theory is particularly concerned with the question of why firms differ in their strategic behavior and economic success in the long term, i.e. why they realize different economic rents even when they operate under comparably competitive conditions and social environments. The issue is framed by the question, "Why do firms differ from each other?"[29] Hult, Ketchen and Slater,[30] as well as Rumelt, Schendel and Teece,[31] regard this question as the most important one to be answered regarding differences in firm performance. Also, the entrepreneurial reality has impressively shown that firms in the same industry differ in either being successful or remaining unsuccessful over time. If conditions are comparable, the differences in strategic behavior and success can be explained by the bounded rationality of managers and employees. This means that they interpret similar situations and strategic options differently, and therefore also act differently regarding strategy. The task of strategy theory is consequently to develop frameworks for explaining differences in economic success.

In this vein, Mahoney and Pandian write, "Strategy can be viewed as a 'continuing search for rent'."[32]

The perspective, which assumes that firms can generate a sustainable rent in a competitive environment, was discussed in economic theory early on. At this point, the Ricardo rent must be mentioned, which is explained by the limited availability of resources under continuing demand. Monopoly rent is explained by power over price. And Schumpeter's entrepreneurial rent is achieved by the risk-taking activities of entrepreneurs acting in complex business environments.[33]

In the next section, following the mainstream of strategy theory today, we will focus on the content-oriented argumentation. It contributes in a substantial way to how value creation occurs in a firm, and attempts to explain the differing strategic success of firms based on firm-specific, sustainable, competitive advantages in the value creation process. This perspective is based on the assumption that firms are different regarding the content of their strategies, i.e. their development differs even though they face the same or similar contextual conditions. The establishment of a sustainable, defensible competitive advantage, and therefore of differences in the firm's strategic success, is influenced by the discretion of managers (actors) making decisions within the value creation process.

Traditional strategy theory offers two basic justifications for these differences: the "industry structure view of strategy" (ISV)[34] and the "resource-based view of strategy" (RbV). In the following paragraphs, we will give an overview of these two argumentations for strategic success and will then elaborate on their basic assumptions. Both approaches provide valuable insights for the development of the stakeholder paradigm that we develop in more detail in Chapter 5 (p. 78).

The strategy theory: the "Industry Structure View of Strategy" (ISV)

Economic theory of competition forms the general theoretical background of the industry-oriented perspective (ISV). The ISV is primarily rooted in Industrial Organization Economics (IO), which is concerned with the behavior of competing firms and how market structures and market forces influence the firm's success.[35] According to Foss, the focus of early IO is clearly described by Bain:[36] "I am concerned with the environmental setting within which enterprises operate and in how they behave in these settings as producers, sellers and buyers."[37]

Strategy theory in the 1970s and 1980s was built on this body of knowledge and this environmental, mostly product market related, orientation.[38] The ISV approach led to a breakthrough in strategy, which has been presented in a comprehensive way by Porter.[39] We hereafter refer to his seminal contributions. "The result of these theoretical breakthroughs in the field of strategic managerial and related disciplines has been a rapid growth in the intellectual maturity of strategic management."[40] Therefore we will discuss the ISV on the basis of its most prestigious representative, Porter, whose research focuses on the ongoing strategic success of firms from the industrial-economics perspective.

What is the purpose of the firm and its underlying principle of value creation?

To Porter, the essence of strategy theory is the following: "To explain the competitive success of firms, we need a theory of strategy which links environmental circumstances and firm behavior to market outcomes."[41] Thereby, the environment is understood as "the industry" and the focus is on the firm and its strategic business units in industry. "The basic unit of analysis in a theory of strategy must ultimately be a strategic distinct business or industry."[42] This leads to the SCP paradigm (Structure–Conduct–Performance) as the basic causality explaining strategic success in the ISV.

The purpose of a firm is seen thereby in an economic sense: "The generation of above-normal rates of return (i.e. rents) is the focus of analysis for competitive advantage (Porter, 1985)."[43] This was recently confirmed by Freeman *et al.*: "The primary and, to some scholars, only important dependent variable was economic performance, typically measured in terms of profitability or shareholder returns."[44] This fully reflects the economic paradigm.

The causalities leading to above-normal economic performance (the conducts) are based on the firm's monopolistic position in the industry. To determine this position, Porter developed the framework of the five forces. It particularly shows the industries' structure, meaning which industries or sections within an industry have a low level of competitiveness and therefore a potential for monopolistic conditions, which increases the industry's long-term potential profitability. The lower the level of these competitive forces, the lower the level of competition. And therefore the higher the attractiveness of an industry and the chance for a firm to find a monopolistic position and thus the strategic potential for success. "Strategy can be viewed as building defense against the competitive forces or finding a position in the industry where the forces are weak."[45] In recent publications, the causality between market orientation and strategic success has been analyzed in more detail, showing that the influence from factors like culture, market information processing, organizational responsiveness, etc. can also influence success.[46]

Based on an industry analysis using the five forces concept, the firm must organize its strategy by choosing appropriate activities in its value chain. This leads to its position in the industry. But a strategic position is not sustainable unless a firm chooses a trade-off with other competitor positions and therefore finds a unique position. Continuity strengthens the strategic position; frequent changes in strategy are costly and confusing for customers and employees.[47]

Who are the actors and who are the owners?

The ISV is characterized by a managerial perspective, and managers are therefore the main actors. The managers' decisions, their behavior and their understanding of the industry determine the strategy. The general managers' core role is to establish, shape and maintain the firm's position in the market. Managers focus on the industry structures and the economic causalities to create, maintain and exploit imperfect competition in order to earn an ongoing strategic rent.[48] Managerial choice therefore is fundamental. "The managerial choices which are made under uncertainty about the future, define the firm's concept for competing (positioning), in configuration of activities, and the supporting investments in assets and skills."[49] Managers should serve the interest of shareholders as Porter sees the meaning of positioning in superior and sustainable financial performance.

As competition is basic for the ISV, the new and incumbent competitors, the suppliers and the customers are the most important constituents. But they are not seen in a stakeholder perspective but much more as rivals in an ongoing struggle, exercising their power against the focal firm and constantly competing for a higher proportion of the firm's rent. The industry structure is important for rent appropriation, i.e. how much rent can the firm retain and how much is bargained away by customers, suppliers or new entrants.

Interestingly enough, and forced by increasing claims for the social and ecological responsibility of firms, Porter and colleagues recently took some first cautious steps toward identifying a broader range of stakeholders potentially relevant to a firm's strategic success.[50] "The moment for an expanded view of value creation has come. A host of factors, such as the growing social awareness of employees and citizens and the increased scarcity of natural resources, will drive unprecedented opportunities to create shared value."[51] The major benefit from these insights is the corporate awareness of social stakeholder potentials, as firms have to take society as a whole into consideration and not merely individual stakeholders.

The chain of causalities explaining ongoing strategic success in the ISV starts with the competitive forces and the activities underpinning it. At this level, there is no link to the institutions or people (stakeholders) providing these activities and influencing the causalities leading to strategic success. Therefore even Porter himself sees the necessity "to push even further back the chain of causality."[52]

What are the main attributes of actors and their behavior?

Based on an understanding of the five competitive forces and the set of activities available to a firm in its value chain, Porter suggests three generic strategies to choose from, namely cost leadership, differentiation and focusing.[53]

In a cost leadership strategy, the focal firm is able to reduce its costs for products or services below those of all of its competitors while still maintaining a comparative level of quality. This generates economic profit available in a dynamic perspective to reduce the threat of each of the five forces and to exploit opportunities offered by change in the relevant industry (e.g. changes in technology or in demand). Differentiation focuses on unique features of products and services compared to the competitors. So the firm can set its price higher than the competitors and, despite some additional costs, obtain above-normal profit, which again is available to reduce the threats of the five forces and to exploit chances resulting from industry development. Finally, focus means concentration on specific market segments, on specific geographical areas or on specific products or services. Compared to non-focused competitors, a focused firm can realize high prices or lower costs with the respective strategic advantages mentioned above.

These three generic strategies typically offer basic trade-offs to a firm's management. Thereby, as we mentioned earlier, the future is uncertain and the relevant causalities (activities) are manifold. In such a situation managerial discretion exists and allows different behavior despite similar conditions. As to the assumptions concerning the actors' behavior, there are no elaborated discussions in the ISV. But given the need to interpret the uncertain competitive conditions and the complexity of the trade-off decisions including managerial discretion, one can conclude that the actors behave and decide somehow under the conditions of intended and therefore bounded rationality. "Strategic choice then expresses the top coordinator's attempt to maximize the rents."[54]

In their latest publication, Porter and Kramer confirmed that the invisible hand of Adam Smith is still in charge but with a broader concept of shared value: "It opens the doors of the pin factory to a wider set of influences. It is not philanthropy but self-interested behavior to create economic value by creating societal value. If all companies individually pursued shared value connected to their particular businesses, society's overall interests would be served."[55] The authors have developed new strategies to address their broader concept of shared values connecting their outside-in view to the value chain.[56] But this concept lacks a connection to the former generic strategies.

What are the conditions of the environment?

As mentioned above, in the ISV the firm's strategic success is explained primarily, or almost exclusively, by causalities leading from the environment to strategic positioning, to competitive advantage, and finally to the ongoing financial success of the relevant unit of analysis.

To show this, Porter refers to some empirical work he has done in different industries in various nations.[57] The content of "environment" is reflected in Porter's five forces of competition (supplemented by government influence in his later publications). This means the "environment" is represented by a few economically and immediately relevant stakeholders such as new and potential competitors, customers and suppliers. Opportunities for successful strategic actions are particularly seen in product market imperfections (e.g. entry or mobility barriers) and not in a firm's resource heterogeneity. "The environment both constrains and influences outcomes."[58]

The applied terms and the developed causalities in this context are overwhelmingly oriented toward competition (*competitive* advantage, *competitors*, *rivalry*, etc.) and not toward cooperation. Only in later publications does Porter discuss competitive advantage resulting from firm agglomeration (clustering) in a nearby geographic environment.[59] Complementers are seen as supporting actors. But the next step, to see complementers as stakeholders providing not only benefits but also influencing risks on both sides (firm and complementer), is not yet discussed in these publications.

The link between a firm's competitive environment and its success in the ISV is understood in a dynamic perspective. Industry changes open opportunities to promising new strategic positions.[60] "Firms create and sustain competitive advantage because of their capacity to continuously improve, innovate, and upgrade the competitive advantage over time."[61] This dynamic perspective relates in a way to an entrepreneurial type of rent.

With time, Porter also expanded from a more local or proximate environment as mentioned above to the broader national environment. He included such factors as demand conditions, supporting industries or factor conditions at the level of a country in which a company is acting,[62] as well as to society.[63] Therefore the dominant factor for strategic success is still the environment.

Final remarks on the ISV

The earlier publications of the ISV are based on theoretical concepts of industrial organization economics but also on empirical research on corresponding mobility barriers or concentration of industries.[64] In a number of later studies, a particular focus was put on measuring the influence of industry classification (industry effects) or of positioning (e.g. market share or effects of business segments) on profit differences between firms. However, the results are contradictory.[65]

The ISV and its environment-success assumptions have been criticized in different respects. First of all, some scholars think that this approach is not in line with the idea of social welfare espoused by economists.

Most authors agree that the original purpose of the structure-conduct-performance paradigm in industrial organization economics was to isolate violations of the perfectly competitive model to address these violations in order to restore the social welfare benefits of perfectly competitive industries ... As applied by strategy theorists focusing on environmental determinants of firm performance, social welfare concerns were abandoned in favor of the creation of imperfectly competitive industries within which a particular firm could gain a competitive advantage ... At best, this approach to strategic analysis ignores social welfare concerns. At worst, this approach focuses on activities that firms can engage in that will almost certainly reduce social welfare.[66]

In recent publications, Porter and Kramer[67] intentionally take society into account. They even claim that, "Profits involving a social purpose represent a higher form of capitalism, one that creates a positive cycle of company and community prosperity."[68] But all the adaptations Porter and Kramer have intended in recent years do not effect the basic assumption they state: "It is not philanthropy but self-interested behavior to create economic value by creating societal value."[69] Moreover, these adaptations or even the formulations of new concepts such as the "shared value" are not coherent with former publications. Such basic critique of the ISV already comes earlier in 1996 from Foss.[70] He compares Porter's publications over time. He claims that, at the beginning, Porter had a clear and economically sound basis in industrial organization economics; IO was a fundamental part of the ISV of strategy.[71] According to Foss, in Porter's later publications,[72] he loses this clear line of thinking and makes a shift toward the complexity of the firm's internal activities.[73] Therefore, the dominant logic of the influence of the environment on competitive strategy suffers; the firm is conceptualized in different ways which are difficult to integrate. Foss criticizes that neither the frameworks nor the underlying theories are well linked. In their latest publications, for example, they make no reference to any theory![74]

Other critical remarks also emphasize the fact that in the ISV external factors almost exclusively determine the strategy. Internal, firm-specific and resource-based causalities leading to strategic success are neglected. This position is justified in the ISV by the assumption that strategic resources are highly mobile and therefore available to all competitors. This assumption eliminates resources as possible sources of competitive advantage. "There is much about the 'environment' but little about the 'company' ... the firm-specific components of competitive advantage are never seriously addressed."[75] These criticisms led to a more resource-based approach of strategy which we will develop below.

The ISV assumes that constant or at least long lasting factors exist, which influence the (market) environment structure. Authors like D'Aveni reject this by emphasizing an environment in constant fundamental and turbulent change, and that therefore it is nearly impossible to sustain advantages over time. He describes this as "hypercompetition."[76] In this context, building or defending a strategic advantage over time seems impossible. Following D'Aveni,[77] firms have rather to create a series of *temporary* advantages. The capability to maintain such a series of short-term advantages in a rather hectic battle is the source of ongoing strategic success in the perspective of hypercompetition. Porter rejected this criticism by emphasizing that hypercompetition may sometimes be a phenomenon at the operational level but not in strategy.[78] And even at the operational level, he thinks behaving in a hypercompetitive way is leading increasingly more companies down the path of mutually destructive competition instead of striving for a sustainable competitive advantage. Based on his empirical evidence, he claims on the contrary that continuity in strategy and sustainability strengthens the firm's successful position. Strategic behavior is still determined by market structure not by market turbulences. This corresponds to the modern ecological movement in society, attributing a high value to sustainability.

Despite these criticisms, the ISV induced a breakthrough in strategic thinking, by addressing fundamental strategic questions of firms, and by contributing, based on economic and market perspectives, to answering the question of the origin of strategic success. It has the potential for further development, e.g. deepening the logic by pushing further back the chain of causalities or broadening it by including a richer set of the firm's stakeholder interactions. Chapter 8 contributes to this development in the perspective of the license to compete.

The strategy theory: the "Resource-based View of Strategy" (RbV)

Apart from the ISV, a resource-oriented causality represents the second main approach of the content of strategy theory.

What is the purpose of the firm and its underlying principle of value creation?

The work of Penrose[79] is often regarded as the foundation for the current discussion on the resource approach. Her ideas were adopted by Wernerfelt[80] in his seminal article "A Resource-based View of a Firm" and were concisely expressed by Grant: "The resource-based view perceives the firm as a unique bundle of idiosyncratic resources and capabilities where the primary task of management is to maximize value through the optimal deployment of existing resources and capabilities, while developing the firm's resource base for the future."[81] Barney identified three categories of resources that may enable firms' value creating strategies, namely physical capital resources, human capital resources and organizational capital resources.[82] Hall emphasizes the importance of intangible resources for sustainable competitive advantage.[83] Over time the focus of the RbV has shifted more from physical resources to intangible assets, especially to knowledge.[84] "We propose that a firm be understood as a social community specializing in the speed and efficiency in the creation and transfer of knowledge."[85] Knowledge is seen as the most important resource of sustained strategic advantage for firms.

As to the principle of value creation, it is assumed that the sustainable strategic success of a firm does not merely depend on industry and positioning – as discussed in the last paragraphs on the ISV – but much more on internal, firm-specific factors. Already Hansen and Wernerfelt noticed that a large part of the differences regarding a firm's success can be explained by intra-organizational factors. They are the preconditions for the choice of a specific market and for creating tangible and intangible assets.[86] Empirical research has originally shown that the firm effect, which mainly affects the available resources as described in the RbV, cannot or can only marginally account for the differences regarding the firm's success. Interestingly, new studies show that firm-specific factors can be very important, if they are regarded in a differentiated manner and with regard to their complementary effect on the industry structure as described in the ISV.[87]

The resource-based view is tied to the Ricardo rent, i.e. to the idea that the availability of resources is limited, which leads to resource asymmetries between firms.[88] With the development of the RbV, authors have frequently commented that the RbV is based on economic theory. An example is given by Barney.[89] In a retrospective on his earlier articles, he writes: "I would link the argument much more closely to other economic traditions, including Ricardian economics and evolutionary economics."[90] And Foss confirms this when he sees his contribution to RbV in a "value maximizing manner."[91] However, the strong alignment of the RbV with the economic paradigm has been critically discussed at an early stage. Mahoney and Pandian, for example, already wrote in 1992 on "the resource-based theorists' dissatisfaction with neoclassical theory of the firm."[92]

The "core competence concept" by Prahalad and Hamel lent a specific impulse to this strategy approach as it is geared to entrepreneurial practice.[93] Resource asymmetries, i.e. core competencies, must have specific characteristics in order to generate a sustainable competitive advantage. Barney points out that resources have to be valuable, rare and inimitable, as well as supported by an adequate organization (VRIO framework).[94] The search for the cause of sustainable resource asymmetries has led to further insight. They can be attributed to social complexity, specificity of resources, causal ambiguity, irreversible investments, cost effects of resource changes, as well as their non-substitutable nature.[95]

Based on this economic background of the RbV, the main purpose of the firm is seen in the creation of an economic rent for the owners. Unique bundles of resources, i.e. heterogeneity and immobility of resources, are in the RbV the preconditions for sustained competitive advantage which allows these rents.[96] In the following statements the basic causalities in RbV are summarized: "A firm is said to have a *sustained competitive advantage* when it is implementing a value creating strategy not simultaneously being implemented by any current or potential competitors and when these other firms are unable to duplicate the benefits of this strategy."[97] Barney adds, "This conclusion suggests that the search for sources of sustained competitive advantage must focus on firm resource heterogeneity and immobility."[98] Heterogeneous and immobile resources thus build the basis for a sustainable competitive advantage. Firms must therefore strive to gain such resources to achieve an above normal economic performance. Sustainable rent therefore depends on the firm's ability to make use of their resources in unique ways.[99] Thus, the argumentation of the RbV is mainly related to the question of strategic success at the firm level: "Resource-based logic takes as its unit of analysis the firm."[100] Most of the main contributors to the RbV confirm this unit or level of analysis.[101]

Who are the actors and who are the owners?

The focus on economic rent as an indicator of a firm's strategic success is located in the traditional RbV, combined with the assumption that the owner (shareholder) is the residual claimant and therefore is earning this rent. "A firm's competitive advantage can be defined with respect to return expectations of that firm's owners."[102] And "this logic ... does not address how the economic rents a strategy might create are appropriated by a firm's stakeholders."[103] Coff follows a similar approach.[104] Managers seeking rents for their owners are the main actors.

In the RbV argumentation, the chain of causalities starts with the choice and combination of unique resources. There is no focus on the stakeholders providing these resources, and how their behavior and the stakeholder network influence the subsequent chain of causalities leading from resources to strategic success.

An important impulse for the development of the RbV in recent years came from the integration of property rights theory into the RbV. Already in 1992 Mahoney and Pandian wrote: "The resource-based view is linked to property rights since delineated property rights make resources valuable."[105] But a breakthrough of these ideas – which also opens the horizon for a stakeholder theory of the firm – took place only around 2005.[106] This is developed in more detail in Chapter 4.

What are the main attributes of actors and their behavior?

With respect to strategic success, it is important in the RbV that management makes appropriate decisions in order to develop and sustainably defend resource asymmetries. In this, managerial discretion can play an important role: "Because of (1) resource-market imperfections and (2) discretionary managerial decisions about resource development and deployment, we expect firms to differ (in and out of equilibrium) in the resources and capabilities they control. This asymmetry in turn can be a source of sustainable economic rent."[107] The result is not a monopoly rent as in the ISV but an efficiency rent (Pareto rent) based on the different efficient use of resources by management.[108] Consequently, the manager is the key actor in the RbV.[109] He is the strategist who decides on the resource deployment in his own or in the owners' interest,[110] and he is therefore an important source of value creation.[111] The RbV moreover intends to support managers in their decisions. Thereby, the manager is not a fully rational actor, which Conner and Prahalad,[112] for example, confirm by referring to Simon's concept of bounded rationality: "As to bounded rationality, we suppose that individuals are 'intendedly rational but only limitedly so'."[113] As a result they possess finite cognitive abilities. In many publications concerning the RbV, the bounded rationality of actors is directly or indirectly assumed.

The dynamic perspective is used in the RbV in a specific way, namely by the concept of dynamic capability.[114] This refers to the capabilities of the managers to successfully influence change. Another interpretation of "dynamic" would be the change of core competencies over time, i.e. a longitudinal analysis of competencies and resources.

What are the conditions of the environment?

The environment in the RbV is essentially seen as the competitors surrounding the firm.[115] The fact that the RbV links strategic success to resources that other firms cannot duplicate (see above, p. 28) directs attention toward competition, which means activities against the competitors and other firms. Competition in the RbV is the dominant principle. Cooperation within the value chain occurs in a RbV only, if this leads to a better use of resources and if this strengthens the core competencies.[116] A certain broadening of this narrow view can be found in recent contributions of some scholars who discuss performance aspects in a network environment.[117]

Final remarks on the RbV

Although the RbV makes an important contribution to the current discussion on the economic aspects of strategy theory, critical objections are raised as well. In particular, the question is raised regarding the strategic importance of resource bundles in a fast changing environment. Altering market and social conditions can lead to a competence trap, if the firm is committed to specific resources and thus is unable to adapt to altering conditions due to irreversible investments.[118] The core competencies can turn into core rigidities.

Porter also criticized the concentration on core competencies to explain strategic success.[119] He pointed out that a sustainable defendable strategic position can only be reached with a coherent system of core and complementing resources, and not by focusing on just a few isolated core competencies. "It can be misleading to explain success by specific individual strengths, core competencies or critical resources." And Porter adds, "The competitive value of individual activities – or the associated skills, competencies, or resources – cannot be decoupled from the system of strategy."[120]

In their critical article, Priem and Butler analyze in detail the RbV[121] as depicted by Barney in his seminal article in 1991.[122] They criticize – among other aspects – that the RbV is tautological and that the role of product-markets is underdeveloped in the argument. Barney has rejected most of these critiques.[123] However, he accepts to a certain extent that market aspects have been somewhat neglected, though less so for the resource markets. Market imperfection and therefore resource immobility are in fact crucial for the RbV. Barney thus admits, "A complete model of strategic advantage would require the full integration of models of the competitive environment (i.e. product market models) with models of firm resources (i.e. factor market models)."[124] And he concludes that resources must always be assessed with regard to the firm and its market environment. This would be a path toward ISV. Foss analyzes the complementarities of the RbV and the ISV.[125] Despite some basic differences in the theoretic foundations, he sees clear thematic complementarities. Nevertheless, his preferences are for the RbV.[126]

An enlargement of a firm's interaction with all relevant stakeholders appears to be less important in the value creation perspective of RbV.[127] There is no elaborate discussion of how stakeholder relations underpin a firm's core competencies, i.e. why and to what extent stakeholders are willing to contribute to the firm's resource development and value creation, and how their behavior influences this process. This is only discussed later in the stakeholder theory of the firm (see Chapter 4, pp. 48–53). Stakeholder aspects are briefly mentioned in the RbV in the context of value distribution,[128] and primarily in the sense that the expected values of shareholders can be eroded by other constituencies (rent appropriation).[129] In RbV there is still a potential for broadening and deepening the causalities, linking resources and more precisely the resource owners to success. We will contribute to this discussion in Chapter 7 on the license to innovate.

In reviewing the RbV it appears to make an important contribution to some of the key problems of the economic theory of the firm in a managerial perspective, and to complement other approaches to strategic management like the ISV. However, the RbV is still anchored primarily in the economic paradigm; it develops economic causalities to explain the strategic success of firms but it is also limited by this paradigm.

The economic paradigm revisited

We can conclude that the economic paradigm of a theory of the firm and of strategy theory offers important explanations of why firms exist and why they are different. Several causalities, explaining the efficient use of resources in a strategic perspective, have been developed in order to enhance the value for the firm's owners (shareholders). However, these models clearly have their limits and weaknesses.

- In a world of complex, dynamic and uncertain interactions, theories that focus narrowly on shareholder value appear more and more questionable: in recent years, this kind of thinking has led to mismanagement, to managers taking excessive risks and to market failures which not only endangered the affected firms but whole industries and in the end the global economy (see Chapter 1, p. 4).

  Despite these developments, the economic paradigm of the theory of the firm is in practice at present still widely acknowledged by management, even though it is well known that its models are not able to deal with realities that are so complex and dynamic that they often are not measurable.[130] Neither are these models suited for problems that are unknown and cannot be captured in simple cause-and-effect measurements. The faith in measurability based on economic models has led to a common saying for management: "You can't manage what you don't measure." Therefore management collects data (measurements), determines how these will be expressed as a standard (metric), and compares the measurement to the benchmark to evaluate progress. Key performance indicators as a result of this thinking are quantifiable measurements, agreed to beforehand, that reflect the critical success factors of an organization such as the firm. The institutes for business cycle analysis serve as dramatic examples of the limitation of measurements.[131] None of them was able to forecast the financial crisis and the subsequent recession. Broader approaches than economic measurements to evaluate value creation are therefore necessary (see Chapter 5, pp. 91–92).

- Moreover it seems important to develop new role models in order to overcome the principle of homo economicus represented by self-interested, opportunistic behavior and the bounded rationality of individuals. Some scholars adhere to this assumption of self-interest but admit that there must be constraints on such behavior if it is to serve the common good. Others take a more basic view; one such attempt was initiated by Ghoshal. After the first waves of corporate scandals, Ghoshal claimed in his seminal paper that we have to change the basic assumption of strategic management, and that amoral business with its negative impact should not serve as a role model.[132] Because "a management theory – if it gains sufficient currency – changes the behavior of managers who start acting in accordance with the theory. A theory that assumes that people can behave opportunistically and draws its conclusions for managing people based on that assumption can induce managerial actions that are likely to enhance opportunistic behavior.[133] A theory that draws prescriptions of corporate governance on the assumption that managers cannot be trusted can make managers less trustworthy.[134] Whether right or wrong to begin with, the theory can become right as managers – who are both its subjects and the consumers – adapt their behavior to conform with the doctrine." In a similar way Bosse *et al.* argue that homo economicus as a self-interested wealth-maximizing individual does not exist.[135] This suggests that the model of the homo economicus is unable to understand the complexity of human beings (see Chapter 4, pp. 60–62).
- In addition, the dominance of the equity owner and therefore of the shareholder is being questioned. Traditional strategy theory, as we have seen in this chapter, is still mainly owner-focused. A formulated definition of "Strategic Management" presented by Nag *et al.* at the AoM Meeting confirmed this.[136] This definition is grounded

on an empirical investigation, where scholars in the field of business policy had to associate characteristic core words with the field of Strategic Management. Based on this analysis, the authors come to the following definition: "The field of strategic management deals with the major intended and emergent initiatives taken by general managers on behalf of *owners*, involving utilization of resources, to enhance the performance of firms in their external environment."[137] As we have already seen in this chapter, it is more and more accepted that stakeholders other than owners are the focus in causalities explaining strategic success. This is especially true concerning knowledge contribution.

To overcome such weaknesses of traditional economic and strategic thinking, leading scholars in the fields of strategy theory (among others Mahoney, Coff, Margolis, Kogut and Henriques) and in stakeholder theory (Donaldson and Freeman) discussed a development of the stakeholder theory of the firm, based on the property rights approach at the Annual Meeting of the Academy of Management (AoM) 2008 in Anaheim. "The strategic management literature has begun to utilize the Carnegie School behavioral theory of the firm as well as both classical (Alchian & Demsetz, 1972) and modern (Grossman & Hart, 1986) property rights theory in recent years, with some of the foundational work by Chi (SMJ 1994), Liebeskind (SMJ, 1996), Oxley (JEBO, 1999), Mayer & Argyres (Organization Science, 2004), Foss & Foss (SMJ, 2005)."[138] "Assumptions of opportunism, self-interest, perfect capital markets, well-defined property rights, bounded rationality and uncertainty" currently used in the strategy literature were questioned and new conceptualizations of business are needed.[139] In this realm, Margolis asked what strategy theory should be guided by, and offers possible answers such as "accuracy, adherence to economic theory or equipping managers for the practical reality."[140]

In this book we aim to contribute to a new paradigm that approaches the challenges stated above. In the next chapter we present relevant insights of stakeholder theory to advance such a paradigm.

3 | Contribution of stakeholder theory to our understanding of the stakeholder paradigm

In the following we give an overview of the current stakeholder theories, which provide the basic body of knowledge for our understanding of the stakeholder paradigm.[1] From the existing literature we have selected elements that seem of special importance in the light of our perspective. To analyze these elements, we rely upon the classification of Donaldson and Preston.[2] According to these authors, stakeholder theory can have three dimensions: a descriptive, an instrumental and a normative dimension.

Descriptive dimension

Donaldson and Preston state that a descriptive approach focuses on the questions of what the corporation is, its characteristics and its observable behavior.[3] The descriptive dimension is justified by the fact that the majority of managers believe that not only shareholders but other stakeholders are to be considered in their business decisions. Post *et al.* refer to a number of empirical analyses and studies showing that managers consider stakeholders in their decisions.[4] Even though managers may not always use the term "stakeholder management," they apply it in practice. In addition, various countries have specifications in their laws that give stakeholders and their interests in a firm a recognized position aside from that of the shareholders.

There is substantial literature on descriptive stakeholder management, which focuses on two main questions: who are the stakeholders of a firm, and what are the interactions between the firm and its stakeholders?

Who are the stakeholders?

An answer to this question can be found either by looking empirically at who stakeholder managers consider, or by analyzing the definitions in the literature concerning stakeholders.

Table 3.1 *The most important*
stakeholders

Stakeholders	Ranking
Customers	1
Employees	2
Shareholders, investors, owners	3
Society	4
Regulators	5
Business partners	6
Government	7
Suppliers	8
Politicians	9
Unions	10

Note: The stakeholder rankings are based on
the accumulated number of mentions: top ten
out of twenty-nine stakeholder categories in the
telecom and financial industry in Switzerland.
Source: Sachs, Rühli & Kern (2009).
Sustainable Success with Stakeholders.
Reproduced with kind permission of Palgrave
Macmillan.

Empirical aspects

In our empirical study, managers acknowledge a broad range of stakeholders. For example, in Table 3.1 one can see the managers' perception of the importance of stakeholders in two industries analyzed.[5]

Five of the top ten stakeholders mentioned belong more to the market
or business area, the other five to the social sphere. This perception of
importance relates to the firms' economic as well as social function and
emphasizes the relevance of social and political stakeholders for value
creation. The customers, employees and owners are ranked on top. We
call them the magic triangle of stakeholder management.[6] They are
stakeholders of primary importance, since no corporation or any other
organization can exist without them. In this sense they are constitutive.

Aside from empirical studies, definitions in the literature also
provide insights as to who the stakeholders are.[7] The literature on
stakeholder identification has focused on examining the two sides
of the firm–stakeholder relationship by addressing how firms impact

stakeholders, and more recently, also how stakeholders influence the firm. The basic fact is that constituencies have a "stake" in the firm. Clarkson defines "stake" as follows: "A 'stake' can be defined as something of value, some form of capital, human, physical, or financial, that is at risk, either voluntarily or involuntarily."[8] Goodpaster makes a distinction between strategic and moral stakeholders.[9]

The strategic dimension in stakeholder definitions

Freeman's hub-and-spoke depiction of the firm and its stakeholders was pioneering, by suggesting that managers take the expectations and needs of different groups into account in their strategizing in addition to the shareholders, and manage these relationships accordingly.[10] Whereby, Freeman defined a stakeholder as "any group or individual who can affect or is affected by a firm's operations in achieving its objectives."[11] Various scholars have a similar firm-centered understanding of stakeholders.[12]

Frooman's study addressed the stakeholder influence on a firm's strategy somewhat differently by adopting the stakeholders' rather than the managers' perspective.[13] Frooman proposed that stakeholders may employ strategies based on their access to resources, and may either directly or indirectly attempt to use these resources to influence the firm's behavior through coalitions with other stakeholders. By flipping sides on the stakeholder–firm relationship, Frooman emphasized the relevance of studying the stakeholders' viewpoint in the stakeholder identification process.

The different stakeholder definitions are classified on the basis of their strategic dimension by Friedman and Miles:

Along the strategic dimension, definitions differ according to a number of factors. We can distinguish definitions with a very high strategic implication that limit stakeholders to those that are critical or affect the very survival of existence of the organization. At the other end are definitions with a very high strategic implication that involve legal or institutional conditions that may force organizations to deal with stakeholders, such as through contracts, explicit or implicit. In the middle are definitions that define stakeholders in terms of their power, influence or ability to affect the organization.[14]

All these definitions emphasize the relevance stakeholders have in strategic management. Stakeholders are seen as those individuals or groups that influence the firm's strategy.[15] In contrast there are definitions of the so-called moral stakeholder that focus on normative aspects.

Normative dimension of stakeholder definition

The definition of stakeholders based on their influence on a firm's strategy as discussed in the last paragraphs might be acknowledged as too broad by some. No specific criteria are mentioned on which to base whether a particular individual or group can be regarded as legitimated to influence firm strategy. Therefore a group of scholars identify stakeholders on the basis of legitimate claims.[16] Friedman and Miles call this a stakeholder definition based on a normative dimension;[17] Goodpaster speaks of a moral dimension.[18] Scholars in search of legitimacy differentiate between categories such as "moral claims,"[19] "risks"[20] or "contracts."[21]

However, all these definitions are considered to be too narrow by Mitchell *et al.*[22] They developed a typology for stakeholder identification based on the three key attributes of power, legitimacy and urgency. In their stakeholder salience model, stakeholders gain priority or salience in the eyes of managers, and thus become definitive stakeholders of the firm when they possess all three of these attributes, i.e. power, legitimacy and urgency.[23] A growing category of stakeholder definitions emphasizes also an integrative view of the strategic and normative dimensions.[24]

What is the interaction between the firm and its stakeholders?

Basically, one can distinguish unilateral and multilateral modes of interaction. This leads to significantly different ways of how firms deal with stakeholders.[25] There is a trend from unilateral (dyadic interactions) to multilateral (networks) forms of interaction, as the complexity and interconnectivity of business activities grows. We distinguish therefore between dyadic interactions and networks.

Dyadic interaction

Scholars in stakeholder theory traditionally discuss primarily the nature of the relations between a firm and a particular stakeholder as interest-guided, dyadic interaction. But interests are not the only factor that matters in explaining differences in stakeholder interactions. Rowley and Moldoveanu add to the interest an identity-based view with which they explain conditions under which stakeholders become active.[26] Interactions occur when stakeholders either see their interests jeopardized or when they intend to identify with other stakeholder groups. Their central claim is that the interest-based view relies on the assumption of narrow rational behavior. But individuals are not completely rational, and have multiple interests and different identities that have to be taken into account. In a dyadic perspective of stakeholder interactions, the stakeholders' identities as well as the firm's identity are relevant. Brickson defines the organizational identity orientation as the perception of the assumed relationship between a company and its stakeholders.[27] Depending on how the organization sees and understands itself, a company will act differently toward its stakeholders.[28]

Turcotte distinguishes between conflictive and collaborative relationships of firms with stakeholders.[29] Butterfield *et al.* suggest how and why stakeholder groups form collaborative alliances in their interactions with the firm.[30] With respect to collaboration, Savage *et al.* criticize that stakeholder theory still understands the corporation "as the focus for stakeholder relationships. Social partnerships, in contrast, are unique as a relational form in several ways."[31] The most important reason for managing stakeholder interactions in a non-"daunting" way, but as a social partnership, is that such partnerships can achieve collaborative advantage.

These collaborative relationships between firms and stakeholders need a concrete understanding of dialogue forms used for stakeholder interactions. We refer to the ladder presented by Friedman and Miles.[32] In their "ladder of stakeholder management and engagement," they distinguish twelve steps, which can be assigned to different levels, describing the degree of influence of stakeholders on business decisions (e.g. informed of management decisions, consulted before making a firm decision, influenced the decision of the firm, involved in decision). While on the first level a one-way communication prevails, the communication on the following levels is bi- and multilateral.

Burchell and Cook claim that dialogue should not present and advocate solutions or give advice, but that it should examine and search for answers.[33] Examples of dialogue forms of interaction are roundtables, which are composed of business representatives and stakeholders, where the corporation and stakeholders work together on agreements. They develop new solutions that integrate the business and stakeholder perspective. In such solutions, the decision-making authority lies not necessarily exclusively with the company. Solutions arise from mutual agreement.

This form of cooperation is a shift in the understanding from the idea that managers control stakeholder relations toward dialogue and exchange between firms and stakeholders in reciprocal engagement.[34] It involves increasing dialogue forms of interaction, which are characterized by openness, mutual interest and respectful treatment.[35]

Stakeholder networks
The forms of collective dialogues as mentioned in the last section go beyond dyadic interactions and emphasize multi-stakeholder settings. With respect to these multi-stakeholder settings, Rowley[36] criticized the original hub-and-spoke model proposed by Freeman[37] for being too firm-centric and for focusing only on the dyadic level of interactions between independent actors. Rowley proposed that firms are structurally embedded in networks of relationships with stakeholders, who are also tied to each other within networks. Thus, Rowley's network argument enlarges the original conception of the stakeholder model and focuses on the structural ties of a firm's stakeholder network. Moreover, other scholars also apply a network perspective.[38] Such a network perspective focuses on embeddedness.[39] With respect to embeddedness, Roloff maintains that stakeholder theory does not sufficiently show what happens in multi-stakeholder settings, because it still tends to focus the attention on the corporation, although it is clear that managers cannot always control their interactions with stakeholders.[40] She makes a claim for a new understanding of stakeholder networks by making a distinction between having and being a stakeholder. Therefore, the firms are the center of a network as long as they have stakeholders, but at the same time they are a part of it.

Our understanding from a descriptive perspective

In our understanding of the stakeholder paradigm, we consider those stakeholders that have something "at stake," namely who have some possibility of gaining benefits or experiencing risk induced by the basic choices of corporate activities in value creation. Therefore many stakeholders – investors, employees, customers – associate themselves voluntarily with a corporation in the hope of obtaining benefits. Others are involuntarily involved with the firm's activities, and seek to minimize any resulting negative effects on their welfare.[41] Consequently, Post *et al.* formulate an integrative definition taking into account strategic and normative dimensions. "The stakeholders in a corporation are the individuals and constituencies that contribute, either voluntarily or involuntarily, to its wealth-creating capacity and activities, and are therefore its potential beneficiaries and/or risk bearers."[42]

The Stakeholder View (SHV), as expounded in the book by Post *et al.* published in 2002 and on which we build, still relates primarily to a focal firm's interactions with its stakeholders. Consequently, the network aspect was not fully integrated at the time; however, it provides an opportunity to extend the stakeholder view by considering value creation based on network interactions. Thus, we understand value creation between firm and stakeholders in the context of relational embeddedness based on mutual and multilateral processes. The network view is a key element of our understanding of the stakeholder paradigm (see Chapter 4, pp. 59–63). We assume that if corporations want to tap their stakeholder potentials as a source of continuous value creation, they need more than bilateral dialogues. Rather they need collaborative procedures to build common ground with their multiple stakeholders in a network view.

Instrumental dimension

Stakeholder theory has also an instrumental dimension. It establishes a framework to examine causalities between the firm's stakeholder management and its performance goals. The widely accepted hypothesis by Donaldson and Preston claims that by adopting stakeholder principles, firms will achieve a better financial performance than without it and will maximize efficiency.[43] And Post *et al.* write in the same vein: "The descriptive accuracy of the stakeholder model as a picture of the modern corporation implies that management policies and practices that take account of multiple stakeholder interests will prove advantageous."[44] As we will show below, there are a considerable number of studies which confirm this.

Stakeholders impact value creation

Again, Freeman must be seen as one of the main originators of instrumental stakeholder thinking on the strategic level.[45] His conceptualization of the stakeholder model was the forerunner in suggesting that firms in strategizing ought to take into consideration the expectations and needs of other groups. In addition to the traditional focus on shareholders, one should manage the relationships to other groups appropriately to enhance the firm's potential for value creation. An instrumental dimension of stakeholder theory is well suited to a comprehensive perspective of stakeholder involvement in strategic management.[46] Other representatives of this line of thinking focus on the particular effects on value creation. For instance they emphasize the risk-avoiding effect, such as the increased pressure of stakeholders on a firm's strategy[47] or the destruction of value induced by stakeholders.[48]

Stakeholders create competitive advantage

Instrumental stakeholder theory also makes the assertion that a firm's relations to its stakeholders leads to a competitive advantage as a result of increased trust and cooperation.[49] Managing the links with key stakeholders proactively or interactively should result in benefits for the firm.[50] It opens a new field for managerial activities and widens managers' discretion by building and using stakeholder interactions to enhance competitive advantages.

As mentioned earlier, scholars[51] in strategy theory increasingly question the dominance of the "Grand-Design Principal-Agent Model" focusing one-sidedly on the owners' investments.[52] In their perspective, other stakeholders also make firm-specific investments that support the competitive advantage of the firm (see Chapter 4, pp. 48–53).

Stakeholder relations pay off

In the instrumental dimension of the stakeholder theory, some scholars emphasize that the corporate financial performance directly depends upon interactions with multiple stakeholders.[53] Over the past thirty years, the possibility that some association might exist between conventional indicators of corporate financial performance and the presence or absence of stakeholder-oriented policies and practices has been extensively explored in academic literature. Margolis and Walsh analyzed more than 120 studies; over 70 disclosed a positive correlation between financial and social performance, 30 a negative correlation and the rest showed mixed findings.[54] The study of Banks and Vera links strategy to performance results as well as to the stakeholder environment.[55] According to them, strategies established on a contract level lead to a stakeholder strategy on the firm level. And firms that adapt their strategies to such stakeholder relations will be more successful in financial and in social terms. Banks and Vera therefore come to the conclusion that stakeholder management has both a positive effect on the firm's financial performance as well as on its social performance.[56]

Our understanding from an instrumental perspective

As already expressed in our understanding of who our stakeholders are, our focus is on value creation in stakeholder networks in a comprehensive sense. A comprehensive understanding of value creation is contradictory to a one-sided and narrow focus on a firm's competitive advantages and financial success. We differentiate the causalities in the value creation process by distinguishing the roles of stakeholders, as benefit provider and receiver and as risk provider or bearer in a network view (see Chapter 4, p. 60). And we will show in more detail with our framework of the three licenses, how benefit and risk potentials can contribute to a comprehensive understanding of value creation (see Chapters 5–8).[57]

Normative stakeholder dimension

Stakeholder theory is also normative as Donaldson and Preston claim.[58] Normative stakeholder management means that the interactions of firms with stakeholders are based on moral guidelines. The literature provides two distinct categories of the normative foundation for firm–stakeholder interactions: the economic and the social/philosophical foundation.[59] In the following we emphasize these contributions, which we have considered in our understanding of the normative core.

Economic normative foundation

The representatives of the economic foundation attempt to adapt the assumptions of usual economic conduct to the corporation's role by including the social context.[60] They try to overcome the so-called stakeholder paradox, which assumes that ethical and business values are not compatible.

Goodpaster introduces the notion of "multi-fiduciary" to discuss ethics in business.[61] This notion means that firms not only have responsibilities toward shareholders, but always toward other stakeholders as well. Responsibility toward stakeholders is not an "add on" to the responsibility toward shareholders, but an integral part of the "multi-fiduciary" concept. From this perspective, the stakeholder paradox does not exist, as ethics in management is automatically based on the ethics and moral behavior of the individual managers. Thus, the conscience of a firm is the sum of the managers' individual consciences.[62]

Hendry aims to offer a pragmatic solution to the stakeholder paradox. In his opinion, the disadvantages of the economic approach are conflicts of values. "Economic morality is the morality of money and power, of egoism and 'might is right'."[63] Thus, an adapted theory must always emphasize relationships with all relevant stakeholders and include ethics and economic aspects. The firm is not described as a nexus of contracts but as a dynamic system of relationships between moral actors.[64]

Apart from this interpretation of the enhanced understanding of the firm's role in regard to its stakeholders, some scholars propose an enhanced understanding of property rights as the basis of a normative understanding.[65] Property rights are the rights to use resources that are protected either legally or by social norms.[66] Donaldson and Preston already claimed that property theory can serve as the normative foundation of the stakeholder theory. Based on their contributions, stakeholders gain property rights and the corresponding normative basis for a fair distribution of outcomes: "For example, the 'stake' of long-term employees who have worked to build and maintain a successful business operation is essentially based on effort. The stake of people living in the surrounding community may be based on their need, say, for clean air or the maintenance of their civic infrastructure. Customer stakes are based on the satisfactions and protections implicitly promised in the market offer, and so on."[67]

With respect to Donaldson and Preston's idea of distributive justice and Phillips *et al.*'s[68] addition of procedural justice that involves the fairness of the rules and procedures of a firm's value creation with its stakeholders, Bosse *et al.* propose further that actors should not be solely self-interested but should adhere to norms of fairness and reciprocity.[69] Building on this implies that "managing stakeholders well" involves delivering fairness to them in distributional, procedural and/or interactional terms.[70] Interactional justice comes from appropriately sharing information and avoiding rude or cruel remarks.[71]

Social/philosophical, normative foundation

Normative foundations in social and philosophical fields are diverse.[72] Evan and Freeman, for instance, suggested a neo-Kantian perspective, in which stakeholders are treated as ends and not only as means.[73] The idea is that a new narrative is needed to understand how joint value creation can be explained. "The very purpose of the firm is, in our view, to serve as a vehicle for coordinating stakeholder interests."[74]

Burton and Dunn make a similar distinction between seeing strategy theory as a masculine theory, in which competition and the pursuit of self-interest dominate, and stakeholder theory with feminine traits such as cooperation and caring for others.[75] They propose a hybrid approach of not harming those stakeholders who are the least advantaged, and treating those stakeholders well with whom the firm has close ties.

Our understanding from a normative perspective

In our understanding, we claim that a new paradigm is about how stakeholders and corporations can work together in value creation.[76] In this perspective, we follow Goodpaster's integral concept of multi-fiduciary toward all stakeholders,[77] whereby we rely on enhanced property rights thinking and assume that participation in value creation leads to appropriate participation in value distribution.[78] Based on the Kantian claim, it is important not to forget that stakeholders are human beings, and not only benefit and risk potentials.[79] Fromm reflects the Kantian categorical imperative within mutual human interaction in the sense of "oneness."[80] Oneness implies that all human beings are ends. Thereby Fromm emphasizes that human beings need to interact with other human beings primarily with active and not only with passive "motivation."[81] The passive motivation focuses on controlling the interaction only to protect property, for instance. The output of these interactions can be described as "having." In contrast, active motivation considers "being" as "process, activity and movement."[82] Fromm describes motivation as an activity between two human beings as follows: "He gives him of his joy, of his interest, of his understanding, of his knowledge, of his humor, of his sadness – of all expressions and manifestations of that which is alive in him."[83] With respect to knowledge, Fromm offers the following examples to contrast the active and passive motivation within human interaction: "*Having* knowledge is taking and keeping possession of available knowledge (information); *knowing* is functional and serves only as a means in the process of productive thinking."[84] Based on active motivation, the caring and cooperative aspects of the interaction between stakeholders are emphasized. In our understanding of stakeholder interaction, we include Fromm's concept of active motivation.

Final remarks

Donaldson and Preston claim that:

The stakeholder theory is managerial in the broad sense of that term. It does not simply describe existing situations or predict cause-effect relationships; it also recommends attitudes, structures, and practices that, taken together, constitute stakeholder management. Stakeholder management requires, as its key attribute, simultaneous attention to the legitimate interests of all appropriate stakeholders, both in the establishment of organizational structures and general policies and in case-by-case decision making. This requirement holds for anyone managing or affecting corporate policies, including not only professional managers, but shareowners, the government, and others.[85]

We build on this claim when we operationalize the stakeholder paradigm with the three licenses in Chapters 6 to 8.

In this chapter, we have emphasized important aspects, opinions and insights of current stakeholder theory. We also clarified our understanding of these aspects, which we will build on in the next chapter and shape our understanding of the three licenses in Chapter 5.

4 | *The stakeholder paradigm*

In this chapter we will first discuss two prominent new theoretical approaches, the "Stakeholder Theory of the Firm" and "Stakeholder Capitalism," both based on revised assumptions compared to traditional economic and strategy theory. These approaches apply a stakeholder perspective. Both claim that stakeholders matter, but from different points of view. We will analyze these approaches and their basic assumptions according to the same criteria as the economic approaches in Chapter 2. Based on the insights of these approaches and the conclusions we draw in Chapters 2 and 3, we then will clarify the basic assumption of our understanding of the stakeholder paradigm.

The stakeholder theory of the firm

Representatives of the stakeholder theory of the firm[1] increasingly doubt that shareholder primacy is the most effective way to understand strategic management. In contrast to shareholder primacy, they assume that different owners of resources, sometimes based on implicit or incomplete contracts, also contribute to value creation.[2] Consequently, Mahoney claimed at the AoM 2008, "The modern property rights perspective of implicit and incomplete contracting provides a solid economic foundation for the revitalization of a stakeholder theory of the firm within the evolving science of strategic management."[3]

What is the purpose of the firm and its underlying principles of value creation?

In the stakeholder theory of the firm, the scholars emphasize that the nature of the firm as a bundle of resources, as mentioned in Chapter 2 on RbV, is changing.[4] Intellectual property, intangible assets and knowledge are becoming more important than financial capital. This also changes the character of property rights.[5] They not only come from the financial capital invested but from any firm-specific investment made by stakeholders.[6] Instead of describing the firm as a nexus of complete contracts with shareholders as the only residual claimants, they define the firm as a nexus of complete and incomplete contracts,[7] or as a nexus of firm-specific investments made by different stakeholders, where these investments create residual value.[8]

In the perspective of this extended interpretation of property rights, Asher *et al.* intend to show that in the reality of today, the assumption of shareholder primacy in the traditional theories is unsatisfactory for answering the two fundamental questions of the theory of the firm: the one of value creation and the one of value distribution.[9] They claim that a modern property rights perspective provides a better economic foundation for a theoretical understanding of firms than earlier approaches: "Seminal works in classical property rights literature include Alchian and Demsetz (1972), Coase (1960), and Demsetz (1967). The modern property rights approach, discussed in Hart (1995), builds on Grossman and Hart (1986) and Hart and Moore (1990). Whereas the modern property rights research literature equates ownership with residual control rights, classical property rights theory defines ownership as residual rights to income (residual claimancy)."[10]

Uncertainties and the unpredictability of future conditions in and around a firm make complete contracting almost impossible. This means that other contracting parties aside from the shareholders are also not fully protected by explicit contracts. Grandori confirms that since contracts are incomplete, firm-specific investments by shareholders or other stakeholders might not be protected.[11] Blair also states that most contracts are incomplete since it is not possible to assign responsibilities and returns for all conceivable situations. In such cases, it is preferable to establish decision rules, based on which the firm can decide how its assets are to be used and how asset owners are to be compensated.[12]

The conclusion is that the firm normally has incomplete contracts with stakeholders other than shareholders, such as bondholders, employees or suppliers.[13] The incompleteness of contracts implies that a variety of stakeholders can claim to participate in the firm's strategic rent. Such a stakeholder perspective therefore broadens the

traditional purpose of the firm and requires that the economic value
of the firm include an economic rent, which may reside not only in the
shareholder value, but also in the suppliers, customers, labor or other
stakeholders.[14] The inclusion of other stakeholders besides the shareholders has important implications for the understanding of value
creation and value distribution processes in companies, as well as for
corporate governance and control, as Asher *et al.* emphasize:

We maintain, however, that there are potential benefits moving towards
the stakeholder view, which we highlight in the text. To balance these
potential costs and benefits may require case specific analysis: there may
not be a single "best" governance structure. Therefore, we are not arguing
that we should abandon the shareholders as an important claimant, but
rather we are arguing that we should at least allow the consideration of
other claimants.[15]

In this context a key question is under which conditions the different stakeholders are willing to make firm-specific investments that
create an economic surplus. Value distribution can have an enhancing
effect: employees, suppliers or other stakeholders, who are attributed
a fair share in value distribution, are more willing to make firm-
specific investments which lead to even higher rents.

Who are the actors and who are the owners?

In the stakeholder theory of the firm, all stakeholders involved in value
creation are considered actors. This is reflected in Blair's "Model of
the Corporation."[16] Similarly Stout writes, "Advances in economic
thinking and recent practical experiences within corporate scandals
in 2003 and the financial crisis in 2007 have made clear that shareholders generally are not – and probably cannot be – sole residual
claimants in firms."[17] Legally, shareholders do not own the corporation and consequently only have limited rights.[18] Stout concludes,
"As a legal matter, shareholders accordingly enjoy neither direct control over the firm's assets nor direct access to them."[19] Asher *et al.*
refer to Stout's argument and add that the shareholder primacy is also
not based on empirical results.[20]

Blair and Stout's team production theory of corporate law
presents an alternative to the principal agent theory.[21] In the team
production perspective, numerous stakeholders make firm-specific

investments. Firms need inputs from different groups to be productive. Blair thinks that this is especially true for employees, as they
develop firm-specific knowledge and skills that the firm depends on.
This also means that it is often difficult for employees to use their
knowledge and skills in other firms because they are so specific. It
becomes a high risk for the employee: the more specific their knowledge, the less marketable it is.[22]

Blair and Stout also point to rethinking the ownership approach
by focusing more on the importance of intellectual capital: "Viewing
the firm as a bundle of assets owned by shareholders also seems odd
once we recognize that one of the key assets a corporation uses in
production is 'intellectual capital' – that is, the knowledge and experience residing in the minds of its employees, rather than the hands
of it shareholders."[23] In the perspective of the stakeholder theory of
the firm, the focus is also on the fact that corporate resources do not
belong to shareholders but to the firm. A mediating hierarchy in the
firm exercises control rights over these resources. Thus, the firm is
rather a nexus of firm-specific investments than contracts. This mediating hierarchy consists of the board of directors. According to Blair
and Stout,[24] team production also emphasizes horizontal relations,
since a mediating hierarchy is implemented, which in turn controls
the rights over the resources.

What are the main attributes of actors and their behavior?

In public companies based on today's legal regulations, a key actor
is the board of directors. The shareholders as owners influence the
firm primarily through the board of directors. The firm's corporate
governance can be described as director primacy and not shareholder
primacy, as the directors run the firm. Shareholders only have three
rights: the right to vote, the right to sue and the right to sell their
shares. These rights do not give shareholders the right to treat managers as their agents having to serve their interests.[25] Team members
of production and shareholders delegate control rights over the firm's
resources to the mediating hierarchy, the board of the directors.
Thereby, self-interest is reduced. Directors can play the role of trus-
tees representing the interests of both shareholders and other team
members. Above all, in this perspective directors must serve the interests of the firm as a whole.

Team production and director primacy are also advantageous for convincing different stakeholders to make firm-specific investments. They are more willing to make such investments, if they know that not only shareholders will benefit but others as well. The mediating hierarchy can thus coordinate these investments and their beneficiaries.

In this realm, the question has been asked whether or not the stakeholders should be part of corporate governance.[26] Blair proposes strengthening the stakeholder role in corporate governance in order to improve the wealth-creating potential of the corporation as a whole. As stakeholders make firm-specific investments, corporate governance ought to be adapted to this fact. Thus, stakeholders should be considered regarding control rights and responsibilities.[27] Blair goes so far as to declare, "Boards must understand that they are the representatives of all the important stakeholders in the firm – all those whose investments in physical or human capital are at risk. Thus, individuals who explicitly represent critical stakeholders should be put on boards, to give those stakeholders some assurance that their interests will be taken into account."[28] There are many questions in this realm that have not yet been discussed in depth (see also Chapter 9, pp. 173–178).

What are the conditions of the environment?

In the stakeholder theory of the firm, the environment is represented by external stakeholders, but the importance of markets and competition to coordinate economic activities is still key: "Market pressure – in the product markets or in the input markets – is thus the most fundamental mechanism in a free market economy preventing business corporations from abusing their power, and the one with the longest pedigree."[29]

However, according to stakeholder theory of the firm, the focus should also be on the internal coordination and functioning of the organization, and consequently on the so-called "internal" stakeholders. The mediating hierarchy, consisting of the board of directors, puts market coordination into perspective, which is necessary to compensate for market inefficiencies and failure. The firm consequently must monitor these aspects that are organized via the market, such as control rights, decision rights and responsibilities.[30]

Stakeholder Capitalism

Final remarks

In the stakeholder theory of the firm, the dominance of the conventional shareholder-owner is enhanced by all stakeholders making firm-specific investments. By including more actors in the value creation process, the firm can achieve an increase in economic value. The understanding of extended property rights takes into consideration that stakeholders involved in the value creation process will still be motivated. The mediating hierarchy by the board of directors serves as an internal and external control mechanism, which reduces the risks for stakeholders and makes the firm the dominant actor of value creation.

However, in this first step toward a stakeholder paradigm, the implicit assumption of self-interest is not abandoned but rather reflects enlightened self-interest due to an extended understanding of property rights. This understanding of homo economicus still does not embrace human nature in its complexity. Furthermore, the overall thinking in the stakeholder theory of the firm maintains that, with a more comprehensive analysis based on a stakeholder orientation, the capability of firms to control reality is enhanced and will generate economic surplus for the firm and the involved stakeholders.

In advancing our understanding of the stakeholder paradigm based on the insights described above, we can conclude that it is still necessary to expand the understanding of value creation from a mainly economic and market-driven perspective to a more comprehensive one. Furthermore, we intend to take a further step in the extension of property rights away from an exclusively firm focused understanding of value creation to a network perspective, in which the roles of the firm as well as of the stakeholders as resource owners are emphasized. Additionally, the complexity of human nature needs to be taken into account.

Stakeholder Capitalism

Freeman *et al.* propose a human-oriented understanding of the stakeholder paradigm.[31] Based on an extended analysis of the environmental trends of current capitalism, and on a broad review of stakeholder theory, they develop their new vision of capitalism. Stakeholder Capitalism[32] is based on libertarian[33] and pragmatist views.[34] Freeman

et al.[35] express the most important assumption of their underst...
ing of a stakeholder paradigm in a set of six "pri...
be addressed according to our four criteria

What is the purpose of the firm and its underlying principles of value creation?

In Freeman *et al.*'s Stakeholder Capitalism,[37] the firm is not only an economic but also a moral and human institution.[38] In their opinion it is not possible to separate the normative from the positivistic question, and it is necessary to avoid thinking in trade-offs in order that innovative value creation can take place. The purpose of the corporation is to create value in both perspectives. A key argument of Freeman *et al.*[39] is that managers as well as academics need to acknowledge that there is no separation of business and ethics, since value creation in business has a human dimension, which is rooted in the fact that business decisions always have consequences for "real live complex human beings."[40] They call this integrated view the "ethics of capitalism."[41] "Value can be created, traded, and sustained because parties to an agreement are willing to accept responsibility for the consequences of their actions."[42]

The assumption underlying Freeman *et al.*'s principle is that "capitalism works because we can pursue our purpose with others."[43] They consequently adopt a cooperation perspective in value creation and emphasize the importance of partnerships in value creation instead of political processes.[44] The cooperation between a firm and different stakeholders is thereby the key source of innovation.[45] Freeman *et al.* conclude, "Business is a source of innovation, and it can be a source of moral innovation as well."[46] However, what the purposes of cooperation might be depends on the different underlying normative cores.[47] In this view, a firm's purpose is not limited to economic considerations, but allows for a differentiated understanding of the human dimension of business activities, and is therefore open to a plurality of values in business.[48]

Who are the actors and who are the owners?

Freeman *et al.*[49] emphasize that over time the different narratives of capitalism have always empowered one stakeholder group as the leading actor, e.g. the shareholders in investor capitalism or the managers in managerial capitalism. This is based on the assumption that firms compete with each other over limited resources.[50] However, in their principle of stakeholder engagement (2nd principle), they propose: "that a large cast of stakeholders are necessary to sustain value creation," as the locus of the action in reality is the stakeholders.[51] New narratives about doing business have to be found that emphasizes the partnership of the firm with all kinds of stakeholders for value creation.

This argument is further strengthened by Freeman *et al.*'s principle of stakeholder cooperation (1st principle). Here the emphasis is on the importance of cooperation between the different stakeholders within value creation, by satisfying the needs of stakeholders based on voluntary agreements. Concerning these agreements, freedom is the central notion and property is a derivative. Value is therefore a social phenomenon and focuses on human relationships and shared sense making.

What are the main attributes of actors and their behavior?

Freeman *et al.* emphasize that Stakeholder Capitalism is not based solely on the self-interest of the actors but on the cooperation and responsible behavior of human beings.[52] Stakeholder engagement requires taking responsibility for the consequences of one's actions. Stakeholders should not be harmed, but in the event that they are, they must receive compensation based on negotiations. Freeman *et al.* call this "collective responsibility" and label it "responsible liberalism."[53]

This understanding of responsibility is mainly reflected in their understanding of joint value creation for stakeholders: "We have also made the point in other places as the need to 'balance' the interests of stakeholders. We prefer the metaphor of thinking about keeping stakeholder interests in 'harmony.' 'Harmony' depicts a 'jointness' to the interests that is perhaps the major contribution of a stakeholder approach to business."[54] The principle of complexity (4th principle) takes into account that people are complex, as already mentioned above: "It is also important to note that since we are complex, we are able to differentiate between consequences based on who is being affected."[55]

What are the conditions of the environment?

In Freeman *et al.*'s approach, the firm is embedded in society and particularly in the capitalistic system, giving primacy to cooperation rather than competition, as "Business should be the best we can create together, rather than about avoiding the worst."[56] Freeman *et al.* further define their view of competition in the 6th principle: "Competition emerges from a relatively free society so that stakeholders have options. Competition is an emergent property rather than a necessary assumption to capitalism."[57] They intend to avoid the zero-sum solution of the economic paradigm, and prefer to make room for new solutions of joint and additional value creation.[58] More detailed interactions of a firm with the product and the resource markets are not discussed in this approach.

Final remarks

In developing our understanding of the stakeholder paradigm in the next section, we will draw particularly on the body of knowledge developed by Freeman *et al.* over the years, as consolidated in their book *Stakeholder Theory: The State of the Art* (2010). We have added our theoretical insights supported by the empirical material that we have collected over the last few years. Thereby we have sought to contribute to the proposal by Freeman *et al.* that further empirical research regarding stakeholder strategies should be initiated (see Appendix, pp. 181–193).[59]

We will also deepen the understanding of the "two sides of the same coin," the individual vs. the community in Freeman *et al.*[60] In a globalized world, human beings are increasingly voicing their interests and purposes in groups or organizations, or are even combining such interests and purposes in new organizational forms.[61] Value creation consequently is more often linked through different interests, knowledge and experience, that in turn also redefine the role of the firm but also that of the stakeholders.[62] In our case research we could see those bottom-up processes developing from the level of individuals to groups and then to communities (see Chapters 5 to 8 for diverse examples). These different kinds of actors build an interwoven network of direct and indirect interactions among each other.

By drawing on the property rights understanding of the stakeholder theory of the firm (pp. 48–53), we extend the property rights in our underlying basic assumptions even more. The firm and the stakeholders are understood as owners of different kinds of resources, which they bring into action in networks of value creation.

In the course of the book, we will work on the idea of a firm's embeddedness in its stakeholder network and the shift from controlling self-interest to mutuality. We expand the understanding of Freeman *et al.*,[63] as we see the firm and the stakeholders as actors for value creation in a network view. This also implies that stakeholders are themselves embedded in the stakeholder network. Although we consider Freeman *et al.*'s notion of jointness, in our understanding of value creation, we differentiate between jointness based on similarities, and take into account the threats of a lack of common ground. Therefore, we prefer the term of mutual value creation to the notion of jointness, especially if striving for solutions in value creation is value laden and these values are non-negotiable for some of the stakeholders (see Chapter 6, pp. 110–111). Moreover, we integrate parts of traditional strategy theory into the stakeholder paradigm in more detail than Freeman *et al.*, as we operationalize these insights by the concept of the three licenses (see especially Chapters 7 and 8).

The basic assumptions for our understanding of the stakeholder paradigm

The clarification of the assumptions of the two approaches to the stakeholder paradigms in the paragraphs above emphasize their strengths but also areas for potential development. In order to further develop our earlier work, we build on the positive potentials of these approaches and enhance them for the purpose of tackling the economic and social change addressed in Chapter 1.[64] In the following, we present the assumptions for our understanding of the stakeholder paradigm according to the same four questions used for the other approaches.

What is the purpose of the firm and its underlying principles of value creation?

The overall basic assumption of our understanding of the stakeholder paradigm is that in a knowledge-based, networked society the purpose of the firm is mutual economic and social value creation with and for stakeholders. The starting point for the understanding of the purpose of the firm is therefore the corporation as an economic and simultaneously social institution interacting with a broad cast of stakeholders.[65] This understanding of a firm's purpose and activities seems obvious for globally active corporations, but it is also of key relevance for regional or local firms in their specific environments. It is linked to our general understanding of organizations: organizations (e.g. corporations, non-governmental organizations, etc.), unlike living organisms, do not have a right to exist and survive per se (see Chapter 6, pp. 95–98). Their justification is to make a useful contribution to the needs of the society through their coordinated activities.[66] In this way, they are transmitters of intentions and purposes.[67] This function is inherent to all kinds of organizations. Human beings form organizations based on common interests in order to pursue a common purpose. The firm is just one possible form of organization where human beings can participate in a value creation process.

Sometimes, stakeholders are active as individuals or in groups; in recent years, they are more often likely to form non-governmental organizations, interstate organizations or civil society organizations, in which they participate in value creation activities. These organizations have increasingly been professionalized and have gained organizational capability (see particularly Chapters 6 and 9). These organizations also illustrate that in a knowledge-based, networked society, an increasing number of people want to be involved in the value creation process as stakeholders based on their values, knowledge and experience. These stakeholder organizations receive or maintain their right to exist by fulfilling the purpose of these human beings. Corporations and their stakeholders have consequently to keep in mind that their purpose is to serve society.

As to the principle of value creation, it is most important that corporate relations with multiple stakeholders are seen as constitutive to maintain and increase the corporation's abilities to create wealth. We emphasize that the linkages between the corporation and its multiple stakeholders in the economic and social sphere are in many ways important vehicles for creating, sustaining and enhancing the corporation's wealth-creating capacity.[68] These stakeholders are also interacting with each other. The interactions of firms with the stakeholders and the interaction of stakeholders among themselves are not only contextual conditions, but determining variables of a firm's strategy in a knowledge-based, networked society. Consequently the firm and the stakeholder embedded in a network view is the focus. In our understanding of the stakeholder paradigm, we assume that the value creation contribution not only evolves in the dyadic relation between the firm and a specific stakeholder, but most prominently within the stakeholder network (network view). We thereby build on the insights of stakeholder theory regarding networks (see Chapter 3, p. 40). This results in a more comprehensive understanding of the unit of analysis in strategy theory than has been the case thus far.

We can summarize that in our understanding the firm is an economic as well as social institution. The purpose of the firm is mutual economic and social value creation, with and for stakeholders (mutuality principle). Stakeholders are indispensable contributors for firms and for each other's value creation (network view). The value arises from their contributions, which constitute the focus for firm's but also for the stakeholders' strategy.

Who are the actors and who are the owners?

As we have seen, the stakeholder theory of the firm considers an extension of the property rights understanding of the traditional theory of the firm, which is based on a financial perspective, to all actors who contribute in a financial or in a non-financial way to value creation. The stakeholders' contributions create property rights of all kinds (e.g. intellectual, organizational, financial, etc.) for the firm, and therefore stakeholders become actors in the value creation process. Although this corresponds to our view, in our understanding the stakeholders are also the owners of resources. Due to their contribution in the value creation process, they potentially create and enhance property rights for the firm as well as for themselves. A broad range of stakeholders are indispensable for corporate operations but also for the stakeholders themselves. This has in fact important implications not only for value creation, but additionally for value distribution. Both are not exclusively of a financial nature but consist of different kinds of values.

Our empirical studies show that firms and stakeholders can contribute in various roles in the value creation processes and thus impact the firm, any other stakeholders or the whole network. Benefit and risk potentials emerge, are influenced, or become accessible by interactions in stakeholder networks. Thereby, we can distinguish the following roles of contributors in networks:[69]

- Benefit providers
  Participants in value creation can contribute in a variety of ways, from emotional engagement to sharing resources.
- Benefit receivers
  Participants in value creation can benefit due to gaining or enhancing their resources.
- Risk bearers
  By making specific contributions, the participants in value creation take specific risks. It may be difficult for them, for example, to apply and evaluate specific knowledge outside the network.
- Risk providers
  Participants of value creation can pose potential threats to interactions in the network and can even destroy value.

We could also see in our empirical research that some of the value creation contributions of a participant in the stakeholder network can be either intensified by an interaction with another participant, or it can be weakened or even destroyed. Therefore, we do not talk about a "nexus of value creation contribution," as does the stakeholder theory of the firm, but of a "stakeholder network of value creation."

We can summarize that in our understanding of the stakeholder paradigm the assumption is that extended property rights are based on different types of contributions (benefits and risks) to value creation by participants in a network. The firm and the stakeholders are consequently understood as owners of different kinds of contributions, causing them to act in the networks of value creation. Knowledge is of special importance as a value creation contribution. This opens a broad spectrum of causalities within the mutual value creation process.

What are the main attributes of actors and their behavior?

Based on the Kantian claim (see Chapter 3, p. 45), we assume that the actors are human beings with distinctive individual knowledge, experience, values, education, personal and family profiles and group affiliations. As we mentioned above, human beings act on their own, build groups or even different kinds of organizations in order to mutually pursue a purpose. The distinct features of human beings have an impact on a group or organization's identity, and therefore also the stakeholders and firm's identity.[70] This identity influences how the individual, the group or the organization perceives benefit and risk potentials for value creation between itself and its stakeholder network. Based on these perceptions, similarities and dissimilarities of the firm and the stakeholders' understanding of mutual value creation may arise. To capture the full picture of the firm and the stakeholders' behavior, we have to understand all of their perceptions. They shape the possibilities of the mutual value creation process.

As mentioned earlier, many stakeholders have developed organizational capabilities in recent years, and consequently they can contribute to value creation in a stronger and more differentiated way than before. We could study such bottom-up processes in our empirical examination.[71]

Figure 4.1 illustrates this line of argumentation. This line of interactions and especially the different perceptions of actors is a key assumption in our understanding of the stakeholder paradigm. Respect for the similarities and differences of the firm and the stakeholder's perception in the mutual value creation also implies that no one, neither the firm nor any other stakeholder, is always in a position to dominate the value creation process. Furthermore, firms and stakeholders have multiple, sometimes conflicting, roles that can change over time in the value creation process that also impact their perceptions.[72]

We conclude that in the stakeholder paradigm the actors are human beings. They are not only driven by the assumption of self-interest, but most importantly by their specific perceptions, which are shaped by individual experience, values, education, personal and family profiles and group affiliations. The fact that stakeholders are human beings requires a profound respect for each other, regarding the similarities and the differences of their perceptions shaping mutual value creation. Our understanding of the stakeholder paradigm considers individual human beings and respect for them, as well as the community, built on the principle of mutuality. This also implies that the participants in networks sometimes play multiple roles that change over time. No

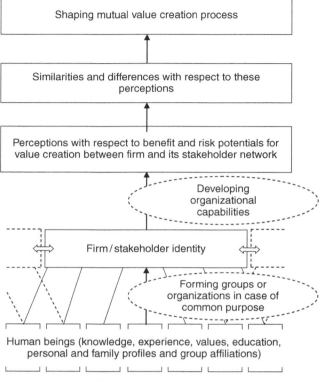

Figure 4.1 Perceptions of firms and stakeholders

one always dominates the stakeholder interactions, neither the firm nor a specific stakeholder.

What are the conditions of the environment?

In our understanding of the stakeholder paradigm, we assume that the environment of firms is represented by stakeholder networks (see Chapter 3, p. 41), where firms and stakeholders are interlinked in value creation. In contrast to this, in economic theory but also in strategy theory, competition is the focus and, therefore, the environment of a firm is represented by anonymous markets.

Thus, the original reason in economic theory to focus on competition was to avoid agreements between competitors, each seeking to enlarge their returns by monopolistic practices.[73] But it is misleading to narrow this idea down to the point of saying that the market solves all problems. This is especially false when markets are not perfect, and when market failures occur by not taking into account externalized costs, as for instance pollution due to corporate activities. In such cases some governmental regulation is necessary to improve general welfare. Stiglitz is asking for a better balance between the market and government, which he formulated after the financial crisis as follows: "One of the lessons of this crisis is that there is need for collective action – there is a role for government, as I have repeatedly emphasized."[74] This understanding of collective action corresponds to our understanding of the stakeholder paradigm. Cooperation with specific stakeholders, as for instance communities or employees, can lead to better solutions than pure competition.[75]

In evolutionary theory it is a central theme that evolution can be enhanced as much by cooperation as by competition.[76] While cooperation often enlarges value creation, competition in our understanding of the stakeholder paradigm is understood as benchmarking. It serves as a comparison between similar kinds of value creation processes to stimulate value creation in the sense of Fromm's understanding of active motivation (see Chapter 7).

We can summarize that the environment is represented by stakeholder networks. With respect to these environmental conditions, we make the assumption that a balance between cooperation and competition enhances value creation between firms and the stakeholders.

The assumptions of different paradigms

In our extended analysis of the underlying assumptions of the relevant theories, we have shown that the basic assumptions of the neoclassical economic theory, based on self-interest, bounded rationality and the market efficiency hypothesis, are also predominant in strategy theory and even partly in the stakeholder theory of the firm. These assumptions seem however to be a hindrance for a comprehensive analysis and understanding of value creation in a knowledge-based, networked society.

We conclude with Table 4.1, which compares the basic assumptions of the economic and stakeholder paradigms, and at the same

Table 4.1 Overview of the assumptions of the most important paradigms and theories

	Economic paradigm			Stakeholder paradigm		Our understanding
	Theory of the firm	Strategy theory		Stakeholder theory of the firm	Stakeholder capitalism	
		ISV	RbV			
Purpose of the firm and value creation						
	• Firm as an economic institution • Total economic value creation for one objective (rent for capital owners) • Optimal resource combination and allocation	• Firm as an actor in an attractive industry • Analysis of competitive environment to find position with low level of competition and high profit expectations • Strive for monopolistic position • Recent reformulation "principle of shared value"[a]	• Firm as a bundle of idiosyncratic resources • Gain and sustain competitive advantage based on resource heterogeneity and immobility • Strive for unique core competencies	• Firm as a bundle of resources with a special focus on knowledge • Total economic value creation and distribution (for all contributing stakeholders)	• Firm as moral and human institution; ethics of capitalism • Common purpose pursued by management with their stakeholders	• Firm as an economic and social entity embedded in stakeholder networks • Mutual economic and social value creation with and for stakeholders (mutuality principle) • Stakeholders as indispensable contributors for firms and each other (network view)

Main actors and owners

• Owners (shareholder) as sole residual claimants • Property rights based on capital investment	• Owners (shareholder) as sole residual claimants • Managers as key actors • Some stakeholders and CSR aspects have complemented the traditional ISV in recent years	• Owners (shareholder) as sole residual claimants • Managers as key actors • Resources as bundles of property rights (addressed in the literature after 1992)	• Stakeholders with firm specific investments • Nexus of incomplete contracts resp. nexus of firm-specific investments • Firm as owner of the corporate resources, not the shareholders • Firm represented by board of directors; director primacy	• Large cast of stakeholders are necessary to sustain value creation • Cooperation between firm and stakeholders as key source of innovation • Freedom as central notion and property as derivative	• Large cast of stakeholders are indispensable contributors to value creation • Stakeholder network of value creation • Participants in networks with different roles (benefit and risk) in value creation • Extended property rights: firm and stakeholders as owners of different kinds of resources

Table 4.1 (*cont.*)

Theory of the firm	Economic paradigm		Stakeholder paradigm		
	Strategy theory		Stakeholder theory of the firm	Stakeholder capitalism	Our understanding
	ISV	RbV			
Main attributes of actors and their behavior					
• Self-interest • Bounded rationality	• Bounded rationality in exploiting favorable position in industry • Managers as strategizers have to create, maintain and exploit imperfect competitive conditions by making trade-off decisions • (Enlightened) self-interest	• Bounded rationality regarding creation and exploitation of unique core competencies • Managers are strategizers deciding on creation and exploitation of unique resources • (Enlightened) self-interest	• Team production including different stakeholders • Bounded rationality • Enlightened self-interest	• Collective responsibility • Complexity of human nature • Keeping stakeholders in harmony (jointness)	• Stakeholders as human beings with distinct knowledge, experience, values, etc. • Respect for similar and different perceptions • No dominance in the network by the firm nor any specific stakeholder • Consideration of the individual human being with respect and the community based on mutuality

Environmental conditions

• Focus on competition (markets) • Further specific conditions in the single approaches (e.g. agency theory)	• ISV explains firm's success based on the (economic) environment • Focus on rivalry; unique positioning against rivals • Product markets as coordination mechanism • Recently resetting the boundaries of capitalism by including social improvements	• RbV explains firm's success with internal factors (core competencies) • Competition (rivalry) as external condition • Resource markets as coordination mechanism	• Representation of the environment by external stakeholders • Market pressure as prevention of abuse of power by the firm • Mediating hierarchy of board of directors as control for market failure	• Avoidance of zero sum solutions • Priority of cooperation • Competition as an emergent property, not a basic element of capitalism	• Environment represented by stakeholder networks • Balance of competition and cooperation in networks

Table 4.1 (*cont.*)

Theory of the firm	Economic paradigm		Stakeholder paradigm		Our understanding
	Strategy theory		Stakeholder theory of the firm	Stakeholder capitalism	
	ISV	RbV			
Impact on firm and key question					
	• Sustainable competitive advantage focused on mainly economic causalities in comparison to the market ⇩	• Sustainable competitive advantage in value creation and distribution based on stakeholder relations to explain the permanent strategic rent ⇩	• Joint (economic and social) value creation for stakeholders ⇩	• Mutual value creation to improve the quality of life for human beings and the sustainability of the natural world ⇩	• Impact on firm and key question
	• Enhance permanent strategic rent compared to rivals ⇩	• Why are firms different in an economic perspective?	• What do firms stand for and for whom are they creating value?	• What are the firm's and the stakeholders' roles in a network view?	
	• Why are firms different in an economic perspective?				
	• Why do firms exist?				

a Porter & Kramer, 2011: 64.

time summarizes the main assumptions for our understanding of the stakeholder paradigm.

In the next chapter we further develop our understanding of the stakeholder paradigm. We analyze in more detail the firm's and the stakeholders' roles in value creation within networks. We also analyze how firms and stakeholders, basing their activities on our revised assumptions, can develop solutions that better serve society than by following the economic paradigm.

PART II

Our understanding of the stakeholder paradigm and its operationalization

5 | Our understanding of the stakeholder paradigm operationalized in the three licenses

Our claim for the stakeholder paradigm

The economic paradigm in an endless series of constraints

According to traditional economic and strategy theories, the firm is mostly seen as a purely economic institution and its actors as driven by self-interest, with society a constraining factor as we discussed in Chapter 2.[1] A firm's total economic value creation, by combining and allocating factors of production in the competitive environment, is oriented to a utility function that focuses on one objective, namely value maximization for the owner of capital (e.g. shareholder value).[2]

If all human beings are modeled as self-interested actors and efficient market functioning fails to occur, there must be additional control mechanisms over a firm's value creation, which is normally in the form of state laws and regulations or in some cases by voluntary self-regulation (e.g. Global Compact). This continuous need for control is even more important as some of the actors are not interested in efficient market functioning.[3]

Moreover, national states are also unable to sufficiently control self-interest, as recently experienced in the global financial crisis and in the BP oil spill in the Gulf of Mexico and in the Fukushima disaster. State sovereignty is limited to its geographical borders, which leaves gaps in governmental constraints on self-interest, especially at the international level where the actors operate across borders. Boundaries and constraints are challenged as a result.[4] New kinds of political unions (e.g. EU, North American Union), institutions (e.g. NGOs, CSOs) and norms (e.g. sustainability or CSR standards) have been created which only partly fill the control gaps. Therefore, today we have a mixture of compulsory and voluntary adherence to regulation. But in a changing environment there have thus far never been sufficient constraints through regulation or standards. We can conclude that there will always be a need for further constraints.

Challenging the dominance of self-interest

Until now the exponents of the theory of the firm and strategy theory (ISV and RbV) have resisted the fact that sufficient control of self-interest is lacking. Only some minor additional regulation has been attempted as described in Chapter 2. The basic assumption of pure self-interest is questioned in various streams of literature in economics,[5] biology[6] and the social sciences.[7] In particular there is no convincing empirical evidence that nature foresees pure self-interest.[8] Other research based on the so-called co-evolutionary approach relies on nature (genetic disposition) and nurture (socialization).[9] Experimental studies have shown that social norms and institutions are reinforced when deviation is punished. This is especially evident in the studies on large groups, in which a lot of differentiated cooperation occurs. In fact in a sufficiently large number of individuals with a strong sense of reciprocity, selfishness is replaced by cooperation for better adaptation, because selfishness is penalized by other members of the group. Furthermore, the internalization of social norms leads to better adaptation, when applied for other than instrumental reasons.[10] These insights are especially relevant in a globalized world where individuals are interrelated through networks. It is against this background that we suggest a complete shift from the economic to a stakeholder paradigm.

This paradigm shift away from pure self-interest to mutuality corresponds to similar shifts in other fields, such as in climate policy for example. The latest Hartwell paper advocates shifting from human "sinfulness" to human "dignity," emphasizing innovative solutions (e.g. new energies) instead of restrictive rules (reduction of CO_2).[11]

The fundamental shift to mutuality in a network view

We therefore question why is it necessary for firms to outperform each other and to be confronted with an endless series of constraints, when they can build on the mutuality of a broad cast of stakeholders for value creation? Instead, we make the claim for a new paradigm that focuses on mutuality, and thereby advocate a network view to create value between firms and stakeholders to enhance quality of life. According to the most widely acknowledged standards (see, for example, the Human Development indices, Human Poverty indices, Happy Planet Index, etc.), quality of life comprises wealth that includes primarily sustainable access to resources, education and health.[12]

The current debate encompasses the notion of the quality of life not only from a human perspective but also from the perspective of the sustainability of the natural world. In the book *Mismeasuring our Lives*, Stiglitz *et al.* reflect on current measurements of GDP and propose a more comprehensive understanding.[13] Thereby, they distinguish three approaches to the concept of the quality of life: the first approach is based on the notion of subjective well-being, which considers the perceptions of human beings in value creation.[14] The subjective well-being requires respecting the similarities and differences of the perceptions of human beings (see Figure 4.1, p. 62). Second, the capability approach emphasizes human life as a combination of various activities and the ability to choose between different activities due to various values and goals. Consequently human beings are ends and not means (see Chapter 3, p. 45). The third approach takes into account the notion of fair allocation and goes beyond monetary dimensions by including the social dimension of value creation (see Chapter 4, pp. 57–59). In the second part of the book, the authors propose sustainability that, in addition to the quality of life of future generations, also considers the sustainability of the natural world.

Stiglitz *et al.* conclude, "For a long time, economists have assumed that it was sufficient to look at people's choices to drive information about their well being, and these choices would conform to a standard set of assumptions. In recent years however, much research has focused on what people value and how they act in real life; and this has highlighted large discrepancies between standard assumptions of economic theory and real-world phenomena."[15] This recognition requires a comprehensive understanding of value creation. In this sense, Putnam proposes avoiding the collapse of the Fact/Value Dichotomy.[16] Putnam consequently refers to Sen for the entanglement of fact and value: "In short, the serious welfare economists have to have a serious acquaintance with the best of contemporary ethical discussion."[17]

In introducing our understanding of the stakeholder paradigm, we rely on such a comprehensive understanding for value creation and contribute to Sen's claim. There are useful elements in the mainly fact driven economic and strategy theory, but also in the stakeholder theory that includes the discussion of values (see Chapter 3, pp. 43–46). Mutuality enhances benefits and reduces risks for the firm and its stakeholders that are embedded in the network, and therefore leads to superior value. We

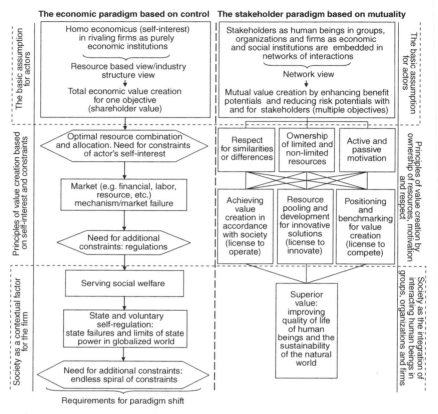

Figure 5.1 Comparison of the economic and the stakeholder paradigm

understand superior value as a continuous search by the firm and its engaged stakeholders to improve the quality of life of human beings and the sustainability of the natural world. Figure 5.1 compares the current economic paradigm with our understanding of the stakeholder paradigm, which we will operationalize in three licenses.

Putting the paradigm into operation: the three licenses

License as entitlement

Since their beginning, firms have been embedded in a legal framework that provides the basic license to operate. This basic license is granted to firms by authorities such as national, regional or local governments, which have the legitimacy to provide or withdraw licenses.[18] These include regulatory agencies for special matters, such as security standards for electricity, fire, employees, etc. Firms that do not fulfill these standards lose their license to operate. In a modern society, firms, which do not obtain or lose such formal licenses to operate, have the possibility to appeal the decision of the authorities, for instance by a court review. In different countries and regions, however, there may be different regulations for granting the licenses to operate in similar fields. There are three specific "conditions" where government must consider a license to operate: (1) decision to license the original grant (charter) – are the applicants trustworthy? (2) challenge the license – reauthorization of an operating license (e.g. telecom or television in the United States); (3) reclaiming a license to operate after it has been taken away, e.g. deep water drilling licenses after the oil spill which was re-granted in 2010 under new conditions.

In our understanding of the stakeholder paradigm, a "license" is not primarily a legal term, but rather a comprehensive entitlement, granted to the firm by its stakeholders. It includes the descriptive, instrumental and normative dimensions that we developed earlier in Chapter 3.[19] The normative dimension of a license incorporates the idea of stakeholders as human beings, which are involved in the process and the outcome of mutual value creation. Therefore, respect for persons, their expectations and perceptions are salient. As human beings are always ends and never means, they are never sources for value creation but owners of different kinds of resources, which they contribute to the value creation process. Thereby, they create and enhance property rights for themselves, as well as for others that are involved in value creation processes.

The descriptive dimension of a license focuses on the role of the firm and the stakeholders for mutual value creation. Firm and stakeholders are thereby embedded in a network. The instrumental dimension of a license emphasizes the influence of mutuality on the enhancement of benefits and the reduction of risks for the firm and engaged stakeholders. And it implies that value creation always acknowledges all perspectives, the firm's and the stakeholders'. As a consequence, value creation is not only measured by financial success but has an economic and social dimension.[20]

According to the entanglement of facts and values, the descriptive, instrumental and normative dimensions of licenses are not separate but interdependent.[21] In our framework of the licenses, the descriptive, instrumental and normative dimensions reinforce each other, and together provide an in-depth understanding of the stakeholder inter-actions for mutual value creation.[22] The licenses are 'managerial' in a broad sense according to Donaldson and Preston, because they offer strategies, processes, structures and attitudes that, taken together, operationalize the stakeholder paradigm.[23]

Licenses stimulate value creation

In the following section we claim that mutuality induces superior forms of value creation between firms and stakeholders, which are striving for solutions to complex projects, difficult issues or innovative products and services. In defining the licenses, according to our under-standing of the stakeholder paradigm, it seems appropriate to draw on the body of knowledge contained in the traditional approaches of strategic management (see Chapter 2, pp. 19–32). We will look at the industry structure view (ISV) and the resource-based view (RbV), and develop them further into the perspective of the stakeholder para-digm. As our previous analysis shows, these two approaches have to be complemented by a social and political view (SPV).[24] Therefore, we distinguish three licenses, namely the license to compete, the license to innovate and the license to operate.

Take another look at the Matterhorn

The three licenses are different but complementary views of the same phenomenon, namely the mutual value creation process in networks. The three views allow a richer insight than just one specific perspec-tive. The following metaphor might illustrate the richness we are able to gain by taking several perspectives into account simultaneously.

One of the most famous mountains in the world is the Matterhorn in Switzerland. In countless journals, media publications and adver-tisements the picture of the Matterhorn is shown as in Figure 5.2.

Millions of people know this picture of the mountain, taken from a specific, particularly attractive and spectacular perspective. If one takes a closer look at the mountain, one can see that four ridges des-cend from its peak and thus also four surfaces, i.e. the rock faces. But the well-known picture (Figure 5.2) shows only two of them. Therefore, another perspective is necessary to capture the whole

Figure 5.2 The Swiss view of the Matterhorn (source: Dreamstime)

mountain (Figure 5.3). This additional perspective shows a different, less spectacular shape. Yet it adds additional topographical and geological insights, giving a full picture of the mountain.

It follows that in order to capture the full picture of this mountain, different perspectives are necessary. Since we are proposing that this is also true for mutual value creation, we have searched for suitable perspectives in the strategy and stakeholder literature that can contribute to a full picture. The overlaps and incommensurabilities that may occur are preferable in our opinion than the disadvantages and

Figure 5.3 The Italian view of the Matterhorn (source: Dreamstime)

imperfections of a one-sided view. We already mentioned the necessity of the multi-perspective view in Chapter 1 (p. 6) for developing the paradigm shift we are proposing.

The economic paradigm focusing on self-interest is a one-sided view comparable to the first picture of the Matterhorn. It is impressive with its elegance and coherency but does not show the full picture. In contrast, the stakeholder paradigm is comprehensive because it takes into account the whole picture with a multi-perspective view. We think that it provides insight so as to make "climbing the Matterhorn" accessible under various conditions and in different ways.

In order to understand mutual value creation in networks, the three licenses provide the multi-perspectives. These licenses, which we develop in more detail in Chapters 6–8, are described in the following overview:

- License to operate
  The license to operate focuses on the role of the firm in society and its acceptance. It includes the social and political stakeholders as indispensable constituencies in a firm's value creation.[25] Market stakeholders can also act as social and political stakeholders as

everybody is part of the society in a network view. Preston and Post already advocated this view in 1975: "Over the long run, the political legitimacy of business organizations depends upon their ability to serve the needs of society, not the other way around."[26] Mutual value creation in networks aims at serving society by improving the quality of life for human beings and sustaining the natural world. This requires mutual respect for the similarities and differences regarding the expectations and perceptions of the individuals as part of organizational entities.[27] Stakeholders can provide but also restrict or even withdraw the license to operate of a firm, depending on the evaluation of its achievements with respect to the social and political dimensions.[28]

- License to innovate

The license to innovate emphasizes the firm's role as an innovator. Innovation is based on the pooling and development of the resources owned by the firm and all engaged stakeholders.[29] Thus, innovation is the result of enhancing benefit potentials and reducing risk potentials by mutual value creation.

Some resources such as water, oil or living space are limited. But in contrast to what traditional economics suggests, key resources in today's world such as knowledge, experience, renewable energies, etc. are not limited.[30] Non-limited resources can be enhanced and improved. Under these conditions, a characteristic of doing business is not merely a fight for limited resources among rivals, but much more a constant striving for the discovery, development and improvement of non-limited resources among firms and stakeholders. These resources are generally not only available in anonymous markets. Stakeholders are owners of these different kinds of resources and are contributing them to the value creation processes. We can conclude that the understanding of innovation in this sense means the superior value creation of firms interacting with stakeholders as resource contributors in a network view. Hence, the firm's license to innovate depends on its ability to motivate and cooperate with stakeholders as resource owners based on the principle of mutuality.

- License to compete

In this perspective, the firm's role within its environment, conceptualized as a stakeholder network, is focused. The firm's positioning in its stakeholder network is salient. These networks not only

take into account direct market participants, but also other stakeholders, who are involved in mutual value creation in a comprehensive sense. Thus the motivation for mutual value creation is for
a better quality of life, and not the fight to reap greater rents (e.g.
quasi-monopoly rent in the ISV) from direct market participants.
Competing is understood as benchmarking between similar kinds
of value creation processes, and serves to increase the motivation
for mutual value creation.[31] In this sense competition is a race in
which the participants spur each other on. Benchmarking between
similar processes and outcomes is essential to motivate superior
value creation rather than outperforming rivals. Consequently,
the license to compete is provided to firms and their stakeholder
network depending on their ability to stimulate value creation in
and between networks. Figure 5.4 gives an illustration of the three
licenses.

Embeddedness in networks

In contrast to the economic paradigm, the stakeholder paradigm is
not focused on the definition of a firm's boundaries, and therefore
the distinction between internal and external stakeholders, but on the
firm's embeddedness in a dynamic stakeholder network. Thereby the
firm and the stakeholders are contributors for value creation which
also implies that stakeholders themselves are embedded in stakeholder
networks (Figure 5.5).[32]

The stakeholder network as resource pool

The illustration (Figure 5.5) shows two firms (A and B), each of which
is embedded in its respective stakeholder network (left and right circle
respectively in illustration). Each stakeholder network, which consists
of all kinds of stakeholders, provides the firm with different resources
(see Chapter 7). The stakeholders contribute to improving and developing the value creation processes, as both firm A and B can tap and pool
the resources together with their stakeholders for innovative solutions.

The reason such a network perspective is important can be illustrated by the experience that Pfizer Switzerland[33] gained with respect
to the issue of developing innovative medicines. In the past, the company did not regard the general practitioners as partners; they were primarily regarded as prescription-givers. However, as new expensively

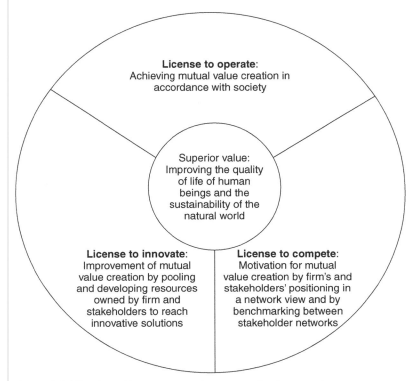

Figure 5.4 The three licenses to analyze mutual value creation

developed medicines are often criticized as "me too drugs" by physicians, healthcare insurers and even investors, the company opened itself to its stakeholder network and initiated a process of discussions. Pfizer started to recognize that the general practitioners among the physicians could contribute valuable knowledge with respect to real innovation, concerning their patients' needs. At the end of the process, the physicians should benefit in the future from innovative medicine more closely tuned to their patients' needs. This is also clearly a potential benefit for the patients. Needless to say, this is also in the interest of the company whose business it is to serve patients with the best products they can provide.[34]

Society as a contributor, not as a constraint
As an extension to the traditional management approaches focusing on market participants, social and political stakeholders ($\otimes$ in

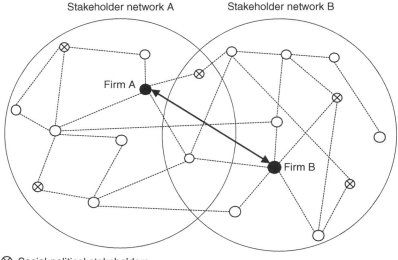

Figure 5.5 Stakeholder networks

Figure 5.5) are considered integral parts of the above stakeholder networks. These stakeholders also have value creation potential and thus are active in a firm's value creation (see Chapter 6). By including social and political stakeholders into a firm's stakeholder network, society is not seen as a constraint or an external factor, but as an indispensable contributor to mutual value creation in order to improve quality of life for society itself and for the sustainability of the natural world.

The "too big to fail" phenomenon in the banking industry provides an impressive example of the meaning of the firm as an integral part of society, and social and political stakeholders being important for firms. In the financial crisis it became clear that some banks were systemically relevant for the economy and society as a whole. The decision of the US government not to support Lehman Brothers and indirectly withdraw its license to operate led to severe effects in its global stakeholder network. Not only other banks but also other companies in different industries and even social institutions were heavily affected by this decision. And because the whole economic and social systems were in danger, citizens were in the end obliged to support other affected banks with their tax money, even though these banks were not state but private banks. It became clear that, in such situations, neither a single nation state alone nor the market can provide the solutions or the necessary constraints. A whole variety of social and political stakeholders became relevant: in addition to shareholders and customers, citizens, nation states, political parties, national banks and international finance organizations were heavily involved. And these stakeholders in the end had to define to what extent the affected banks are systemically relevant and whether to support them or not.[35]

Positioning and benchmarking

Figure 5.5 also shows that in the context of their stakeholder networks a firm's positioning occurs in two different ways: the firm needs first to position itself in its stakeholder network, i.e. vis-à-vis its different stakeholders to enhance value creation (left and right circle respectively in Figure 5.5). As an example, a bank, ZKB, in our empirical case studies was striving to establish cooperation with the World Wildlife Fund (WWF) to have a better position for developing sustainable financial products for their customers. This cooperation was favorable for mutual value creation for all three involved stakeholders (bank, clients, WWF).

Sometimes the participation in one stakeholder network excludes the participation in another, for example if partners ask for exclusiveness. But sometimes, as Figure 5.5 shows, some stakeholders are stakeholders of more than one firm (intersection of the circles). Thus, some stakeholders are common to two or more firms. Positioning occurs also vis-à-vis the common stakeholders. In the recently liberalized market of the telecom industry in Switzerland, the newcomers Orange and Sunrise had a weak position in the stakeholder network, as the established firm Swisscom had already had interactions with the most important common stakeholders over a long period of time. The newcomers had first to establish interaction forums with these stakeholders (e.g. the regulator). As we could observe in our case studies, this drive for positioning strongly challenged the newcomers, but at the same time enhanced not only their own value creation but also that of some of their stakeholders.[36] Also one needs to remember that stakeholders do not necessarily contribute identical resources to different firms.[37]

A second dimension is the positioning of the firm and its stakeholder network vis-à-vis other, similar stakeholder networks. This second dimension is primarily seen as benchmarking to motivate the process and outcome of both firms and their stakeholder networks for superior mutual value creation. This took place in the pharmaceutical industry as we mentioned above; they had to change their business model to improve the production of more innovative and accepted medicines. In our Pfizer case study, for example, this was achieved by first conducting comprehensive interviews with Pfizer's senior management team and the firm's stakeholders to evaluate their perceptions of the issue. In a next step, a workshop with Pfizer and one of their focal stakeholders, a health insurer, was organized in order to discuss their perceptions of innovative medicines and particularly the similarities in their perceptions. Thus, the workshop provided a platform for Pfizer and the health insurer to increase their mutual understanding of their different approaches to common issues. Based on the results and insights of the workshop, Pfizer decided on the necessary strategic adaptations, such as changing its whole sales model to a stakeholder-oriented one.[38] Based on this mutual value creation process, it contributed to improving the benchmark for the whole industry with regard to innovative medicine, which in turn produces better quality of life for patients.

Positioning in the two ways mentioned above is especially relevant in the perspective of the license to compete (see Chapter 8). Firms that are not able to strive for superior value creation will be challenged sooner or later by their stakeholders, e.g. customers, employees, investors, interest groups, etc., and their licenses questioned.

Stakeholder licenses

The three licenses are not only salient for the firms but also for all engaged stakeholders in mutual value creation. Stakeholders such as shareholders, customers, suppliers, NGOs, etc. have to be aware that as participants in a stakeholder network they can enhance or weaken the potential of the network but also of their own projects, issues, products or services. In doing so, they also need entitlement for their contributions. This may be even more important the more professionally the stakeholders are organized. However this thinking is not yet sufficiently anchored in the literature and in practice.[39]

Based on our understanding of the stakeholder paradigm, we make a strong claim for stakeholder responsibility from the perspective of the three licenses. Shareholders' responsibilities, for example, are sometimes challenged by engaged shareholder movements.[40] Financial intermediaries, such as pension funds or investment funds, are especially important actors regarding shareholder engagement, as they contribute important resources to value creation. A research-driven company may be under pressure when major shareholders as resource contributors demand short-term profits, instead of focusing on long-term benefits. This pressure may negatively influence the research and development of the company, as it may have to reduce investments in these areas. The consequences are fewer innovative products on the market and also lower profitability of the firm. Other consequences might be that such a company impacts the performance of pension funds, which in turn could lead to lower rents for the insured individuals. Retirement funds, as resource contributors, need to take responsibility by being in close and proactive contact with the firms they invest in.[41]

Stakeholder responsibility was also a focus point for NGOs in the case of Brent Spar in 1995.[42] At that time Greenpeace was confronted with a shrinking European membership. At the same time they were well acknowledged for their capabilities regarding ecological issues, which they had built up since the 1960s. Therefore, they looked intensely for a "target" to prove to their members that their activities and capabilities were still needed in Europe. Shell was the perfect "target" for such a campaign, since it was the market leader at the time and it had not developed strong competences to act on "soft issues," such as the disposal of the oil platform required.[43] Even though the impact on Shell of the Brent Spar issue evoked a positive change in the industry as a whole, and one could say that Greenpeace fulfilled a stakeholder responsibility, the way in which Greenpeace went about inducing it remains questionable.

Another example of stakeholder responsibility concerns the customer, who is often considered king. But especially big and important customers (e.g. lead users) have to be aware of their responsibility toward their stakeholder network. Their position in the network allows them to influence the whole network.[44] One example is McDonald's in its role as a customer of meat suppliers. Its demands not only influence future animal husbandry but also innovative solutions on this topic, which include important responsibilities.

Multiple roles of stakeholders

One important observation we made in studying our cases is that stakeholders often play more than one role in the mutual value creation process. Many firms have stakeholders with multifunctional roles. They are for instance customers, suppliers and investors at the same time, which implies multiple social identities.[45] Multiple social identities, well researched in social sciences, emphasize the tensions evoked by the different identities of a person, group or organization, and the lack of transparency for those interacting with them.[46]

One example can be derived from the financial industry: the bank ZKB that we analyzed has different types of stakeholder with multifunctional roles. On the one hand, the bank is publicly owned, and on the other hand, members of the public are customers of the bank and quite a number also work for the bank. Thus, they are owners, customers and employees at the same time, which again concerns all three licenses. The bank is well aware of these multiple roles, but this might not be true for all of the stakeholders. In our case it appeared that members of the public were often unconscious of the different roles, and also the influence they might have on the bank. Therefore the bank is challenged to make the multiplicity of roles more transparent to the stakeholder network.

Based on such multiple roles, a stakeholder is part of the cast of a firm's stakeholders for a variety of reasons and appears differently in the perspectives of the three licenses. A one-sided perspective of stakeholders is too narrow.

Common dimensions of the three licenses

The specific characteristics of the three licenses from the point of view of mutual value creation in networks will be analyzed in more detail in Chapters 6, 7 and 8. But before doing so, it seems useful to clarify the dimensions common to all three licenses. Value creation with and for stakeholders is the focus of each of the licenses. All our empirical cases have these dimensions in common, independently of the industry, the size of the firms or the characteristics of the human beings involved, either as firm representatives or as stakeholders. In the following chapters, we have organized the argumentation with respect to the three licenses as follows:

Content of the licenses

Each chapter starts with a short overview of the specific content that is emphasized by the respective license, concerning mutual value creation and embeddedness in a network.

The cast of relevant stakeholders

The cast of stakeholders of a firm includes everyone who is involved in mutual value creation.[47] The stakeholder paradigm acknowledges a broad variety of possible stakeholders, which may vary according to the interpretation of the three licenses.

In identifying the cast of relevant stakeholders of a firm, we first of all identify stakeholders as owners of limited or unlimited resources which they contribute to the value creation process. This is based on an extended view of property rights (see especially Chapter 7).[48] Second, the cast of stakeholders is also influenced by the fact that the firm can have different and changing positions in its environment, and is always embedded in evolving stakeholder networks (see especially Chapter 8).[49] As these stakeholders are interrelated with other stakeholders, sometimes they contribute not only directly to the value creation process but also indirectly.[50] Third, some of the stakeholders, e.g. employees, contribute voluntarily to value creation. Some do not (e.g. neighbors) but are forced to contribute or cannot abstain from contributing.[51] This is quite often true for social and political stakeholders (see especially Chapter 6). In response, these involuntary stakeholders have specific expectations of a firm's value creation process, and sometimes even have the power to influence it.

Mutuality as a value creation principle also emphasizes the need for the stakeholders to adhere to their own three licenses as already claimed above (pp. 86–87). The analysis of the three licenses helps to clarify the cast of relevant stakeholders from different perspectives.

Contributions to value creation

Each license can shed light on specific benefit and risk potentials regarding mutual value creation. They might occur due to the expectations of the social and political stakeholders (see Chapter 6), the nature of limited or non-limited resources owned by the stakeholders (see Chapter 7) or the positioning in the stakeholder networks (see Chapter 8). The benefit and risk potentials within these interactions may be seen differently from the corporate or the stakeholder perspective.[52]

The benefit and risk potentials are not only salient for the firm's licenses but also for the stakeholders'. If for instance a specific stakeholder contributes or challenges the firm's license to operate, at the same time its own licenses are impacted. The above mentioned example of Shell's Brent Spar illustrates this; not only was Shell's license to operate challenged but so was that of Greenpeace.

Value distribution

Value creation in the sense of mutuality is at the heart of our understanding of the stakeholder paradigm, and enhances ownership of the firm and the engaged stakeholders in proportion to their contribution to the benefits and to their adoption of risks in the value creation processes. But there are times when one of the participants of mutual value creation takes more of the value added than they deserve. In these cases, value distribution in proportion to contribution comes into play.

How much of these values will be appropriated to the firm or to the capital owners in the classical perspective, and how much will be appropriated to other involved stakeholders depends on the social processes among the firm and its stakeholders.[53] In the stakeholder paradigm, value distribution appears not to jeopardize, but on the contrary to stimulate, future contributions of stakeholders to improve superior value creation.

Value distribution, and particularly the question of who should participate and to what extent, can be reviewed in the light of all three licenses, from the firm but also from the stakeholders' perspective. This also includes indirect stakeholder contributions that occur, for example, when a stakeholder – e.g. a patient organization – transfers the experience of another stakeholder – e.g. patients – to a firm, such as Pfizer. This impacts not only Pfizer's licenses but also the patient organization's licenses.

Firm and stakeholder strategies

The principle of mutual value creation and distribution challenges firms and their stakeholders to engage in specific kinds of strategic activities. Strategies consider common actions of firms and stakeholders in a network view. The three licenses emphasize different aspects of firm and stakeholder strategies. With regard to the license to operate, a comparison of the similarities and differences between the firm and its stakeholders' perceptions, regarding common issues, projects, products or services, reveals different solutions for firm strategy (Chapter 6). From the perspective of the license to innovate, capabilities such as resource pooling, resource development and motivating stakeholders are elements of a firm's strategy (Chapter 7). The license to compete emphasizes strategies for cooperation, coopetition and competition that enhance benefit potentials and reduce risk potentials within and between the stakeholder networks (Chapter 8).

Evaluation of mutual value creation

Traditional strategy theory normally evaluates value creation by the surplus of economic rent. Strategic success due to competitive advantages based on positioning (ISV) or core competencies (RbV) is mostly expressed in financial terms, as discussed in Chapter 2.

In our understanding of the stakeholder paradigm, value creation takes place within a network of stakeholders of which the firm is a part. From this perspective, it is not only the outcome for one stakeholder (e.g. shareholder) that is the focus, but the mutually defined value for all stakeholders. Value measured in financial terms is often the top priority of business, but it does not necessarily reflect the full picture. Value in the stakeholder paradigm is consequently not understood only in financial terms, but encompasses a broader understanding of financial and non-financial components, as is the case in the three perspectives of the licenses. Moreover, we propose that the notion of value cannot be defined in a general way in the perspectives of the three licenses and for all situations, issues and specific contexts. The parties involved in a given value creation process have to define what they mean by value, and which components are to be included or excluded.[54] The mutual value creation and distribution process is not only efficient for the firm in an instrumental sense, but also creates motivation and satisfaction for the stakeholders. In this context, we refer to the differentiation of Fromm's active motivation (process) and the passive motivation (outcome).[55] This understanding

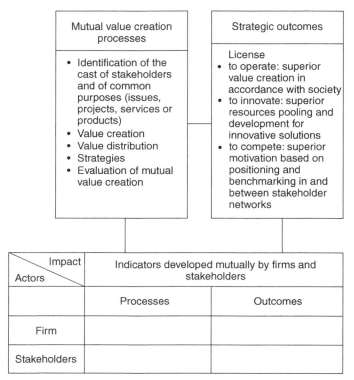

Figure 5.6 Evaluation concept (we thank Ruth Schmitt, Tom Schneider and Michael Sitte, with whom we are collaborating on a research project concerning evaluation of stakeholder engagement)

corresponds to the original meaning of "value" since it implies estimation in a general way.

The definition and evaluation of value creation can lead to differences that are induced by the different stakeholders involved. Such differences cannot be resolved by a one-sided financial perspective, rooted in the illusion of the efficient market hypotheses. Social processes are inevitable.[56] In such processes, firms may sometimes be able to manage their stakeholder interactions, but very often they are just a part of the stakeholder network.[57] For both situations, firms need to understand the similarities and differences of the stakeholder perceptions of value to recognize the common ground for solutions.[58]

We can conclude that in evaluations, the process is as important as the outcome (see Figure 5.6).[59] The evaluation standard "AccountAbility" also relies on this distinction of process and output: "Such 'engaged

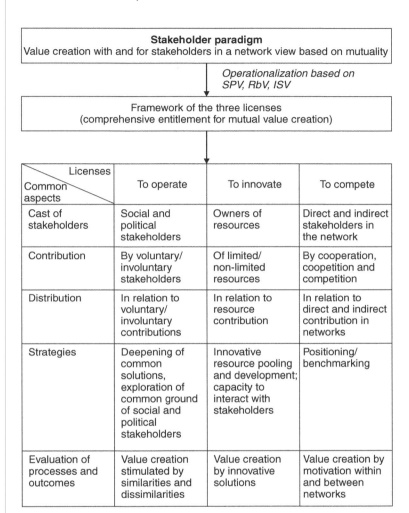

Figure 5.7 Key elements of the three licenses (we thank Jean-Paul Thommen for stimulating the discussion leading to this figure)

learning' is built on the notion that stakeholder engagement is both high quality (i.e. the process is fair, transparent, inclusive and responsive) and outcome-based (i.e. it makes a difference)."[60]

To evaluate the process of mutual value creation as well as the outcome requires an assessment of the benefits and risks, which differs according to the perspective of the three licenses. In concrete situations, the firm together with its stakeholders will need to develop indicators for the evaluation of mutual processes and outcomes. Based on this broad assessment of indicators, benchmarking between different stakeholder networks and their value creation capacity can be made. And given these benchmarks, the stakeholders can decide if they want to stay with a certain firm and its network or change to another.

In the next chapters, we will operationalize what the stakeholder paradigm means for mutual value creation between firms and stake-holders along the dimensions of the three licenses. Figure 5.7 gives an overview of the key elements.

It is important to note that the discussion of the three licenses in the following chapters is the result of initial work and is not complete; considerable work remains to be done.

6 | *License to operate*

The content of the license to operate

The license to operate perspective focuses on the role of firms in society and society's role in the value creation of firms in stakeholder networks. On the one hand, the firm has to contribute to the quality of life in a society. On the other hand, social and political stakeholders, aside from economic stakeholders, are indispensable contributors to the mutual value creation of firms.[1] The perception of a firm's activities and its relevance in society may depend on different factors:

- Size of the corporation
  Large corporations, like Nestlé, Philip Morris, General Motors or Wal-Mart with many thousands of employees and activities and assets worldwide, are more closely watched than small ones. NGOs, for example, concentrate on large corporations, and the press reports daily on large corporations. The reason lies in their market power and the extent of their social impact (e.g. laying-off thousands of employees, mergers and acquisitions or strategic failures with consequences on tax income or communities). The more stakeholders are dependent on a corporation, the higher the standards are for retaining a license to operate. Given the economic and social challenges that were evoked by the financial crisis in 2008, and particularly the requests for public funds for firms "too big to fail," the license to operate of banks has become of tremendous importance. The phenomenon of "too big to fail" implies the existential relevance of one single corporation not only for the financial system, but for the whole economic and social system.
- Public exposure
  Depending on different events or issues, firms have higher or lower public exposure and are faced with various levels of critique. Labor relations are often particularly closely watched by society. Orange Switzerland,[2] one of the telecom firms we analyzed, had

such an experience. In the beginning, when it entered the market after deregulation, as a newcomer it profited from an enormous growth rate. However, after a few years the market became saturated, and the growth rate slowed considerably. In the end, the firm had to close a call center and dismissed hundreds of employees. Without informing its employees adequately in advance, several hundred employees were laid off. This caused protests not only from the employees but also from unions and the media. The status of the employees also changed. In the beginning, they were highly regarded and provided with a luxurious work environment. When the firm faced financial problems, the employees suddenly became a cost factor that needed to be cut. The firm then realized that it had made a mistake, and established an employee forum. Its aim was to regularly inform employees regarding developments in the firm, and to improve the cooperation and communication among the parties involved.[3]

- Complexity of value creation
  Companies with complex value creation activities, that are even obscure for those outside the company, present more opportunities for anxiety and criticism, and do not have transparent stakeholder relationships. They often arouse suspicion if they are involved with new technologies (e.g. genetic engineering).[4]

- Degree of sensitivity
  In the public awareness of firms, there are basic differences regarding the various kinds of value creation. Entertainers as a rule are seen positively.[5] In contrast, those whose products are judged to be "socially sensitive" are regarded critically. Yaziji and Doh regard products to be socially sensitive that can threaten or save lives.[6] Examples are weapons, tobacco, alcohol or pharmaceutical products, as well as products sold in delicate markets, such as to children, the poor, the poorly educated, etc. Such products and services quickly raise the suspicion of "profit versus people." The image of an industry substantially influences individual perception of a firm, and also investors.[7]

- Property
  In Europe, publicly owned companies are seen differently than privately owned ones. Swisscom is an example of a firm mainly owned by the Swiss government. For this reason, the public regards itself as part owner of Swisscom, and has a closer relationship to it than

to other firms. Moreover, the obligation of companies listed on the
stock market to report publicly means that more information about
them is available to the public.[8]

Based on the growing trend toward more transparency in society,
the "license to operate" of firms will be increasingly scrutinized in
the future, especially for those firms not dealing appropriately with
stakeholder concerns. For example UBS, Switzerland's largest bank,
experienced such a challenge from its customers in the financial crisis
of 2008. UBS underestimated the concerns of their retail customers,
who reacted by withdrawing their money and closing their accounts.
According to the UBS Annual Report 2009, before the crisis the bank
had a net inflow of CHF 125 billion in 2007.[9] This changed dramatically in 2008 and 2009, when the bank suffered net outflows of
CHF 107 billion and CHF 90 billion respectively. This affected UBS's
license to operate substantially, and it could only be maintained by
credit from the national government.

The overwhelming importance of social and political stakeholders
to a firm's value creation also became evident in the case of the BP oil
spill case in 2010, when all the media reported in detail on the accident. In a survey in June of that year, 70 percent of Americans wanted
President Obama to intervene by being tougher on BP.[10] As people
become more dissatisfied with business, a new debate on regulation
and self-regulation, and on ethical, moral and community standards,
is likely to ensue in the coming years. In this context, the claim that
a firm needs the acceptance and the legitimation, not only of a broad
range of economic but also of social and political stakeholders, is of
high priority.[11]

The legal framework is still the important part of the license to operate. However, some additional agreements are also relevant. Already
Preston and Post have advocated, "*Public policy* – the principles that
guide action relating to society as a whole – may be made explicit in
law and other formal acts of governmental bodies, but a narrow and
legalistic interpretation of the term *policy* should be avoided. Implicit
policies – policies that can be implemented without formal articulation
of individual actions and decisions – may be even more important."[12]
Today social and political groups, with their multifaceted interests,
purposes and perception, are gaining increasing importance within
these processes, as Porter and Kramer also state: "Every company

needs tacit or explicit permission from governments, communities, and numerous other stakeholders to do business."[13]

As one can see from the examples above, the social and political environment is not only a constraint on a firm's activities. As the firm is an integral part of the society, social and political stakeholders provide necessary contributions for superior value creation between firms and stakeholders.

Not only firms but also stakeholders, including social and political ones, have to earn their license to operate, as already proposed in Chapter 5. This is particularly obvious for stakeholders that are highly professionalized and organized, such as powerful global NGOs (e.g. Greenpeace) or powerful media organizations (e.g. CNN), and that have developed a high level of organizational capability.[14]

The cast of stakeholders: society as an end and value contributor, not as a constraint

In the perspective of the license to operate, the cast of relevant stakeholders is that which contributes to the mutual value creation between the firm and the stakeholders, and serves society as an end. Reich closes his book *Aftershock* with this insight: "The most fortunate among us who have reached the pinnacles of power and success depend on a stable economic and political system. That stability rests on the public's trust that the system operates in the interest of us all."[15]

Research concerning social and political aspects of firm–stakeholder relations has increased in recent years as Mattingly and Greening state.[16] On a generic level, stakeholder theory focusing on the social and political stakeholders often speaks about "the public," "society at large," "civil society" or the "government." Both "public" and "public interest" are often mentioned in the context of public affairs[17] and community relations;[18] however, the terms are hardly ever defined in stakeholder theory. "Society at large" as a category of stakeholders is criticized as a useless term, because it is conceptualized at a different level than "government," or it is too comprehensive as a residual pool of stakeholders.[19] "The public," divided into different stakeholder groups, with highly differentiated characteristics, seems to be more appropriate.[20] From these different parts of society, only those stakeholders who can organize their "stake" are effective.[21] The other "stakes" are often invisible and ineffective, and are also referred to as "silent voices."[22]

"Civil society" is an increasingly important term in stakeholder theory, and it is often used in the realm of NGOs (non-governmental organizations) and CSOs (civil society organizations).[23] According to Yaziji and Doh, the number of NGOs increased from 52,000 to 1.4 million between 1993 and 2001.[24] NGOs are seen as the "tangible manifestation of civil society."[25] Thus, as Yaziji and Doh state, individuals are grouping around common ideas, causes or needs in order to promote collective benefits.[26] Forming into groups is crucial for individual social actors in order to be capable of action (see Chapter 4, p. 58). Thus, CSOs and NGOs have indirect, representative stakes.

Sometimes "the government," including its different departments, is also considered as a stakeholder;[27] however engagement explicitly and primarily with government is rather rare.[28] Therefore, Galang distinguishes the role of the government as enforcer and enabler for a firm's activities, thus directly linking this role to the formal license to operate.[29] Government as an enforcer is a powerful and coercive stakeholder from the perspective of the license to operate. Its main instruments are laws and regulations, which in the case of the non-compliance of a firm can lead to costly sanctions or the loss of the legal license to operate. The government is often a multifunctional and complex stakeholder, providing infrastructure besides laws and regulations. Government, including legislative and executive bodies, acts at different levels (local, national, international).[30] Governments as enablers provide conditions that may bring firms and stakeholders advantages or disadvantages. Firms and stakeholders can push for favorable policies through lobbying.[31]

Furthermore, government as one actor in multi-stakeholder constellations is prominently discussed in the global governance debate (see also Chapter 9, pp. 173–178).[32] Through regulation, governments often pave the road for firms' breakthrough products and services (e.g. automobiles, the Internet).[33] Innovations can lead to adaptations both in the respective industry and in society, as they become part of everyday life. As Wilson *et al.* claim, "Integrating these innovations into mainstream use requires the involvement of many and varied partners from government agencies, nonprofit organizations and commercial firms."[34]

In a broader perspective, the government is part of the political system.[35] However, the politicians are often following self-interest instead of public interest due to short election cycles.[36] They receive their license to operate from the electorate. Since political groups and parties can have a great deal of influence on business (e.g. legislation), firms exert as much influence as possible on politics through lobbying, the main task of the public affairs departments of most firms.[37] At times firms also financially support political parties or their candidates.[38]

The interaction between business and politics is often limited by deficiencies. Before the financial crisis politicians failed to exercise sufficient influence on this industry, thereby laying the groundwork for the crisis. In the United States, for example, the Glass-Steagall Act, which called for the separation between investment and commercial banking, was repealed due to political pressure. In addition, the Securities and Exchange Commission neglected its duties, and home ownership was encouraged by lowering mortgage rates beyond a healthy limit. Questionable in this realm is also the steady exchange of personnel such as between Goldman Sachs and government (revolving door).[39] We can conclude that the political stakeholders need to find a way to balance their supervisory duties and their contribution to value creation in a stakeholder network.

A further important social and political stakeholder is "the media." Sometimes it is characterized as an intermediary between other stakeholders.[40] Although the media is mentioned in this way, it is usually not discussed in depth in stakeholder theory.[41] When it is mentioned, then it is mostly as a risk provider for firms.[42] Moreover, the media tends to play a minor role in stakeholder theories. Perrin made a detailed study of the role of the media based on its dual structure as publisher and editor.[43] She was able to show that the one-sided role as risk provider in stakeholder theory does not correspond to the complex role of the media. Perrin's case study of the pharmaceutical company Pfizer unveiled that the reports in the media about the company were mostly neutral, and only critical regarding current but not firm-specific scandal topics such as manager salaries.[44] Against this background, the media as legitimacy provider and its own "license to operate" needs to be questioned. It is far more likely that the media, similarly to other private companies, is striving to secure its own economic success.

Table **6.1** *Most important social and political stakeholders*

Stakeholder	Frequency of mentions
Regulators	115
Society	107
Politicians	64
Government	64
Union	40
NGO	34
Media	33
Social partners	24
Local communities	16

Note: Clear differences are shown in the frequencies (in absolute numbers) with which the interviewees in the telecom industry mentioned the respective potentials.

The importance of social and political stakeholders is also supported by our case studies. Managers often mention "regulators" and "society" as the most important social and political stakeholders of a firm. This was particularly salient in our case studies in the telecommunications industry (see Table 6.1).

Not surprisingly, the regulator played a dominant role in the newly liberalized telecom industry, as it had to build and monitor the new market conditions. Therefore, all firms we analyzed in this industry agreed on the salience of the regulator for themselves and the whole industry. Additionally, after liberalization the society also became an important stakeholder for the telecom firms. The reason was that firms had to deploy a whole series of antennas, which were and still are strongly opposed by the residents (see p. 107).[45] An interviewee of a telecom firm stated:

The antenna problem is still critical for us, since we need them to send signals in order to phone. But it is like highways: everyone wants to drive on highways but no one wants a highway in their yard.

In our research we also looked at firms that were not founded by entrepreneurs, but by the state during difficult economic times. Up to the present time, they still have a public mandate (e.g. employee insurance in Switzerland). For this type of firm, the legal license to operate is based on a broad stakeholder orientation. In such cases, political decisions are more important than market forces or investor decisions. And the managers of such firms see their responsibility primarily toward society, not toward capital markets.[46]

Besides the typical social and political stakeholders discussed above, all kinds of stakeholders may entertain social and political expectations regarding value creation. In the case of Monsanto, shareholders made a claim for the appropriate handling of the issue of "gene technology."[47] Institutional investors such as pension funds have also begun to represent social and political expectations, and contribute to mutual value creation of firms with their knowledge and experience to develop innovative solutions for a sustainable quality of life.[48]

Furthermore, all kinds of business partners can address social issues by not doing business with firms that neglect important social aspects. This is especially true for the choice of suppliers. Companies often choose only those suppliers who follow principles accepted by their social stakeholders.[49] For instance, after the issues arising from Brent Spar and Nigeria, Shell formulated a special area of responsibility in the realm of doing business with business partners: "Shell companies insist on honesty, integrity and fairness in all aspects of our business and expect the same in our relationships with all those with whom we do business."[50]

Mutual value creation with and for social and political stakeholders

To better understand mutual value creation it is salient to analyze how the interactions between the corporation and the social and political stakeholders take place.[51] In what follows, we will differentiate between the corporation and the stakeholder perspective.

Corporation perspective

Various approaches to a firm's interaction with social and political stakeholders are discussed in the literature.[52] From her empirical insights, Sloan emphasizes three aspects as especially important for successful engagement between firms and social and political stakeholders in a partnership mindset.[53] Management has to take into account, first, the inclusion of the stakeholders; second, collaboration by learning; and third, integration in the core business and the strategic processes.

With respect to these social partnerships, Savage and colleagues focus on multi-sector, inter-organizational collaborations, which aim to solve "messy problems" that cannot typically be solved by an organization acting alone.[54] Thereby they advocate a collaborative advantage similar to Sloan.[55] In such collaborations a distinction between intra- and inter-organization partnerships in labor relations can be made according to Park-Poaps and Rees: "Internal direction characterizes a firm's intra-organizational orientation toward commitment to fair labor conditions throughout the supply chain. External partnership conceptualized as cooperative and collaborative inter-organizational management of labor issues in the supply chain."[56] Such typologies are relevant in a stakeholder perspective as they show the great variety and complexity of the social and political interactions a firm has to consider.

The interest of business in developing partnerships with social and political actors has increased in recent years, leading to the creation of PPP, public–private partnership.[57] This interest has resulted in a growing number of common projects of firms with public institutions, and in the foundation of various organizations such as the World Business Council for Sustainable Development (WBCSD). In addition, the UN and other global organizations have developed numerous public–private partnerships.

However, the financial crisis of 2008 showed that there were few attempts to solve the issues arising between the finance industry and the social and political stakeholders on the basis of mutual value creation. Following on from the financial crisis, however, a fast growing number of appeals in parliaments and in the media in different countries are urging governments to intervene and regulate the financial sector. At present, a wave of regulation is being discussed, with remarkable differences between the various countries. The result is that in many countries (particularly in the United States and Europe) new government regulations are in the making, to compensate for the lack of consideration of the public interest on the part of the financial industry. This could have been prevented if the financial industry and its stakeholder network had developed common solutions earlier.

Such cases (see also pp. 106–108) lead to the claim that in the future firms need to analyze more systematically and professionally the benefit and risk potentials of social and political stakeholders, in order to avoid value destruction and to enhance value creation for the firm and for stakeholders at the same time.

Stakeholder perspective

The key problem from the social and political stakeholders' perspective is how to have a "voice" in the interactions with firms. Friedman and Miles[58] see the mobilization of groups as a central condition enabling stakeholder interactions with firms to take place.[59] Besides mobilization, stakeholder collaboration is often mentioned as an important condition for stakeholder interaction.[60] Some scholars have analyzed in more detail the conditions that are necessary to establish interaction among stakeholders.[61] One of the critical points is the organizational capability of stakeholders (see Chapter 4, pp. 61–62).[62] The interests of stakeholders need to be organized, in order to have a voice and to be responded to by others. Public opinion can be expressed by different civil-society stakeholder groups, the focus being on the action and mobilization of these particular groups. Thus, exactly this grouping and sorting of stakeholders, and the avoidance of the abstract term "society at large," is distinctive for the stakeholder perspective.[63] The public has to be understood as different subunits, and is thus operationalized. The problem that then emerges is the question of the representation and legitimacy of such groups.[64] This emphasizes the importance of our claim that stakeholders also have to strive for a license to operate (see p. 98).[65] The question of whether they represent the public interest they claim to, is an essential part of their license to operate.

We observed such an example in our case research. Patient organizations and the pharmaceutical company Pfizer conducted a multistakeholder dialogue regarding the issue of health literacy. Both sides agreed on the importance of the issue and also saw the benefits of cooperation, as a win-win situation could result from it. However, the patient organizations did not act in unity, but instead several factions pursued their own particular interests, each differing considerably from the others and not necessarily representing the patients' interests. In addition, many patient organizations are rather small

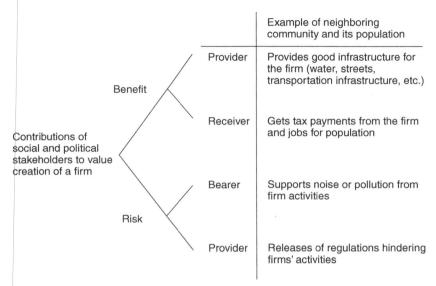

Figure 6.1 Types of social and political stakeholders' contributions

and their organizational capability is not yet advanced. Both circumstances contributed to the fact that the patient organizations did not appear on the stakeholder radar of the pharmaceutical company before the multi-stakeholder dialogue, although they could obviously make valuable contributions to developing solutions for health literacy, and thus improving the quality of life of human beings.

Important benefit and risk potentials from the perspective of the license to operate

In the firm's relations to social and political stakeholders, four basic types of contributions to mutual value creation exist.

Figure 6.1 illustrates these contributions of a social stakeholder, namely the neighboring community, to the value creation of a firm.

In our empirical case research, managers of firms in the telecommunication and the financial services industries assessed the benefit and risk potentials (Figure 6.2, p. 106) they expected, if they interacted with social and political stakeholders.

The benefits of the firm's political cooperation, its social responsibility, as well as the risks of a high exposure, are clearly mentioned

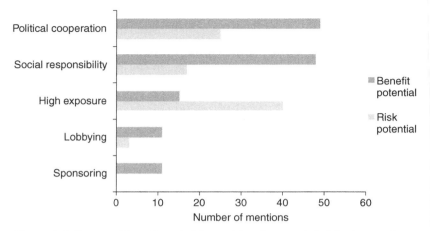

Figure 6.2 Expected benefit and risk resulting from stakeholder interactions (this figure shows clear differences in the frequencies (in absolute numbers) with which the interviewees in the financial and telecom industry mentioned the respective potentials)

as most relevant, when firms interact with these stakeholders. One of our interview partners mentioned that, based on its competencies and social responsibilities, his firm is highly regarded by the regulator, which represents a benefit potential and certainly strengthens the firm's license to operate:

Regulators refer to us as a credible partner, because of the work we do. We are regarded as a source of information. We have a lot of very talented people in this firm who have become specialists. The regulators have come to trust their opinions.

Cooperation like this between a firm and a regulator can without doubt be advantageous for both sides. However dependencies between regulator and firm must be avoided so that they do not find themselves under the same blanket.

In the following we illustrate further benefit and risk potentials, as well as some aspects that might strengthen and secure a firm's license to operate:

• After the wake-up calls of Brent Spar and Nigeria in 1995 that challenged Shell's license to operate, Shell came up with the term "listening and responding" to stakeholders (see p. 102).[66] With this term Shell initiated a new process that was explained in its report "People, Planet and Profits,"[67] one of the first comprehensive sustainability reports. Furthermore, Shell hired former Greenpeace employees to use their capabilities to interact more beneficially or less riskily with social and political stakeholders.

- If firms know and systematically consider the expectations of the social and political stakeholders, they are better prepared to deal with upcoming issues. They run a lower risk of ending up in a crisis affecting their license to operate. As we mentioned earlier, the two newcomers, Orange and Sunrise (formerly Diax), to the Swiss telecom market after liberalization in the 1990s had to deploy large numbers of antennas in order to offer mobile phone service to their customers (see p. 101).[68] Both firms were faced with resistance from residents, who were afraid of health risks such as insomnia, headaches, etc., if antennas were to be built in their vicinity. Sunrise refused to discuss the problem with their stakeholders, and in the end all involved parties appealed to the government and went to court to pursue their claims. The conflict was finally resolved and Sunrise's license to operate was saved, when all parties agreed to make concessions. For Sunrise, the one-year fight resulted not only in a delay in building its antennas, but also in negative national press coverage and damage to its reputation. Orange chose a different, proactive strategy in order to avoid similar difficulties. The firm discussed its intended locations for antennas openly and respectfully with the affected residents, explaining its position (that it was forced by law to build antennas) but also listening to the residents' concerns. The firm's goal was to find a compromise among partners and not to just insist on its formal rights. Thanks to such discussions, mutually acceptable solutions were found without delay for the antenna locations.[69]

- Firms can draw on resources, such as the infrastructure, knowledge and experiences, of the involved social or political stakeholders as benefit potentials. These resources can be especially crucial for new and upcoming issues. As mentioned above (see p. 109), Pfizer was looking for solutions to health literacy by cooperating with patient organizations as social stakeholders.

- Companies are sometimes pressured by social and political stakeholders to carry on despite economic difficulties, in order to avoid loss of value for other stakeholders in the network. An example is not closing plants or reducing jobs despite financial losses. The case of Opel, the General Motors' subsidiary in Germany, showed that the social and political stakeholders were able to pressure the company to maintain the location and the jobs until economic recovery is reached (see also Chapter 8, p. 151).

- In an extreme way, the license to operate "on probation" became a topic in the international financial crisis of 2008. In some cases, countries prevented the risk of bank failures with very high public credits. These banks were "too big to fail" and their collapse too high a risk for the economic system as a whole (see p. 95). During the crisis countries kept such banks in business through financial aid and support. This was a conditional continuation of the licenses to operate, as the aid was linked to a variety of obligations for the firms and the expectations of recovery. Social stakeholders were obliged to involuntarily support the banking business. UBS, for example, had to be bailed out by the Swiss government; it agreed to support the bank with up to USD 60 billion. This corresponds to over 10 percent of Switzerland's GDP. The government regarded the aid to UBS as so urgent and important, that the emergency measure was decided on without consulting parliament or the population. The government support was intended to protect the entire economic system of Switzerland. After intervening in the crisis, the Swiss parliament and the public discussed the measures that needed to be developed so as not to be dependent on a dubious license to operate. Partial solutions are tightening the regulations for the banking sector, and the demand that the future goal must be sustainable value creation.
- The license to operate can be threatened, even when it succeeds in fulfilling legal obligations and meeting social expectations, but fails to fulfill the expectations of its business partners (e.g. suppliers). The license to operate can therefore extend beyond company borders over numerous links in the chain of value creation. The company is held responsible by social and political stakeholders for the complete picture, as the example of the intolerable working conditions of Chinese workers for the suppliers of Honda and Apple show (see Chapter 7, p. 129).[70]

Value distribution to social and political stakeholders

There are spectacular cases of value distributions to social and political stakeholders by owners of firms, such as the donations of Bill Gates and Carlos Slim announced in 2010. Each of them donated 50 million dollars to the health systems of countries in Central America (e.g. Mexico, Guatemala).

But the value distribution problem to social and political stakeholders is not limited to the voluntary redistribution of capital that the sponsors earned from their firms' profit. Our understanding of the stakeholder paradigm, under the consideration of the extended property rights concept, includes value distribution to the stakeholders, including social and political ones, who engage in the mutual value creation. In our cases, we found various examples of value distribution of firms to social and political stakeholders. Some firms – usually state owned or partially state owned – have conducted fair value distribution of this kind since their founding. The publicly owned bank ZKB, that we analyzed, is obliged by law to distribute value to society. However the firm does more than that, by distributing large parts of its profits directly back to the local and regional governments. Moreover, it has implemented a generous plan of public welfare spending, which includes the support of sports or other leisure activities.[71]

Aside from the bank we analyzed, another example of transparent value dissemination of a corporation to economic and social stakeholders is Novo Nordisk (see Chapter 7, pp. 114–115). The firm set up an "economic stakeholder model," in which it reports the total sum of salaries paid to employees, the sum paid to suppliers for their services and products, the taxes paid to the government and the dividend attributed to the shareholders, etc. Novo Nordisk's credo is that customers and society should be included in the value distribution process, and that this should occur in a transparent way.[72]

In some cases, firms are forced to distribute value to involuntary stakeholders. This can be illustrated with the example of the BP oil spill in 2010 in the Gulf of Mexico. The US government forced BP to pay USD 20 billion into a fund. The money was then quickly distributed to victims of the oil spill, i.e. to fishermen who lost their income. This was done to compensate for the hardship suffered by those living along the Gulf Coast and to save them from having to sue BP for damages.[73]

Strategies from the perspective of the license to operate

The special aspect, which the license to operate perspective contributes to the strategic management, is the systematic inclusion of the perceptions of social and political stakeholders in strategy formulation and implementation. The similarities and differences of these stakeholders' perceptions must be collected and taken into account systematically, if in the long run the license to operate is to be guaranteed.

In our action research (see Appendix, pp. 186–188), we developed a process to clarify similarities and dissimilarities between firm and stakeholder perceptions.[74] As we could see, the perceptions of the participants in a stakeholder interaction can be shaped by individual experience, values, education, personal and family profile, and group dynamics. Sometimes these result in big differences. The precondition for the clarifying process requires that the firm and stakeholders are willing to listen to each other, and to acknowledge that solutions can be found even when perceptions differ.[75]

Firms and their social and political stakeholders naturally do not always agree on whether cooperation should take place or what degree of cooperation is desirable.[76] Similarly, stakeholders among themselves may have different perceptions on common issues, projects, products and services.[77] But the level of agreement or disagreement influences the strategic activities of firms and stakeholders. Being aware of this in our action research, we identified three possible situations with corresponding impacts on strategies (Table 6.2, p. 111).

If the involved parties have similar perceptions of an issue, these perceptions can be deepened, which in turn leads to a strengthening of one's own perception. This means that common solutions can be found. If perceptions are partly similar and partly different, there is common ground to start on. Cooperation in areas of similarities can enable the parties to develop common rules to develop solutions. This cooperation allows learning from each other and is especially promising for innovative solutions.[78] Later, such rules can be transferred from the areas of similarities to the areas where the perceptions are different. If no common perceptions exist, the limits of interactions and problem solving become apparent. These situations are the most

Table 6.2 *Strategic activities based on similarities and differences of stakeholder and firm perception of an issue*

Perceptions of firm and stakeholders	Strategic activities
Similar perceptions	Deepening of common solutions
Some similar, some different perceptions	Exploration of common ground for solutions
Different perceptions	Recognition of the limits of interactions and lack of solution

challenging, particularly if they are rooted in value differences, which is often the case with social and political stakeholders. In this realm, a distinction is made between value laden issues that are still negotiable and protected values where negotiations are not possible.[79] If issues are value laden or if new situations develop, in which the involved stakeholders do not yet have any experience of interacting with each other, it might be important for the firm and the involved stakeholders to clarify, evaluate and compare not only their perceptions but also their values.

Comparing and discussing the perceptions of an issue thus helps the firm and the stakeholders to better perceive and appreciate the partners' perspectives, values and their "world" in general. This serves as a basis for developing strategies. In one of our ongoing cases, we can observe a firm searching for common ground with two social stakeholder organizations. This stimulates the development of capabilities of all participants, which in turn can be used to shape their distinct strategies.

Evaluation from the perspective of the license to operate

In the research to date, a distinction between the financial and social performance of the corporation is made.[80] With regards to CSP (corporate social performance), Carroll emphasizes the importance of stakeholders.[81] Similarly, Rowley and Berman come to the conclusion that CSP must be regarded in relation to the firm's stakeholders and their needs.[82] Stakeholders such as NGOs and communities, but also shareholders and customers, are increasingly interested in the social engagement of firms. This has led to a substantial growth in rating agencies, which assess the firms' social and environmental performances and are calling for "One report," which implies sustainable reporting.[83] Examples include the UN Global Compact, KLD (Kinder, Lydenberg, Domini Research & Analytics), the Dow Jones Social Index or International Integrated Reporting Committee (IIRC). Estimations indicate that approximately 2,000 firms and 150 NGOs assess the CSR activities of other firms.[84] However, with so many rating agencies in the market, it is hardly surprising that no agreement exists on the characteristics that are to be assessed and the weight they should be given in the CSR reporting.

The findings on the financial consequences of corporate social performance are mixed.[85] Freeman *et al.* challenge stakeholder theorists in this realm: "However, this approach simply tries to patch up the old model. It falters on the question of determining what counts as 'economic' versus 'social' performance."[86] To find a new approach, recently some authors have not focused directly on social performance, but on the reasons why companies increasingly engage in social action and in new forms of partnerships with social and political stakeholders.[87] Marquis *et al.* emphasize that orienting according to local "peers" is a strong factor, which explains why companies engage in specific social action, and also what forms of social action they pursue.[88] The more an activity becomes accepted, widespread and institutionalized, the more it becomes legitimate. Or it may even be mandatory to be aware of the license to operate: "As a form gains legitimacy, more and more companies adopt it, until it eventually emerges as a dominant practice."[89]

As we have seen, cross-sector initiatives and partnerships have developed involving both businesses and other actors. They also have to be evaluated, as we know little about the impact of such partnerships on the involved actors.[90] Therefore, new impact assessment methodologies are necessary to evaluate how such partnerships work.[91] The acceptance of such impact assessments depends on who conducts the assessment. The results will differ significantly, since every stakeholder involved is interested in telling his own "truth" based on his particular perceptions (see pp. 110–111). Furthermore, the partnership may result in simultaneous gains and losses for the same stakeholder.[92]

In our case research, we could see some first attempts for broadening the evaluations. In order to evaluate the cooperation with its social and political stakeholders, Pfizer developed indicators to measure the impact of such stakeholder interactions. The indicators were defined in cooperation with the stakeholders and linked to the benefit and risk potentials of the corresponding stakeholder relation. For its relations to the regulator, as an example, the indicator measured the time needed for new medicines to achieve market approval. Such indicators are useful for both firms and stakeholders as they provide them with an instrument for communication. This in turn helps the company in its mutual value creation process.[93]

Concluding remarks to the license to operate

The concept of the license to operate, which suggests professional and systematic interactions between firms and social and political stakeholders, challenges the issues for both sides in the coming years. The firm and stakeholders' role as integral parts of society seems not to be readily understood by many firms as well as by the stakeholders. More research and practical experience are needed to clarify what mutual value creation between the firm and its social and political stakeholders means from the perspective of the license to operate. A key problem for research is the development of accepted processes and methods for the evaluation of social action and management.

The identification of relevant social and political stakeholders, and the assessment of their benefit and risk potential to enhance or destroy value creation, is a particularly difficult management task. It presupposes social and political knowledge, and the capability to assess the firm's impact on society and the importance of social and political stakeholders for mutual value creation. To improve this capability, and depending on the situation and the relevant issues, firms sometimes elect former politicians to their boards or individuals with special relations to the social and political sphere, in order to gain knowledge pertaining to the social and political stakeholders and to sustain the firm's license to operate.

A key challenge for the social and political stakeholders seems to be establishing organizational structures and procedures, in order to have a voice. Concerning their own license to operate, they have to be able to bear responsibility in a mutual value creation process with firms and other stakeholders.

7 | *License to innovate*

The content of the license to innovate

Sustainable value creation of firms under rapidly changing conditions depends on ongoing innovation.[1] The license to innovate emphasizes the firm's role as an innovator based on its interactions with stakeholders. Furthermore, the license to innovate implies that stakeholders also have a key role as innovator in a knowledge-based, networked society.

Innovation is salient for the traditional RbV that we analyzed in detail in Chapter 2. The traditional RbV relies on the basic assumptions of self-interest, and focuses on the exploitation of bundles of unique resources in order to create superior financial value for one specific resource owner, the shareholder. Recently, this thinking is being questioned increasingly by scholars of the stakeholder theory of the firm, discussed in Chapter 4, on the basis of what they consider to be enlightened self-interest.[2] They consider stakeholders making firm-specific investments, and their entitlement to participate in value distribution based on their contributions.

The license to innovate incorporates elements of the traditional RbV, namely the key importance of resources for innovation. But the license to innovate considers further that the firm and the involved stakeholders are pooling and developing resources in value creation processes.[3] Thereby, the firm and the stakeholders can own different types of resources, e.g. physical assets, intangible assets, financial and social capital, services, components of products and – most importantly – knowledge. Mutuality in resource development enhances benefits and reduces risks for the firm and the stakeholders, thus leading to superior value and therefore to the improved quality of life for human beings and greater sustainability of the natural world.

This corresponds for instance to the understanding of innovation of Novo Nordisk. This company enhances the pooling of knowledge from a broad cast of stakeholders to develop new solutions for diabetes, which ultimately improves the quality of life for patients.[4] In this understanding, value creation in a firm is a process, in which a broad cast of stakeholders are involved in differentiated ways, as resource owners to create superior value. These stakeholders provide the firm with the license to innovate.

The same is true for the stakeholders involved in value creation. They can also acquire a license to innovate from their own stakeholders including firms, as the following example of patient organization emphasizes. In some countries direct communication with patients is legally limited for pharmaceutical firms. In such cases, patient organizations are important contributors of knowledge for pharmaceutical corporations concerning the patients' needs and experiences. Therefore the license to innovate of patient organizations is at stake: they need to provide knowledge and experiences, which are essential for the patients. Mutual value creation between the patient organization and the pharmaceutical corporation enhance the firm's capabilities to discover innovative medicines, which provide a better quality of life for patients.

The cast of stakeholders: from the resource-based view to the resource owner view

Stakeholders as resource contributors

In the traditional RbV, the focus is on unique combinations of resources as a basis for a firm's economic success. Therefore it is assumed that the firm selectively acquires such specific resources from anonymous factor markets, and can then combine them to unique and inimitable core competencies.

The stakeholder paradigm opens a somewhat different perspective: it emphasizes that important resources, which make up unique core competencies of a firm, are rarely if ever acquired from anonymous factor markets, but rather are the result of interactions between firms and stakeholders as both are owners of different kinds of resources. "All of the firm's resources are represented in some way by various stakeholders, and it is the firm's relationships with stakeholder that make resources available to the organization. Similarly, customers, suppliers, regulators, and other players will be more (or less) collaborative,

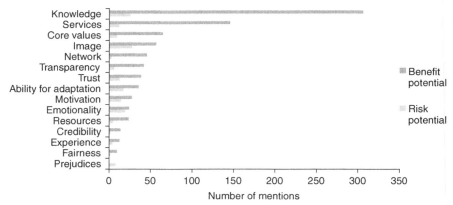

Figure 7.1 Benefit and risk potentials as perceived by managers (this figure shows clear differences in frequencies (absolute numbers) with which the interviewees in the industry mentioned the respective potentials)

supportive, and reliable in their dealings with the firm depending on the kind of stakeholder relations the firm has developed with them."[5]

In our case research, we could observe that if mutuality between firms and stakeholders exists, then it leads to superior value creation for the firm and their stakeholders. As an example, an interviewee from a telecom firm speaking about customer relations mentioned:

When we acquire a customer for the first time, it is important that we provide a benefit for him. I think in the long run we have a good chance to establish a partnership, particularly with large companies, which represent a corresponding value, i.e. banks and insurances with whom we already have a relationship. On the one hand, we help them to improve their services; and on the other hand, they help us actively to improve ourselves, be it services or support. They make presentations for our technicians, for example about what it means for them if a branch of their bank has to be closed, and why they expect a corresponding service from us. I think this is where we have interactions, which lead to mutual improvements.

In the perception of the managers in the two analyzed industries (telecommunication and financial services), the risk and benefit potentials in the RbV were highly ranked (see Figure 7.1).

The outstanding importance of knowledge as benefit potential is evident. As an example, the benefit and risk potentials of a firm's customer are illustrated in Figure 7.2.

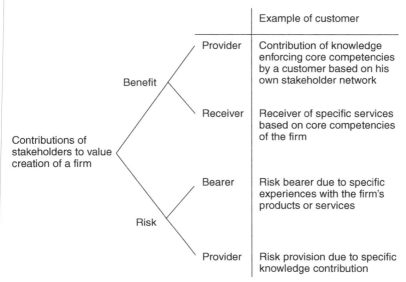

Figure 7.2 Types of stakeholder contributions

As the above example shows, a single stakeholder, in this case the customer, can exhibit all four types of contribution. It is therefore important for firms and stakeholders to recognize and consider all these possibilities. From a resource perspective, the roles of the "benefit provider" and "risk bearer" may often be in the foreground of the perception as our cases revealed.

These types of interaction are also valid from the point of view of a firm's stakeholders in their interactions with their own stakeholders, including the firm. As an example in our case study of Pfizer, a broad cast of stakeholders see each other as important knowledge providers and risk bearers in the process of enabling access to innovative medicines.[6] Physicians in their own stakeholder network often see scientific experts as the most important knowledge contributors. As our studies showed, physicians value the opinion of these experts more than the opinion of the representatives of the pharmaceutical firms. Therefore, Pfizer changed their approach to physicians, and no longer accessed them from a market-driven but instead from a stakeholder-oriented approach as knowledge partners. For example, a physician is now always visited by an expert of certain diagnostic indicators and no longer by product specialists (see Chapter 5, pp. 82–83).[7]

Stakeholders as providers of non-limited resources

In the perspective of the license to innovate, the distinction between limited and non-limited resources is relevant. Non-limited resources (knowledge, experience, etc.) can be further developed in the interaction between the firm and their stakeholder.[8] From this perspective it is important to be aware that the focus is not mainly – as economic theory sometimes assumes – on limited resources that must be optimally allocated. By considering the non-limited resources which are decisive in a knowledge-based, networked society, these resources are not only combined in a better way but can also be developed further, creating innovative solutions with respect to issues, projects, products or services. This thinking has already been realized by the innovative product development of Novo Nordisk, as mentioned above (see pp. 114–115), and by Pfizer as seen before (see Chapter 5, pp. 82–83).

Besides knowledge, important raw materials, construction parts and highly specified services, which are often the source of a firm's unique core competencies, are mostly defined and developed, sometimes even discovered, in differentiated interactions with suppliers. The interaction process with the respective stakeholders is the key. In these processes, the stakeholders (in this case with the suppliers) as owners of all kinds of resources are indispensable contributors to core competencies as one interview partner emphasized:

> The suppliers are creative and often involved as they try to find new solutions for the market … They act as an accelerator who gives us new ideas … And very often the supplier is also a strategic thought leader, two years ahead.

Our case research clearly shows that in such interactive processes, firms and stakeholders can motivate each other in the contribution of resources.

However, it is also noticeable that as far as we can see today very few firms and stakeholders systematically put these contributions to use. There exists an untapped potential for all involved parties. With respect to this systematic approach to stakeholders' resource contributions, it is important to keep in mind that stakeholders are ends and not means. This was emphasized by an interviewee as follows:

Employees as stakeholders play an integral role because if you treat employees as interchangeable commodities, that can just be switched in and out, you're never going to get the transfer of knowledge; and you're never going to achieve the real efficiency, that you can with the development of knowledge and expertise.

In order to mutually develop non-limited resources, the capability of the firm to stimulate and motivate mutual value creation is crucial, especially to gain above-the-norm resource contributions from stakeholders. "Above-the-norm" as we use it in this context refers to resource contributions exceeding contractual obligations.

Some particular aspects of above-the-norm contribution of resources have been discussed already in the literature. For example, the so-called lead user concept focuses on the extraordinary knowledge contributions of front-running customers to a firm's innovations.[9] Lead users are particularly progressive customers (users or buyers), who have the qualifications and mindset required for change. Lead users are customers with needs which will be marketable broadly only in the future. In many ways, the concept of the lead user is in accordance with the idea of the customer as a stakeholder contributing non-limited resources. The lead user becomes a valuable partner to be taken into account in the firm's process of value creation.[10]

Peter Drucker already stated that "the basic economic resource – 'the means of production' to use the economist's term – is no longer capital, nor natural resources (the economist's 'land'), nor 'labor.' *It is and will be knowledge.*"[11] As knowledge is crucial for many firms, an increasing number have established knowledge management of some type. In close cooperation between firms and stakeholders, knowledge can be transferred, exchanged and enhanced. The mutual value creation benefits both sides: firms develop new ideas and products; stakeholders as contributors can improve the quality of their products or improve their processes; customers can buy products and services that better suit their needs; and patient organizations can enable access to more innovative medicines.

The importance of knowledge is also confirmed in our case studies, as it is acknowledged as the second most important benefit potential after cooperation by our interviewees in an overall perspective (see Chapter 8, Table 8.1, p. 142) and the most important in a RbV. Motivating resource contributions may require considerable effort

on the firm and the stakeholder's side, as the example of Pfizer and
a healthcare insurer illustrates (see Chapter 5, p. 86).[12] The healthcare industry in Switzerland was broadly challenged on how one
could come to grips with costs and benefits, and was confronted
with the accusation of making pseudo innovations when bringing
new drugs on the market. In an attempt to solve this problem, Pfizer
decided in a first step to collaborate with one of its major stakeholders, a leading healthcare insurer. However, the breakthrough, which
helped them to develop a more beneficial way to interact with each
other, was only achieved when they concentrated on the common
benefit potential of combining resources such as experiences and
knowledge.

Stakeholders as direct and indirect resource contributors

For the firm and the stakeholders as resource owners, the value creation process is not just about the direct resource deployment in the
traditional economic sense. Both firm and stakeholders contribute
directly but also indirectly. Also in this perspective, stakeholders'
contributions to and participation in mutual value creation are the
results of differentiated social processes among the various parties
involved. In the same sense, Nahapiet and Ghoshal claim that knowledge and knowledge capabilities come about through a social process
in which the various actors take part: "Knowledge and knowing capability of social collectivity ... created through a process of combining
the knowledge and experience of different parties ... occurs through
social interaction and coactivity."[13]

With respect to the direct resource contributors for the firm,
broad access to differentiated resources is important to be capable
of developing innovative products or services or solutions for issues
and projects. It allows firms to "pool imperfectly tradable resources
in order to gain greater efficiency in the use of existing resources
as well as opportunities to create new resources."[14] The focus on
differentiated stakeholder interactions also allows the development
of products, services and solutions for issues and projects. These
can achieve wide acceptance due to the fact that such solutions are
innovative not only for the specific firm but from the perspective
of the contributing stakeholders. Therefore, the identification of
stakeholders, which directly contribute to mutual value creation, is

a key in strategic management. Relevant stakeholders can be identified based on an in-depth analysis of specific value creation processes, such as for example the nature of a firm's production process (e.g. innovative medicines) or a concrete common issue (e.g. health costs).[15]

Indirect contributions occur if a given stakeholder influences or is influenced by another based on the network interactions. His influence takes a detour (see also example patient organizations, p. 115, or Zurich Airport, p. 112). These indirect contributions are challenging for the firm and the stakeholder, as these indirect contributions are not always transparent and can cause risks instead of benefits, such as misunderstandings or misinformation. Patient organizations for pharmaceutical firms are an obvious example. It might be unclear for pharmaceutical firms, whether the patient organizations represent the real needs and experience of the patients or just the organizations' own interests.

Stakeholders as voluntary and involuntary resource contributors

Prominent voluntary stakeholders are shareholders, customers, employees or suppliers, but also other stakeholder groups may become involved in a voluntary way, such as NGOs, media, etc. They can mainly decide if and under what conditions they want to engage in mutual value creation, and thereby provide their resources to the firm. And if they are already a stakeholder of a firm, they can choose to leave or stay in the network.

Voluntary stakeholders have an active interest to cooperate with a firm or another stakeholder, and even to take the initiative to cooperate. They are those who are interested in finding innovative solutions for new products or for an issue. In our case research, we have seen how the WWF contributes know-how to the bank ZKB to create sustainable products for the bank's customers, and also contributes to innovative solutions with regard to the issue of climate change (see Chapter 5, p. 85).[16]

However, not just those stakeholders who voluntarily contribute resources to value creation are important, but also those who are affected involuntarily by the activities of the firm (noise, air pollution, mental effects, etc.). Often, they have no exit strategy and are not able to leave the network. They cannot avoid the negative effects of value creation, but can only seek to have a strong voice in matters so that their demands receive consideration. They have to be taken into account due to the concept of extended property rights, since as risk bearer and sufferers they are also involuntarily contributing resources to value creation. This shows that value creation is not always a win-win process, and not only contributed to by motivated stakeholders, but also by stakeholders who pay the price of suffering. However, in the long run sustainable value creation has to be mutual and acceptable for all participants in the understanding of the stakeholder paradigm (see pp. 123–125).[17]

The example of the neighboring communities of Zurich Airport illustrates how important the involuntary value contributions by stakeholders can become if they are neglected by a firm.[18] As the landing corridor for Zurich Airport extends beyond the Swiss–German border into the southern part of Baden-Wuerttemberg in Germany, Switzerland had to find an agreement with Germany to protect citizens on both sides of the border who were involuntarily suffering from air traffic at Zurich Airport. In the face of demands for reduced noise pollution for their citizens, Germany requested substantial changes in the existing treaty with Switzerland. However, the Swiss authorities resisted making these changes. The German government, pushed by its citizens, unilaterally declared new restrictive regulations regarding flight altitudes and landing times. These restrictions were put in effect unilaterally by Germany within several weeks, since a mutual understanding between Switzerland and Germany was not foreseeable in the near future. In this situation, the neighboring population and communities as involuntary stakeholders became of strategic importance for Zurich Airport, since they could leverage their right to live with bearable noise emission through the political power of the German government. The example of Zurich Airport also illustrates the importance of a firm's ability to interact with its stakeholders. This capability can become a kind of meta core competence.

Exploring and considering the specific nature of stakeholders (direct/indirect; voluntary/involuntary), and of the resources (limited/non-limited) based on the necessities of the given situation, is part of a firm's and stakeholder's responsibility in achieving the license to innovate. This reshapes the perspective of the traditional RbV to a resource owner view.

Mutual value creation

The motivation of stakeholders to contribute resources

When the relevant resource contributors have been identified, the next question is how firms and stakeholders can motivate each other to contribute their resources to the value creation process. From a purely economic perspective, resources are acquired by the firm in return for payment in resource markets, based on a complete contract between the firm and the resource owner.

In the stakeholder paradigm, the contributions of the stakeholders to value creation are not seen as completely determined, meaning that incomplete or even implicit contracts exist. Asher *et al.* comment on this: "Fundamentally, incomplete contracting occurs because making (ex ante) complete contingent claims contracting is too costly, if not outright impossible, to achieve."[19] Therefore, the question of why and how the stakeholder as owner relinquishes resources is placed in a broader framework than in the traditional RbV.

Moran and Ghoshal mention three conditions that must be satisfied for an exchange of resources.[20] First, an opportunity must exist; second, parties must expect such an exchange to create value; and third, those involved must be sufficiently motivated for a knowledge exchange and combination. The motivation of stakeholders to contribute resources to value creation therefore becomes a key question of our understanding of the stakeholder paradigm that recognizes firms and stakeholders as owners of resources. Often stakeholders can be motivated to make contributions of various kinds, sometimes even above-the-norm:

- Employees can be motivated to spend a part of their own time and also money to develop skills (e.g. training), which increase their professional capability and therefore their resource contributions above the norm. This often implies that this kind of knowledge is firm-specific and cannot be applied easily in other workplaces. The firm has to acknowledge the limited transferability of these firm-specific resources with respect to value distribution.
- Customers, especially lead users, can be motivated to make their experience with the firm's products or services available to a firm as a specific type of resource. This makes customers "co-entrepreneurs" as they enable innovative products or services that comprise superior value for both sides.

- Suppliers can be motivated to develop products or services for the exclusive use as resources of a company. In doing so, they bear risks. Or suppliers work without remuneration on a project in order to submit an offer to the firm. This implies that firms acknowledge specific conditions also on the part of their suppliers.

Based on good experience in the past and faith in the future, various stakeholders may be willing to maintain their loyalty to a company, even bearing benefit-losses or higher risks, if the company is going through a difficult period or has had to accept setbacks and losses. Shareholders for example can be convinced to maintain their investment, even when no dividends are paid or the share price falls. Customers can maintain their brand or firm loyalty. Unions can refrain from social demands and seek constructive solutions to conflicts in order to avoid damage to the firm. Policy-makers and regulators can be motivated to maintain supportive relations, etc. In such cases, anonymous market mechanisms are replaced by highly differentiated stakeholder interactions. These stakeholders are prepared to contribute above-the-norm, not only for monetary compensation. Other motivating factors are also at work, such as human commitment, sense of obligation, trust, loyalty, enthusiasm for particular technologies, etc.

However, above-the-norm contributions by stakeholders may reach their limits when contributions are too risky, compensation is lacking for too long a time, or if one stakeholder category is favored systematically in value distribution (e.g. managers). An example for above the norm contributions causing risks for stakeholders may be offshoring for employees in industrialized countries. Globalization has opened markets, which gives firms the opportunity to produce their goods and services abroad, particularly in countries such as China and India, where wages are considerably lower than in Western countries. But offshoring may not just cause problems for the employees in the home country, but also in the country to which jobs are transferred. This can be illustrated with by protests of the Foxconn and Honda workers in China in 2010 (see Chapter 6, p. 108).[21] The employees fought for higher wages and decent working conditions, as they realized that their contribution involved high-risk potentials such as intolerable stress conditions, separation from their families, etc.

From a strategic perspective, firms not only have to ask what the core competencies of their corporation are today and in the future, and what resources they rely on. They also have to clarify the conditions under which stakeholders, as resource owners, are motivated to contribute resources. The goal is to be able to create core competencies that will in return create value through innovative solutions for the stakeholders and the firm.

The stakeholders themselves also have to be aware of the fact that, while being involved in the mutual value creation process, their own license to innovate is challenged. In our empirical investigation we could see that stakeholders experienced such challenges. Sometimes new interaction with their stakeholders had to be found. As a stakeholder of the pharmaceutical companies, Swissmedic, the Swiss agency for therapeutic products, provides such an example.[22] They institutionalized interaction with their own stakeholders to enhance their understanding of how access to innovative medicine is perceived by their stakeholders. This is part of their license to innovate.

The dynamics of resource contribution

The relevant stakeholder network and the interactions between firms and stakeholders are not static.[23] This is a most important factor in a stakeholder perspective. Interactions change over time due to driving forces in and around the firms. Similarly, the significance and role of stakeholders as resource contributors can change.

We observed such changes for example in our empirical studies of stakeholder relations in connection with the privatization of the telecommunication industry in Switzerland.[24] The former state monopolist Swisscom was suddenly confronted with a competitive environment that fundamentally challenged its traditional resource contributing stakeholders. Some of the traditional interactions with these stakeholders that had been sustained over decades even became obsolete; new interactions had to be developed with new stakeholders. The stakeholder network of Swisscom changed dramatically. Four types of changes in the stakeholders' roles and positions as resource contributors in the network could be observed in this case: privatization first affected a change in the importance (strengthening or weakening) of some of the existing stakeholders as resource providers (e.g. enhanced importance of contributors of marketing knowledge). Second, new risks arose for some stakeholder categories (e.g. enhanced risks for employees without competitive experience).

Third, the existence of competition challenged a new interpretation of the role of the previous stakeholders (e.g. the state as the former sole owner became one investor alongside others), and finally privatization led to an extension of the networks through new resource providing stakeholders, which had not existed before the privatization (e.g. external shareholders).

As to the dynamics of stakeholder interactions, a dilemma between "continuity" and "change" was emphasized in the interviews with the corporations. On the one hand, strategic persistence over time can facilitate the building up of sustainable core competencies in harmony with stakeholders. On the other hand, continuity can turn into core rigidities.[25] Firms need to find answers to these contradicting and difficult challenges.

One can observe this clearly in the BP oil spill issue[26] in 2010, which in many respects is similar to Shell's Brent Spar issue in 1995.[27] In both cases, the two oil companies relied on their technically oriented core competence for drilling oil. In both cases, there was a concentration on a very narrow economic and technical perspective of value creation with few stakeholders (e.g. shareholders, customers and suppliers). Both companies underestimated the social dimension of value creation due to a lack of knowledge of and experience with several important stakeholders, even though both of them claimed to have contact with these stakeholders. The original core competence, which was based on few stakeholder interactions, turned out to be a core rigidity, not only with respect to the superior value of innovative solutions but also finally with respect to the financial bottom line.

Furthermore, the dynamics of stakeholder relations are often considered positive as they can open opportunities to access untapped resources. But changes in the stakeholder network do not only affect changes in the resource pool. Long-term collaboration of firms with stakeholders creates social contracts, which in turn can influence access to resources. They have value in themselves, as they regulate and simplify the interactions. For instance, as trust is built based on such social contracts, knowledge and experience sharing are more likely to occur than in new interactions. The newcomers in the telecom industry experienced the importance of such social contracts, as the traditional monopolist had well-established relations with the regulating authorities (see Chapter 6, p. 107). Obviously history matters as an interview partner pointed out:[28]

On the one hand, I have to say that Swisscom as former monopolist has relations to numerous people who are closely connected to parliament. They have so many advantages, that we as newcomers could never make up for, even if we had had countless people for this job.

Frequent change from one resource contributor to another or exit strategies of stakeholders may destroy values, as this disrupts social contracts and benefit potentials, such as trust or credibility. Instead new risk potentials can arise and strongly influence the sustainable value creation of a firm. The literature on the effects of mergers or layoffs on motivation documents this with respect to employee relations (e.g. survivor sickness).[29]

A further aspect that can emerge from a dynamic perspective is the change in the role of a firm or a stakeholder in the network over time. In certain phases of the stakeholder's resource contributions, the firm may be able to lead the interaction process; in other phases a stakeholder may take the lead and the firm's influence is limited. The idea that stakeholder relations are always "managed" over time by the firm does not correspond to the challenges of the knowledge-based networked society.

The so-called Camisea project of Shell, starting in 1994 and ending in 1998, illustrates this impressively.[30] During this time, an ongoing process of interactions between Shell and a whole variety of stakeholders contributing resources (knowledge) took place. These activities exceeded the total and undisputed control and dominance by Shell. "Although a firm does not naturally possess a sovereign position but has to earn it, it can be reasonably assumed on the ground of the Camisea case that a focal actor can indirectly but imperfectly influence the process of relationship building."[31]

From a dynamic perspective also the identification of the relevant cast of stakeholders contributing resources is not a mechanistic-economic decision that can be made *uno actu*. It results from ongoing social processes, and from the discretion exercised in the decision-making of the managers and the stakeholders. As the above mentioned Camisea case demonstrated during the issue solving process, stakeholders can withdraw from or enter in the stakeholder network as late contributors. Closing the stakeholder identification at the beginning of the process runs the risk of missing the chance to gain the full cast of important resource contributors in an ongoing process.

The fact that from the perspective of the stakeholder paradigm the dynamic of change is of major importance makes the discussion on "dynamic capabilities" seem particularly relevant for this approach, all the more if it is extended to a broader than purely economic perspective.[32]

When the stakeholder relations are seen dynamically, then the question arises of how a firm or its stakeholders are able to make valuable estimations to consider future developments and conditions in resource contribution. Future stakeholder relations can hardly be fully recognized, understood and handled *ex ante*. This means that stakeholder relations cannot be completely "managed" in advance in a conventional sense, but may come about or change unexpectedly in the course of the mutual value creation process. These changes in the interactions and dealing with them require that the firms as well as stakeholders continually develop their capabilities to interact. In our empirical studies it was evident that the cultures of the firm and of the stakeholders have to be open for change in this realm. Whereby, situational factors (e.g. national cultures) can also be relevant.[33]

This means that in the complex and interactive processes of motivation and organization of stakeholders' resource contributions, managerial discretion will lead to different solutions despite similar situations. Different solutions include different benefit and risk potentials and have different effects on value creation. The capability to interact with resource contributing stakeholders can become a (meta) core competency itself.

Value distribution to stakeholders from the perspective of the license to innovate

As we mentioned earlier in Chapter 2, in the traditional RbV the economic rent is the indicator of a firm's success. The shareholder (owner) is the only residual claimant and therefore earns the whole rent. In recent publications on the RbV, first steps are being made toward a broader perspective of value distribution. Wang and Barney see value distribution to employees making firm-specific investments as follows: "The rents generated by these firm-specific investments are often shared between a firm's employees and its owners ... and, thus, can be a source of wealth for both the employees and the owners."[34]

The perspective of the stakeholder paradigm is that if stakeholders as owners contribute resources to a firm's value creation, they also participate accordingly in value distribution.[35] Therefore, mutual value creation inevitably raises questions of the rent that could be acquired by a firm or any other stakeholder.[36] A well-known example of employees participating in the value distribution is compensation plans. In our case research, we found a variety of examples.[37]

The principle for value distribution is also important for above-the-norm contributions and residual profits. Novo Nordisk, for example, accounts for its value distribution in detail to employees, suppliers, governments, shareholders, etc., as they have all contributed to the development of Novo Nordisk's innovative products for diabetes (see pp. 114–115).[38] Furthermore, some insurance corporations grant their customers a premium bonus after a good business year. Similar value distributions based on financial success have been announced in 2010 by German firms like Siemens, BMW and Porsche. Value in the form of a loyalty bonus is also given to long-term customers.

There are no limits to the ideas providing employees the opportunity to participate in the value distribution of a corporation in general or in the residual profit in particular, as an interviewee in one of our cases said:

Three years ago, we made an extraordinarily high profit and we paid almost 500 millions into the pension fund without being legally obliged to do so. But our opinion is that it was the right thing to transfer this money from the shareholders to the employees.

Strategy and core competencies from the perspective of the license to innovate

As we have seen in this chapter, in order to enhance its license to innovate, a firm can have access to resources contributed by stakeholders according to three types of core competencies.

- Innovative resource pooling
  The resources contributed by the different stakeholders can be combined and bundled with those of the firm that form capabilities which enable firms to find innovative solutions. An example of this is Shell after the Brent Spar case (see Chapter 6, pp. 106–107). Based on knowledge that Shell acquired in dealing with NGOs through

stakeholder roundtables, the firm achieved a capability in dealing with messy issues, which Shell could later use in the Camisea case (see p. 127).[39]

- Innovative resource development
  Based on the contribution of resources by different stakeholders, the firm and the stakeholders can be motivated to mutually develop these resources. The bundling of such developed resources forms new core competencies with which innovative solutions for mutual value creation can be found. The firm Novo Nordisk that, together with various patient organizations, developed and extended knowledge on diabetes is an example of this (see p. 129).

- Capability to interact with stakeholders
  Firms and stakeholders are able to structure and handle the stakeholder interactions in order to motivate innovative solutions within mutual value creation. Interactions of firms with resource contributing stakeholders can become a meta core competency. By approaching physicians as partners and no longer via conventional marketing, Pfizer developed a new interaction capability (see p. 120).[40]

These three categories of firm core competencies are founded in the different roles of stakeholders as resource contributors, the different kinds of contributions and the different nature of resources. Analogous forms of core competencies can be developed from the perspective of stakeholders.

Figure 7.3 displays these contribution possibilities, which firms and stakeholders can apply to develop such competencies.

In the process of strategy development and implementation, firms and stakeholders have to assess the different types of core competencies and decide to what extent they can be part of their strategy for mutual value creation.

Evaluation from the perspective of the license to innovate

Evaluation in the perspective of the license to innovate has to focus, on the one hand, on the social processes of resource contributions mentioned above. It includes the fact that innovative solutions are not only created by the firm, but are also supported by stakeholders

Stakeholder contributions \ Core competencies	Role of resource contributor: • benefit provider or receiver • risk provider or bearer	Kind of contribution: • voluntary/ involuntary • direct/indirect	Kind of resources: • limited • non-limited
Innovative resource pooling			
Innovative resource development			
Capability to interact with stakeholders			

Figure 7.3 Possible contributions by stakeholders to core competencies

with relevant resources. The processes of identifying and motivating stakeholders to contribute resources to value creation have therefore to be part of the evaluation.

On the other hand, the outcome of the mutual value creation processes is important. It relates to the improved value creation of the firm and its stakeholders, which arises from the pooling of resources, the stimulation of resource development and the unique stakeholder interactions. Criteria or indicators for assessment have to be defined by firms and the contributing stakeholders according to the issues, projects or products and services.[41]

Concluding remarks to the license to innovate

Compared to the traditional RbV the perspective of the license to innovate deepens the causalities of value creation, since it introduces stakeholders as resource owners and contributors (see Figure 7.4). It also broadens the horizon as it enlarges the value creation and distribution processes to all relevant types of resource contributors, and does not limit them to a small set of market participants.

A comprehensive cast of stakeholders as human beings have to be motivated to provide their resources for mutual value creation with the firm. Not only economic and instrumental, but also normative

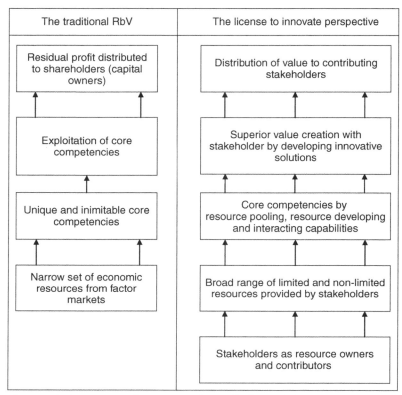

Figure 7.4 Comparison between traditional RbV and the license to innovate

and social aspects matter. Providing these resources, the stakeholders also participate in the value distribution based on their resource contribution.

As to the firm's strategies, the perspective of the license to innovate offers three types of core competencies: resource pooling, resource development and interacting capabilities. This allows superior value creation with and for stakeholders by developing innovative solutions. In the perspective of the license to innovate, the resource-based view (RbV) is developed to a resource owner view.

8 | *License to compete*

Content of the license to compete

From the perspective of the license to compete, the focus is on the roles of the firm and its stakeholders in their environment. In the traditional strategy theory, an environment-oriented perspective is taken by the ISV, which is concerned with the positioning of competing firms and how market structures and market forces influence the firm's success. The firm is seen as an actor in an economic environment, more precisely in an attractive industry; stakeholders are not the focus as we discussed in Chapter 2.

In the perspective of the license to compete, we consider some elements of the traditional ISV. We rely on the concept of positioning and on the importance of the environment. The environment and especially the markets are not anonymous institutions, but are represented by different human beings forming groups or organizations as stakeholders (see Figure 4.1, p. 62). The firms and the stakeholders are interrelated by mutuality in networks, which implies various forms of positioning and cooperation between the firm and its stakeholders. The environment is consequently represented by stakeholder networks.

Environmental interactions are not seen as a fight between firms to reap economic rents from market participants, to threaten the actors in the industry and to strive for a quasi-monopoly in a zero-sum game.[1] Instead they are understood as a constant search to improve value creation for the firm and the stakeholders. Competition is considered as a source of active motivation not as threatening of competitors.

The cast of stakeholders: from the industry structure view to the dynamic network structure view

The nature of stakeholder networks

In the traditional ISV, the focal firm aims to find imperfect markets in an economically attractive industry, where competition is low and the chance of a monopolistic rent high. Five forces characterize such industries in the ISV, representing the threats of four types of stakeholders (new entrants, suppliers, customers, incumbents) and a more technical relationship, namely the substitution of products and services. The focus is on rivalry. These five forces challenge firms to reduce the bargaining power of suppliers and customers, hinder new entrants and oppose existing rivals from securing their own rents, and thus reflect a threat and reap mentality. Society is seen as a constraining factor on competition.

In their more recent publications, as already mentioned in Chapter 6, Porter and Kramer, the main representatives of the ISV, make a claim for a more comprehensive view and are searching for interdependencies between firms and the society.[2] But they still focus on trying to reduce constraints on competition in order to gain additional competitive advantages against rivals. From a similar perspective, other authors suggest cooperation as a source of competitive advantage.[3] However, the central argument of all these positions remains the same: the most important thing a corporation can do for society is to contribute to a prosperous economy by outperforming rivals.

With regard to the environment, in our understanding of the stakeholder paradigm we extend this view in two ways (see Chapter 5, pp. 81–82):

• First, we focus not only on the attractiveness of industries but on the attractiveness of stakeholder networks.
• Second, we assess the attractiveness of networks from the firm's as well as the stakeholders' perspective.

Thus, a firm may influence its network but the stakeholders in the network may also influence the firm.[4] These interactions are the essence of mutuality and an important strategic asset for firms and stakeholders.

The interactions may open benefit and risk potentials that can be included in a value creation between firm and stakeholders. Examples for benefit potentials are access to high quality information, identification and use of complementary benefits, risk reduction, differentiation potentials, economies of scale, access to competencies, cost reduction, loss prevention, innovation, trust enhancement, stimulation of motivation, etc. Risks in a network configuration can be cultural differences, opportunistic partners, different strategic interests, knowledge leakage, disproportional advantages, structural differences, barriers to exit, etc. Benefiting from the advantages of the stakeholder network includes the consideration of these risks. The license to compete perspective offers the opportunity to look more closely at the network view.

The attractiveness of stakeholder networks

The firms and stakeholders are challenged to build and to sustain an attractive network together. Sometimes they can choose with whom they want to interact, and which interactions and potentials they aim to base mutual value creation on. Sometimes the choices are inevitable, such as with local community or government agencies. In our case analysis in the telecommunication industry, we saw that the firms could not in fact build their antennas for the mobile phone network without cooperation with local citizen organizations and representatives of the environmental protection movement (see Chapter 6, p. 107).[5]

Thus, the attractiveness of a network is shaped by two aspects: first, the stakeholders, who the firm or any stakeholder can choose or who they have to accept; and second, the kind of relationships that can be built by positioning in of the network.

An example for this is the pharmaceutical firm Pfizer that we analyzed. As the pharmaceutical industry is highly regulated, the firm has "compulsory" stakeholders, such as the regulator or the agency for authorizing and reviewing therapeutic products. On the other hand, the firm has interactions with such stakeholders as physicians, patients, organizations or experts, which it is mostly free to choose. In order to better position itself in its stakeholder network, the pharmaceutical firm aimed to intensify the cooperation with some specific groups of physicians (see Chapter 5, pp. 82–83).[6]

As a firm normally belongs to a certain industry, its stakeholders typically act in or around this industry. However, the focus is not the industry but the network, which can include other industries or segments of society beyond the industry. This relativizes the focus of the traditional ISV on a specific industry. The healthcare insurer Suva, as an example, attempted to build a comprehensive network for its patients. It included not only physicians and rehabilitation specialists but also lawyers, the employer and the patient's family in the recovery and reintegration process (see pp. 148–149). Thus, stakeholder networks are often complex, as illustrated in Figure 5.5 (see p. 84).

The following characteristics might influence the attractiveness of a network for a firm or a stakeholder and are important for building it up and extending it:

- Size of the network
  Large networks usually contain more differentiated value creation activities than small ones. In large networks, there are also more indirect interactions among stakeholders, which can again contribute to value creation. However, there are possibly also more risk potentials. As an interview partner in the pharmaceutical industry confirmed:

From the perspective of our firm, an area of conflict is that on the one hand, cooperation with network partners promises reducing risks, but on the other hand, important stakeholders have reservations regarding the pharmaceutical companies as true cooperation partners.

- Importance of the stakeholder network
  Stakeholder networks can achieve varying degrees of acceptance, legitimacy, power and influence in the industry.[7] The newcomer Orange was part of a large international network in the liberalized Swiss telecom market. Thanks to its embeddedness in this network, Orange was able to be innovative and to quickly bring new products to the market.[8] One of the interview partners of the firm stated:

I think the group we belong to is very important for innovation. Clearly this group is necessary for giving us input, because our competitor also has access to a large international network.

- Form of interactions
  Networks have different forms of interaction among stakeholders such as communication, consultation, dialogue, partnership, etc.[9] Applying such highly differentiated forms of interaction influences the value creation of a firm and its stakeholders. The significance of a differentiated approach was also emphasized by one of our interview partners, as indicated by the following quote:

We have the task of looking at the whole customer relationship; we don't just look at the customer–supplier relationship but also the reverse. This means involving ourselves in partnerships with these customers.

- Embeddedness and match quality
  Embeddedness in a network can be based on various types of exchanges, such as information, material, experiences, emotions, etc. Network participants may complement each other in these respects by sharing skills and activities.[10] The better the expectations and potentials of the actors match and the better they know each other, the closer the ties between them are.[11] However, relations that are too close can lead to "network rigidities" (see p. 145).[12]

- Configuration of the network
  A network may be strongly oriented to a dominant participant or may be composed of equal stakeholders.[13] This impacts also the question of leadership (see Chapter 9, pp. 167–171). In our empirical studies it was obvious that in cases in which value creation is intense and heavily exposed to public view, it is necessary that the firm and the stakeholders regard each other as equal partners.

- Value creating capability of individual firm and stakeholders
  Participants in a network fulfill a specific function in connection to each other. Those with specific value creation capability can increase the worth of the network for the others; weak ones can decrease it.[14]

- Stability and durability
  Long lasting relationships with positive past experiences can enhance the network ties among the constituencies, and therefore lead to economic and social advantages.[15] However, such ties can also suffer from fast and frequent changes in the stakeholder network. For example, the frequent entering and exiting of stakeholders in networks causes uncertainty, and is especially worrying for employees and investors of specific interest groups. Such unstable social contracts might negatively influence mutual value creation. In contrast, stable networks are important assets,[16] as the following quotation of an interviewee confirms:

We see the suppliers as partners and together we want to achieve as much good as possible. A supplier has truly to disappoint us before we exclude them. We build up partnership relations over long periods.

Continuous reinforcement of the network ties becomes an important task for participants.
• Threat or support
  In a stakeholder network, the different members can be more
  or less willing to make contributions and enhance mutual value
  creation.[17] Accordingly, different emotional forces, such as trust,
  mistrust, enthusiasm, etc., impact the mutual value creation of
  the stakeholders. In our interviews we observed that there is a
  growing awareness to engage with such emotional forces:

I think we can create the expertise and dedicate resources, which means
dedicating people to talk and to work with the different stakeholders ...
with people who would be really committed to developing relationships
and understanding and to working together on a common strategic project
or on a common vision.

Dynamics of stakeholder networks

As mentioned in Chapter 7, stakeholder networks are not static
and stable structures. Our case analyses showed that a significant
dynamic occurs and influences the license to compete. This was also
obvious in the telecom industry, when it was privatized (see also
p. 144). Stakeholder relations come about, evolve and sometimes dis-
appear over time.

The beginning and evolution of stakeholder networks can be
described along three distinguishable phases: "Negotiations to create
the network, enforcement and enlargement."[18] The network continuously evolves when stakeholders enter or exit the network. In addition, changes can occur regarding the ties, and the intensity and the
type of stakeholder contributions. Both the membership and boundaries of stakeholder networks are accordingly dynamic.

By analogy and concluding from successful mergers and acquisitions, we expect that firms and stakeholders that have positive experiences in building, adapting and handling networks are in a better
position to pursue mutual value creation with others than those who
have no such experience and knowledge or have experienced risk in
such networks.[19]

By extending the environmental perspective of the ISV, as mentioned
above, a broader and changing range of stakeholders is considered.

The traditional industry structure view becomes a dynamic network structure view.

Mutual value creation: positioning in and among stakeholder networks

Forms of positioning

The environment seen as stakeholder network implies a more comprehensive understanding of positioning than is understood in traditional strategy theory. In Chapter 5 (pp. 82–83), we mentioned two basic positions a firm or a stakeholder has to consider:

• Position in a stakeholder network
  The firm or stakeholder can have different and changing positions and relations to other network participants. In large networks where complex direct and indirect relations exist, neither the firm nor any other stakeholder is by definition always the center of the stakeholder network.[20] The position in a network can change over time. Firms and also stakeholders need to interact in order to clarify their positions and the changes in the networks.
  In this realm, Butterfield *et al.* discuss how and why stakeholder groups form collaborative alliances by taking into account the motivation of the stakeholders and the development of the alliances.[21] Savage *et al.* emphasize three general factors that motivate organizations to seek partnerships, namely achievements that could not be accomplished in any other way, mutual problem solving and an adaptive advantage.[22]
  Firms and also stakeholders sometimes have to position themselves vis-à-vis stakeholders who are part of a competing stakeholder network. Two pharmaceutical companies may have relationships to the same physicians. In this case, it is important that the focal firms can motivate the physicians to contribute to product development. Thus, the goal is the motivation of mutual value creation for a better quality of life and not the fight to reap rents.

• Positioning between the stakeholder networks
  This relates to the comparison of similar value creation processes among the participating stakeholder networks. It means a new interpretation of competition in comparison to ISV, namely

benchmarking between networks. The goal of this benchmarking is different from pure competition. First of all, it should stimulate motivation for improving the value creation of the networks; rent reaping should not be the center of attention. Further, this benchmarking is not focused only on monetary value, but rather includes all the benefits and risks of the participants. In this way a high degree of transparency is achieved regarding the quality of value creation for the participating networks. On this basis, firm and stakeholders can decide which network they prefer, where they can best actualize their potential and in which network they are better able to follow their goals. Networks that fail to attract, or lose, important stakeholders due to a lack of quality must massively improve their attractiveness or they will be eliminated sooner or later. Their contribution to the quality of life is judged to be insufficient.

The financial crisis has shown, dramatically, how complete and primarily transparent benchmarking between banks and their networks occurs. When, during the crisis, more complete and transparent information on the partly unfriendly behavior toward stakeholders became apparent, the stakeholders drastically changed their priorities regarding the various banks. For example, on the basis of its mistakes, which were suddenly transparent for the stakeholder, UBS experienced a large drain of capital as well as employees. In addition, investors pulled back so that its stock sank to one-fifth of its previous value.[23] Important shareholders changed to other, less negatively regarded banks. UBS would have even gone bankrupt, had the Swiss government not made the decision to support it, as it was considered too big to fail (see Chapter 6, pp. 95–97). Only the intervention of the state gave the UBS network the opportunity to improve the quality of its value creation and thus continue to exist.

Making comparisons between different stakeholder networks is undoubtedly demanding, and thus far we do not have much experience. However, such comparisons are necessary in order to avoid one-sidedness, mistakes and bias.

Benefit and risk potentials in stakeholder networks

From the point of view of a specific firm or stakeholder, the value creation contribution of individual network members can be evaluated by an analysis of the benefits and risks that stakeholders can potentially contribute. For example, in one of our case studies, the following risk and benefit potentials on the basis of stakeholder interactions (Table 8.1, p. 142) were frequently mentioned by the interviewees of Pfizer, regarding the issue "access to innovative medicine" (see Chapter 5, p. 86).[24]

To illustrate Table 8.1, an interviewee of a pharmaceutical firm explained:

The prominent benefit potential lies in the opportunity for better cooperation with the partners in the stakeholder network. But the gap between the possible and previous cooperation potential is still conspicuously large.

As an example, the benefit and risk potentials of a firm's supplier can be shown as in Figure 8.1 (see p. 143).

Network participants can contribute directly to each other, or indirect effects can occur. A network participant can, for example, (positively or negatively) motivate another stakeholder, and therefore can indirectly affect a firm. When Shell wanted to dispose of Brent Spar in the North Atlantic, Greenpeace stepped in and prevented the sinking of the storage buoy (see Chapter 6, pp. 102, 106–107).[25] Based on this intervention other stakeholders (e.g. customers and even governments) reacted negatively, which in turn affected Shell.

Moreover, benefits and risks result not only from the interactions among the stakeholders, but also from the characteristics mentioned above of the network as a whole (see pp. 136–138). For example, if the size of a network increased, then this could lead to changes in the benefits and risks of the individual members of the network.[26]

Network connections therefore have many positive and negative effects on mutual value creation. It is important for the firm and its stakeholders to clarify the benefit and risk potentials connected with direct and indirect interactions, and to consider them when developing strategies.

Multiple roles of stakeholders

The complexity of a stakeholder network is particularly increased, if individual network participants carry out more than one role in the network, as we already mentioned in Chapter 5 (p. 88).

Table 8.1 Benefit and risk potentials

Benefit potentials	Number of mentions	Percentage of mentions	Risk potentials	Number of mentions	Percentage of mentions
Cooperation	151	43	Cooperation	59	20
Information	71	20	Possibility to influence	37	13
Building trust	24	7	Dependency	33	11
Possibility to influence	21	6	Transparency	25	8
Improved service quality	16	5	Information	23	8
Image	10	3	Image	12	4
Credibility	9	3	Credibility	11	4
Lobbying	9	3	Building trust	8	3
Transparency	8	2	Economic contribution	8	3
Political cooperation	7	2	Political pressure	7	2

Note: Table 8.1 shows the top ten benefit and risk potentials out of some twenty in absolute figures (number of mentions) and percentages of mentions by the interviewees of Pfizer regarding the issue "access to innovative medicine."

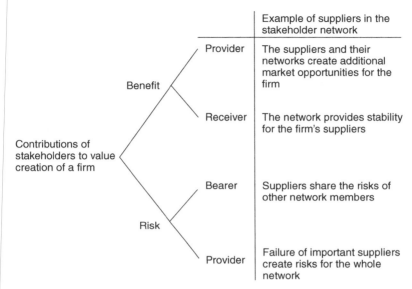

Figure 8.1 Types of stakeholder contributions

Multifunctionality leads to multiple positioning. In such cases, the important question is how multifunctional stakeholders organize and use their multiple and partly contradicting roles in the network to reduce complexity and contradictions. Other questions that may arise are how these stakeholders avoid conflicts of interests and contradictions in their behavior, and how these multiple roles are coordinated by the stakeholders or the firm. And finally, it is also important to assess how other strategically important stakeholders perceive the multifunctional stakeholder's potential to impact the network. As an example in the case of Swisscom, the national government plays three different roles for the newly privatized telecom firm. At the same time, it is the major shareholder, the regulator and one of the most important customers, so that the perspective of all three licenses is relevant. The firm was well aware of this fact but did not consider it to be a problem as the relationships were institutionalized through different units, tools and processes. For some time, this multifunctionality did not pose any problems as the government did not interfere with the firm's business decisions. However, it turned out that the firm had underestimated this multifunctionality: a few years later, the tables turned as the government vetoed the firm's plans to acquire another telecom firm and to expand abroad. The government based its decision not only on its role as the major shareholder, but also enforced by its power as key customer and as regulator.[27]

Therefore, it is relevant to clarify whether there is multifunctionality in the stakeholder relations, and whether there are complementary or conflicting benefit and risk potentials in the network for mutual value creation. For example, we have seen such conflicts in our case research with the bank ZKB. Should this firm, when contracting with suppliers, consider whether a potential contractor is one of its customers, or not? In the case in which a potential contractor is a customer, should it turn down a better offer from a non-customer?[28]

Positioning on the continuum between cooperation and confrontation

The original ISV focuses on confrontation. In this perspective firms are intent on outperforming rivals. In contrast, the license to compete concentrates on the idea of mutuality in stakeholder networks that asks for a new understanding of competition and cooperation.

Within the continuum between total confrontation and complete cooperation, among firm and stakeholders there are zones of common interests. Within them many moderate forms of cooperation are possible, which promise a superior value than the extremes. In any given situation, firms and stakeholders have to identify these zones, to expand them and encourage interactions with each other in these zones. They must find a balance between total confrontation and total cooperation in their interactions. The necessity of such a balance was confirmed by an interview partner who was faced with a powerful competitor:

It is a fact that one cannot act without taking one's biggest competitor into consideration. This means finding a fine balance between the competitive challenge and how one can get along with a very powerful partner in a somewhat friendly atmosphere ... This means that one cannot drive the competition beyond reasonable limits.

The degree of cooperation that best suits value creation not only depends on the interest of the firm but also on its stakeholders. As already presented in Table 8.1, our research has shown that in the perception of the firms, the potential of cooperation was identified as the most important source of benefit in the perspective of the license to compete (see p. 143).

Cooperation may not only lead to benefits but may also be connected with risks; therefore cooperation partners are not only benefit, but also risk providers. Possible risks include opportunistic behavior at the expense of others, cultural differences, knowledge and core competence leakage, heterogeneous priorities, etc. Uzzi even believes that network relations that become too close will decrease the diversity of the network partners and therefore its value.[29] Too close relations can lead to "network rigidities." "Network rigidities" can appear if some network partners oppose necessary adaptations; for instance, if they hinder stakeholders with new ideas from entering the network, or if they oppose the exclusion of network participants. This harms the network's license to compete.

Among others, Brandenburger and Nalebuff, in a purely economic perspective point out that competitive behavior not only brings about advantages but also costs and risks, which could be avoided through cooperation.[30] For example, they mention the hidden costs of competitive behavior, such as falling prices and margins, which will then serve as benchmarks for both customers and new competitors. Therefore, they see a mix of cooperation and competition, called coopetition, as the better solution.

From the different aspects and examples discussed in this paragraph, with regard to positioning between confrontation and cooperation in stakeholder networks, different solutions represent varying degrees of cooperation. They represent the different positions and outcomes, from which management must choose in developing strategy, thus influencing to a large extent the firm's and stakeholders' license to compete.

Value distribution to stakeholders from the perspective of the license to compete

Following our understanding of the stakeholder paradigm, the value creation of a firm impacts the value distribution for engaged stakeholders. In the perspective of the license to compete, the value distribution aspect can be exemplified by looking at how in the

traditional ISV strategies the values of the most important stakeholders, such as customers, employees and investors, can be affected
differently:

• From the point of view of investors, positioning for example as a
  cost leader can be attractive, if it leads to an improved profit margin
  and finally to an improved residual profit. For employees, positioning as a cost leader may result in stressful performance pressure
  and low pay.
• Positioning as a differentiator can open attractive professional
  development opportunities for employees. However it can be
  unattractive for investors, when instead of paying out dividends
  the firm has high research and development expenditures, in order
  to achieve a level of differentiation that is attractive for employees
  and customers.

As to the residual profit, the traditional ISV follows the economic
theory of the firm by considering exclusively owners (shareholders) as
receivers. In the newer publications on ISV, a first step is being made
in the direction of broader value distribution so that society can benefit from the firms' potentials.[31] Thus, the relations between firms and
society not merely prevent harm but improve social conditions. But
despite the acceptance of the community as a benefit receiver, value
distribution to all stakeholders in the firm's network has not yet been
considered in these newer publications.[32]

In contrast to this rather narrow understanding of value distribution, we could observe other kinds of value distribution to stakeholders in the firm's network. As an example, since their founding, state
or partially state-owned firms have at times, and due to their specific
position, implemented value distribution to a wide range of stakeholders. As a result of high profits, the accident insurer Suva, one of
the firms we analyzed with a public mandate, reduced the premiums
of its clients by 5 percent, with the clear intention of letting them
participate in its annual profit.[33] But there are also private insurance
corporations that grant their customers a premium bonus as the result
of a good business year. Value in the form of a loyalty bonus is sometimes also given to long-term customers. From the perspective of the
license to compete, the portion a participant receives in value dissemination is based on the contribution made, based on the position in
the network.[34]

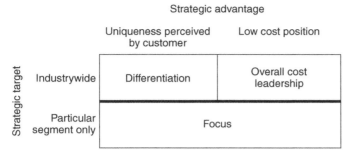

Figure 8.2 Three generic strategies (source: Porter, 1980: 39)

Generic strategies from the perspective of the license to compete

In the traditional ISV it is assumed that the strategic success of a firm, aside from the attractiveness of the industry, also depends on the trade-off decisions of the management, which are expressed in the choice of activities in the generic strategies of cost leadership, differentiation or focus on market niches (see Figure 8.2). These three strategic options refer exclusively to the customer perspective. "At the heart of any strategy is a unique value proposition; a set of needs a company can meet for its chosen customers that others cannot."[35] Strategies bring the customer either the lowest prices, the functionally best product or serve niches that had previously been neglected. For each case, the customer is the decisive factor for the type of strategy in the ISV; therefore this perspective addresses one specific stakeholder.

Extending these three generic strategies of the traditional ISV in the perspective of the license to compete, one can develop the following strategies for mutual value creation:

- Risk reducing strategy

  The firm and stakeholders can keep the sum of the risks as small as possible. Costs for the firm are not the only criteria, as was the case in the original cost leadership strategy of the ISV, but rather all the categories of risks of the relevant stakeholders in the network. Orange, one of the telecom firms we analyzed, discussed the strategy of locating new antennas together with the residents, thus trying to find solutions that were acceptable for both parties. Such a solution reduced the risk of the residents to suffer from negative effects, and on the other hand, reduced the costs for the firm that would have resulted from a legal battle and the ensuing image loss (see p. 136).[36]

- Benefit enhancing strategy
  Extending the original differentiation strategy of traditional ISV, the strategy is characterized not only by the specific characteristics of products or services from the perspective of the customer, but by the total benefits for the firm and all its relevant stakeholders. Suva, the insurance company we analyzed, implemented so-called New Case Management as we already mentioned above (pp. 135– 136). When customers have an accident, in addition to receiving the best medical care, their families, their employers, the physicians and hospitals, and the case manager are all involved in the recovery process. Thanks to this approach, accident victims are able to retain their jobs and to be re-integrated into the work process more quickly and comprehensively than before, benefiting not only the patient but also the firms and society.[37] Figure 8.3 illustrates the stakeholder value chain of Suva's New Case Management, embedded in its stakeholder network.

- Focusing on specific stakeholder categories
  The original niche strategy of the ISV can be extended in that it increases benefits or reduces risk for specific segments of stakeholders. These stakeholders previously received little notice, but are of special importance for a network or are related to a specific issue. An example of a focus strategy for a specific segment in the financial sector, are institutions that provide microfinance (MFIs) in poor areas of the world. Through this kind of focused financing, new stakeholder groups can be bound into mutual value creation, and thereby open largely neglected market niches. Thanks to MFIs, people can develop financial literacy, a livelihood, and organizational and technical skills for professional services.
  In the course of our research, we had the opportunity to see that microfinance takes place in very specific network structures. Three different stakeholder environment sectors can be distinguished in the microfinance stakeholder network. First, the professional environment represents the business world that supports the function of MFIs to provide loans and services to the poor. Second,

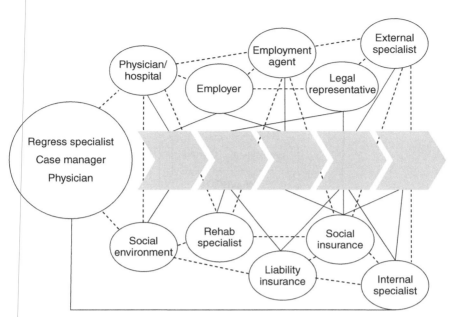

Figure 8.3 The stakeholder network of Suva's New Case Management (source: illustration by Suva)

the customers' environment is reflected in the self-help groups and their families. And third, the network consists of social stakeholders who are representatives or advocates of the society at large, such as the government or the media (see Figure 8.4).[38]

All three of the above mentioned strategies aim at achieving superior value in the stakeholder network through mutual value creation. In the perspective of the license to compete, the traditional generic strategies of ISV can be developed further. This can be illustrated as in Figure 8.5, analogous to the illustration of the traditional ISV (see p. 147).

Evaluation from the perspective of the license to compete

As already shown in Chapter 2, the original ISV was oriented to finding strategies that increase and protect the financial strategic rent of the firm: "Industry structure, as manifested in the strength of the five

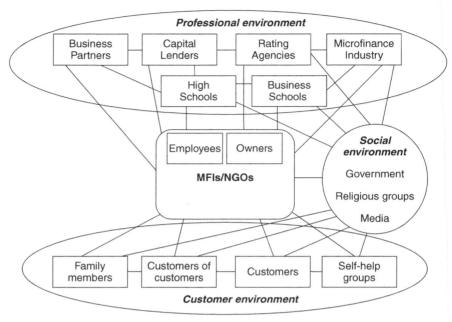

Figure 8.4 Stakeholder network of microfinance institutions (MFIs) (source: Sachs, Rühli, Moser, Krishnan & Lakshman, 2010: 2)

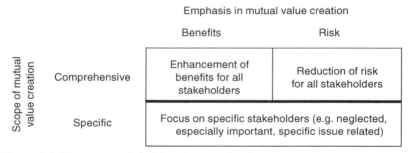

Figure 8.5 Focus on stakeholders in mutual value creation

competitive forces, determines the industry's long-run profit potential because it determines how the economic value created by the industry is divided – how much is retained by companies in the industry versus bargained away by customers and suppliers, limited by substitutes or constrained by potential new entrants."[39]

As mentioned in several places in this book, the stakeholder paradigm sees the evaluation of mutual value creation not only from the perspective of economic rents for the providers of capital, but in relation to the engagement of all the stakeholders in the network. From the perspective of the license to compete, the evaluation includes a wider spectrum of benefits and risks, which are connected with the positioning of every stakeholder (see Figure 8.5). Thus, when the values of certain strategies or types of strategy are to be judged, the mutually agreed components of values for all contributing stakeholders in the network are to be considered. The same type of evaluation counts also for the appraisal of the output of specific strategic issues in a firm, such as cost reduction programs involving laying-off employees, outsourcing or mergers and acquisitions. Once again monetary benefits for a single or for a few stakeholders (e.g. managers or investors) are not the focus, but rather the broad value creation effects in the whole network. For example, when GM in the United States decided to close some plants of its subsidiary Opel in Germany at the beginning of 2010, the criteria of success for doing so could not just be reducing costs for the benefit of the owner, in this case for the parent company GM (see Chapter 6, p. 108).[40] This case rather shows that such strategic measures must also include the loss of manifold know-how potentials, the breaking of social contracts, image damage to GM, and even the disadvantages of a political conflict between the United States and Germany. Such aspects must also be part of an accurate appraisal of the situation.

Aside from the outcomes, the processes in relation to positioning in networks are also part of the evaluation in the perspective of the license to compete. These parts of an evaluation are not yet developed in depth, neither in research nor in practical application. We suggest that two aspects be taken into consideration in this realm: first, positioning and repositioning of the firm and the stakeholders in a network view; and second, benchmarking to compare the value creation process between different stakeholder networks.

Concluding remarks on the license to compete

Our understanding of the stakeholder paradigm conceives the firm's and stakeholders' positioning in networks, which broadens and

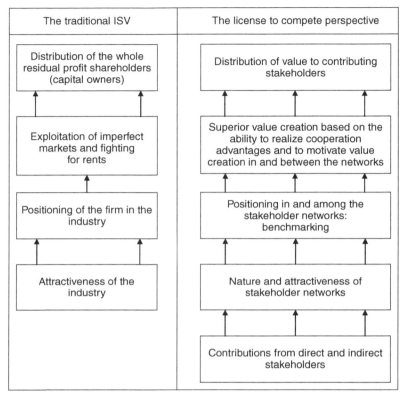

Figure 8.6 Comparison between traditional ISV and the license to compete

deepens the causalities considered in the traditional ISV and adds new perspectives (see Figure 8.6).

In the license to compete perspective, the environment is conceptualized in a network view. The participants in these networks are firms and their stakeholders who are involved in the value creation, and consequently in value distribution based on multiple and changing positions.

Positioning in the environment is no longer a fight against rivals in the industry to eliminate competitors and reach monopolistic advantages. It is characterized by mutuality and the striving for benefits with and for stakeholders, improving the quality of life of human beings and the sustainability of the natural world. Based on these insights, the three former generic strategies of the ISV can be extended to strengthen the license to compete and to contribute to a firm's mutual value creation with and for its stakeholders. The former industry structure view of strategy is developed to a dynamic network view of strategy.

9 | *Challenges resulting from a paradigm shift*

In the course of this book, we have shown how different contributions in the research literature and empirical studies have stimulated our understanding of the stakeholder paradigm. We have also seen various aspects and examples of mutual value creation between firms and stakeholders that conform to this new paradigm, which we developed in more detail in Chapters 6 to 8. The questions remain how such a paradigm shift can occur within the present economic system, and what the main challenges of such a course might be. A vision for a strategy to achieve mutual value creation in society is required, and our aim is to contribute to it (see Chapter 1).

What are the main challenges for the required change?

We are aware that such a paradigm shift not only means changes for firms and stakeholders, but also impacts the economic system. Without doubt such changes and challenges will not only find support, therefore some hindering factors also need to be considered. The *Wall Street Journal* published a statement that emphasizes one such factor, namely a narrow economic view: "In the end, social responsibility is a financial calculation for executives, just like any other aspect of their business. The only sure way to influence corporate decision making is to impose an unacceptable cost – regulatory mandates, taxes, punitive fines, public embarrassment – on socially unacceptable behavior."[1]

We have developed a possible agenda for change and the impacts of a paradigm shift. In the following, we discuss this as shown in Figure 9.1. In the next section, we first look at possible patterns and processes of change. We then focus on some economic, cultural and structural impacts that the change toward a new stakeholder paradigm may induce, and connect them to avenues of future development (Figure 9.1).

154

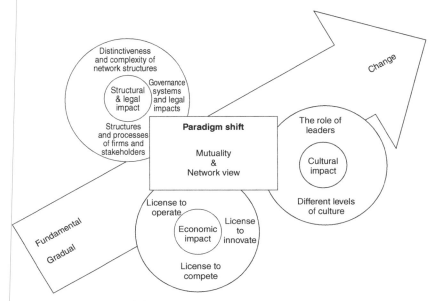

Figure 9.1 Impacts of change processes

What are basic change patterns and processes?

For a deeper understanding of how necessary changes can occur, we refer to evolutionary theory.[2] We apply the insights of the various evolutionary theories (biological, economic and social), not by emphasizing their analogical aspects, but by considering their underlying principles.[3]

General principle of change

Evolutionary theory provides a basic and essential way of thinking about how firms and stakeholders can foster greater mutual value creation in the twenty-first century. Two patterns of evolution are fundamental to our thinking: continuity by gradual change,[4] and discontinuity by fundamental change.[5] Also social evolutionary theories focus on understanding and explaining change of organizations and the inertia hindering it.[6] Hannan and Freeman[7] presuppose that the adaptability of organizations is always limited, due to pushing or inhibiting factors that can enable or hinder change processes.[8]

Depending on these factors, organizations tend either toward iner-tia or an ability to learn.[9] Previous developments that explain path dependencies of organizations regarding inertia or an ability to learn are studied in this literature.[10] Path dependencies refer to the interac-tions between patterns of changes from the past and those from the present or the future.[11] Initial events can stimulate or restrain pre-sent and future patterns of evolution. Continuous gradual changes are compared to discontinuous and fundamental changes of organi-zations. The different kinds of changes of any kind of organization, including firms and stakeholders, offer insights on how a paradigm shift can take place, such as we propose in this book.

Gradual change

Indicative of continuous and gradual change is the survival of organi-zations that develop continuously in small steps.[12] Quinn, studying strategic change of firms, calls this type of change logical incremen-talism, which means purposeful, gradual strategy implementation by experimentation and learning from partial commitments. Several conditions and forces can be relevant for gradual, non-disruptive change (uncertainty, acceptability, experimentation possibilities, pol-itics, etc.).[13]

In our longitudinal case studies we could observe that since the early 1970s there has been a continuous increase in the consideration of an ever-broader cast of stakeholders by firms. Due to environmen-tal and social concerns and to globalization, new forms of organiza-tions such as NGOs and CSOs have evolved and become established. Furthermore, new kinds of tools (e.g. stakeholder mapping), depart-ments (e.g. public affairs) and processes (e.g. stakeholder engagement) have been developed. Corporations have started to publish sustain-ability reports (e.g. Global Reporting Initiative[14]) and signed stand-ards (e.g. Global Compact[15]) or founded roundtables (e.g. corporation 20/20[16]).[17] In the area of undergraduate, graduate and executive pro-grams in business schools, new courses for sustainability, CSR and stakeholder management have been established. In a similar way, other kinds of organizations, such as NGOs, the media, etc., have developed greater organizational capabilities in recent years, and have involved themselves with a broader cast of stakeholders to pursue their purposes (see Chapter 6, pp. 98–102, 104).

However, these gradual and continuous changes often remained within the narrow limits of the economic paradigm and were often labeled as add-ons[18] or window-dressing activities of firms.[19] Nevertheless, over time, gradual and continuous change can lead toward the stakeholder paradigm.

Fundamental changes

Indicative of discontinuous and fundamental change is the inertia of basic structures of organizations, also called "deep structure" by Gersick,[20] despite radical changes in the environment.[21] The inertia theory explains the increased resistance to change in some cases by the advanced age of organizations.[22] One important explanation is that over time successful organizations tend to reinforce their values and norms with strong myths and legends so that adapting to changing conditions becomes difficult.[23] Sometimes, organizational routines are created to which the members of an organization resort, especially in uncertain situations.[24] Thus, uncertainty can be reduced and anxiety can be controlled by routine actions.

However, inertia can lead to a situation becoming entrenched. It can result in the demise of the organization, or the situation is overcome by an act of fundamental change. Johnson *et al.* have observed this phenomenon in the perspective of corporate strategy and call it strategic drift: "the tendency for strategies to develop incrementally on the basis of historical and cultural influences but fail to keep pace with a changing environment."[25] This concept is similar to what Leonard-Barton calls core rigidities,[26] and can occur if former core competencies are not adapted to new situations.[27]

Regarding the inertia of organizations, we emphasized in Chapters 1 and 2 that the basic assumptions of the economic theory are a strong determinant of the deep structure of today's firms, and shape the current understanding of strategic management. The successful development of firms, and the growing economic prosperity over decades in a Western context, is an example of a successful development, leading to inertia that impacts the whole economy. Despite increasing criticism of neoliberal economic systems, necessary changes have not taken place. The inertia of deep structures of the economy was even reinforced by the fall of the Berlin Wall, considered a symbol of the victory of the free market over Communism.

When in recent years new challenges arose in the form of social expectations, especially as a result of corporate scandals and the financial crisis, members of organizations mostly tended to rely on the deep structures that had been successful in the past. In this sense over the last decades, firms experienced that the orientation to the goal of making profit for the financial owner was the driver for growing prosperity, in what Reich called the Golden Age.[28]

Thinking in the economic paradigm not only applies to firms, but has been extended to the whole society, and is called economic imperialism.[29] The deep structures of the economic paradigm are primarily present in the pressure for quantification and measurability, which led to the short-term orientation of corporate financial reports that have to be presented every three months. In recent times only those solutions were considered successful that could be quantified. This has also impacted on other kinds of organizations, such as the media, or non-profit organizations, such as hospitals, that are under increased pressure to perform successfully also in financial terms.[30]

Evolutionary research has shown that sometimes systems destroy themselves by applying their behavioral principles in an exaggerated manner. Excessive short-term shareholder-value thinking can also prevent necessary adaptations and lead capitalism to destroy itself.[31] This primarily quantitative understanding of welfare is now criticized even by economists.[32] And CEOs, such as Jack Welsh or Paul Paulson, have started to doubt the adequacy of the shareholder value orientation.

As the current economic paradigm is challenged by fundamental developments in society (see Chapter 1, pp. 1–6) the question arises if we are not at a crossroad. And the way to overcome the inertia of firms and other organizations is to make a disruptive paradigm shift instead of marginal adaptations.

Three basic learning processes

With respect to gradual and fundamental change, we developed three types of learning processes.[33] These processes offer possible ways for a shift toward the proposed new paradigm to take place:

- Adaptive learning involves adjusting routines and practices to avoid known mistakes and taking advantage of recognized opportunities. Processes and behavior are modified within an essentially unchanged configuration of corporate strategy, structure and culture. These learning processes are based on the corporation's traditional core values, which also influence whether or not the firm strives for a stakeholder orientation within value creation. Adaptive learning typically consists of multiple and continuous single learning loops.

The learning process we have observed so far of the finance industry after the financial crisis seems to be adaptive. As an example, UBS, the largest bank in Switzerland, induced a reduction of its total assets and risks, reformed its system of compensation, focused the investment banking on customer oriented activities, reduced proprietary trading and strengthened internal controls regarding compliance with regulations. These measures lessened some of the weaknesses, but the basic problem remains. A bank of this size is existential for the economic and social system; it is "too big to fail" (see Chapter 6, p. 95). Suggestions made by experts to change the basic structure of the company were not accepted. Which parts of it (e.g. investment banking) could go bankrupt, while other parts of the company (e.g. wholesale banking) could survive?[34]

• Renewal learning involves evolutionary and proactive behavior, including the re-examination of assumptions and cognitive frameworks. Basic values and goals may be pursued in new ways, involving noticeable changes mostly in strategies and structures. The expectations of relevant stakeholders can induce this type of learning processes. Renewal learning consists of both single- and double-loop learning.[35] This type of learning can therefore be seen as a step between transformational (see below, pp. 160–161) and adaptive learning. Renewal learning can be differentiated from adaptive learning, by including double-loop learning and changing one or two of the corporate core's elements respectively (strategy, structure). And it can be differentiated from transformational learning, in that one of the core elements, primarily culture, remains mostly unchanged. Change remains gradual and does not affect the core values.

As we mentioned in the previous chapter, until recently pharmaceutical corporations such as Pfizer did not systematically regard their stakeholders as partners. The relationships to the stakeholders were kept to the minimum required by government regulations. Due to increasing pressures in the healthcare system, but also because of criticism outside the organization, Pfizer decided to react (see Chapter 5, p. 86).[36] In order to ensure a continuous flow of new medicines, they realized that contributions from their stakeholder network were particularly important. Due to these learning processes, Pfizer adopted a broader, stakeholder-oriented strategy and reformulated its vision and procedures accordingly. The process is still underway to implement a broader stakeholder orientation and to adapt the core values, in order to make the step from renewable to transformational learning.[37]

• Transformational learning involves fundamental change within the organization, to increase the probability of success within a changing environment. Often transformational learning is induced by wake-up calls. This type of learning may lead to substantial, even disruptive change of the deep structure within an organization, including change in core values. Significant discontinuities can force such learning, and may induce changes in an organization's strategy, structure and culture.[38] Transformational learning is characterized by higher level learning,[39] meaning that norms, assumptions and frames of references are questioned. Such double-loop or even deutero-learning is necessary, in order to implement generative change in all three elements of the corporate core.[40] This type of learning is necessary for a fundamental change toward a new paradigm.

For many years, corporations in the oil industry have been confronted with wake-up calls: Exxon Mobil with the Valdez disaster in 1989, Shell with the planned sinking of the Brent Spar oil tanks in the North Sea in 1995 (see Chapter 6, pp. 106–107) and recently BP with the explosion of the drill platform Deepwater Horizon in the Gulf of Mexico in 2010 (see Chapter 6, pp. 109–110). The comparison of Brent Spar (Shell) with Deepwater Horizon (BP) reveals a number of parallels: in 2010 the British firm BP was the leading oil producer in the United States and in the Gulf of Mexico. In 1995 Shell was the largest European corporate group and one of the largest multinational corporations (MNC) in the world. In the company report of 2009, BP described, "working in the border areas of the energy business" as its core competence, and was regarded as an ecologically aware oil company. Before 1995, Shell was also considered to be an efficiently run oil firm, with outstanding technological abilities and particularly conscientious regarding ecological sustainability. The positive image of Shell as well as BP was destroyed in one blow. In these crisis situations, both corporations were unable to adequately address human beings and their concerns. Both corporations apologized and adopted new tactics, only after massive pressure from social and political stakeholders. After 1995 Shell embarked on a process of transformational learning.[41] It remains to be seen whether BP will also go through a transformational learning process. In both cases, adaptive learning does not appear to be enough. Not only are the oil companies challenged to undergo transformational learning processes, but also other stakeholders (suppliers, business partners, political authorities, etc.) involved in value creation in the field of energy, in order to keep their licenses.

All kinds of change (strategy, structure and culture) also influence the firm's and stakeholders' embeddedness in the stakeholder network. Whether change is gradual (adaptive, renewal) or fundamental (transformational), it is always path-dependent as stated above.

The fundamental changes we suggest can hardly be fully realized by adaptive learning of firms or stakeholders. A fundamental rethink in the sense of transformational learning is indispensable, at all these levels including that of the economic system. In this respect, Lenssen *et al.* point out that, "A 'plumber's fix' approach to a flawed system can at best give only temporary relief."[42]

A paradigm shift is also advocated by Stiglitz from a similar perspective:

We now have the opportunity to create a new financial system that will do what human beings need a financial system to do: to create a new economic system that will create meaningful jobs, decent work for all those who want it, one in which the divide between haves and have nots is narrowing, rather than widening; and most importantly of all, to create a new society in which each individual is able to fulfill his aspiration and live up to his potential in which we have created citizens who live up to shared ideals and values, in which we have created a community that treats our planet with respect that in the long run it will surely demand.[43]

We can propose that a combination of forces is needed in society in order to move the world toward the stakeholder paradigm. Choices are being made every day that reinforce this trend and more are needed. Mutual value creation becomes a more powerful idea with each crisis, and more successful as a strategy as leaders in firms and in stakeholder organizations understand that value creation is fundamentally about mutuality. The continuing challenge of securing a license to operate, a license to innovate and a license to compete in a world of more people, organizations and purposes is moving people and organizations inexorably toward a new stakeholder paradigm.[44] In Chapters 6 to 8, we propose new perspectives and elements in firm and stakeholder strategies. But the realization of the stakeholder paradigm also requires the development of economic, cultural and legal/ structural aspects.

Economic impacts

Based on our reflections, we support the idea that there is a need to adapt the economic system as already proposed by Freeman *et al.*[45] and submit the following requirements.[46]

Requirements in the perspective of the license to operate

- The economic system must serve the society
  The society is the end and the economy is the means for mutual value creation. The economy exists to serve the quality of life, and not to exploit human beings. For example this requires new incentive structures in firms and even in stakeholder organizations, replacing the one-sided financial incentives.
- The economic system must support the firm and the stakeholders' professionalism to contribute in networks
  Firms and stakeholders do not always possess the necessary organizational capabilities to fulfill their expectations and potentials in mutual value creation. The fostering of organizational capabilities of all involved parties in stakeholder networks is thus fundamental for mutual value creation.
- The economic system must support sustainability and inclusiveness
  The forms and kinds of products and services, and the solutions of issues, should reflect the sustainable improvement of the quality of life for all human beings and the sustainability of the natural

world, and not a systematic advantage for firms or one stakeholder over others, for long periods of time.

Requirements in the perspective of the license to innovate

- The economic system must stimulate innovation by including a broad cast of stakeholders
  The development of innovative products and services, as well as solutions for all kinds of issues, has to be seen as the result of mutual value creation between firms and stakeholders in network structures. The economic system should facilitate bottom-up processes, and not only the voices of a few privileged stakeholders, but the expectations and potentials of the whole cast of engaged stakeholders.
- The economic system must acknowledge diversity as a driver for innovation
  The diversity of human beings and their respective interest and purposes must be respected and supported within the development of innovative solutions between firms and the stakeholders.
- The economic system must be rooted in extended property rights thinking
  The firm and the stakeholders are understood as owners of different kinds of resources, which they bring into networks of value creation. The ownership of those contributing has to be respected. Additionally, the value created is to be distributed between the firm and its stakeholders based on the participants' contributions of resources.

Requirements in the perspective of the license to compete

- Motivation to cooperate must be intensified by the economic system
  Both firms and stakeholders should have opportunities and incentives to contribute their potentials to mutual value creation in order to develop superior value for all involved parties.
- The economic system must focus on competition in the sense of benchmarking
  Developing transparent benchmarks of stakeholder networks is essential so that firms and the stakeholders can favor specific

networks for superior value creation. Competition is seen as a stimulant for the parties involved.

- The economic system must facilitate the idea of mutual value creation

  Mutual value creation means the interaction of a cast of stakeholders as indispensable contributors and receivers of benefit and risks. A one-sided orientation toward competition based on reaping rent has to be overcome in all markets.

Economists and regulatory policy-makers are challenged to create and support a coherent and accepted economic system that includes the requirements mentioned above. But also the way we theorize has to be adapted and we have to leave the "intellectual comfort zone" as Corley and Gioia are challenging the new generation of theories.[47]

An important focus has to be on ownership, as we have mentioned in several contexts. Thus far, traditional property rights theory concentrates on two elements: residual control and residual rights to income.[48] According to our extended property rights understanding, the orientation is to motivate more people and organizations to contribute to value creation as everybody is understood as an owner. Contribution can be in the form of transferring, exchanging or even enhancing resources that are owned by firms or stakeholders. Value distribution includes different forms of financial, material or immaterial compensation or any form of recognition. The focus on motivation for mutual value creation offers an enriched understanding of the multifaceted dimension of ownership, instead of concentrating on residual control rights and legal sanctions. Kim and Mahoney encouraged economic theory to move in a similar direction, as they submit an extension of the property right that offers an understanding of the value of knowledge, shared ownership, etc.[49]

Future research should provide more insights on how the requirements mentioned above can be realized in the economic system. And as Stiglitz states above, we now have the opportunity to do it.[50]

Cultural impacts

Pirson and Lawrence emphasize that corporate culture is interrelated with the paradigm that business is built on.[51] In the following we discuss how culture might support or hinder a shift to a stakeholder paradigm from two distinct angles: the levels of culture and the types of leadership.

Different levels of culture

We see different levels, namely the region, the industry, the firm and the group (department/business units), where cultural patterns exist that can influence a paradigm change in the understanding of mutual value creation:

- Region level

    With respect to the region level, Hofstede's[52] studies showed that values differed significantly across countries, since it is unlikely that there are universally accepted cultural norms.[53]

    In the case of Swiss Re, from a stakeholder perspective, three regionally oriented cultures co-existed in the company at the time of our investigation in 2003: the Swiss, the Anglo-Saxon and partly also the Asian. The Swiss have the European cultural focus on the customers and employees, while the Anglo-Saxon culture concentrates on earnings and the financial bottom line. The different cultures emerged as the business activities included increasingly different stakeholders, as a result of a global expansion and diversification strategy. The main challenge was to maintain some common core values for the company as a whole, while adjusting to local circumstances.[54]

    Regional differences in culture have been confirmed by an INSEAD empirical study based on the perceptions of managers, showing different cultural positions. German managers think that the firm has to concentrate on production to create value. Japanese counterparts focus on the employees and society as key stakeholders. American managers focus most clearly on shareholders.[55]

    Regional cultural differences also impact the importance attributed to mutuality in the value creation between firms and stakeholders. Veser shows in an empirical study that there are large differences between various regions with respect to the openness for mutuality.[56] Asian regions tend to be based more on mutuality, while Western regions tend to be based more on self-interest. Our research project concerning microfinance with Indian colleagues supported this tendency regarding the openness of firms and stakeholders, such as NGOs, for mutuality.[57]

- Industry level

  Christensen and Gordon[58] state that a lot of research indicates that organizations within different industries share distinct cultural values that are not random, but arise from similar industry demands.[59] In our empirical studies we also found such differences: the three firms in the telecom industry that we analyzed ranked innovation and the technological orientation of their culture first. The firms in the financial services industry had a predominantly sustainability orientation. The differences concerning industry cultures shape the way firms and stakeholders create value together.

- Organizational level

  At this level culture comprises a set of values, beliefs and behavior patterns.[60] Hall even identifies the corporate culture as a highly important intangible resource.[61] In our empirical research, we analyzed the basic orientations of the firms' culture. Some common patterns of cultural orientation turned out to be of similar importance for the different firms we interviewed, such as success and performance orientation and stakeholder orientation. With respect to stakeholder orientation,[62] the importance of the magic stakeholder triangle – customers, employees and shareholders – was also emphasized by all our cases for firms and stakeholder organizations.[63] Additionally, the importance of the local community orientation was emphasized.

  But there were also differences at the firm level: in our cases, old companies emphasized sustainability as their cultural orientation and also highlighted the importance of knowledge orientation, while young corporations were seeking brand orientation. And as young companies are often acting in rapidly changing environments, they do not yet have an established culture in the way older firms in the same industry have. These differences are also path dependent and represent driving or buffering factors for change in a firm's culture. Due to the insights of the social evolutionary theory mentioned above, one can assume that such path dependencies might be important for stakeholder organizations too.[64]

- Group level

  With respect to group level, there can be cultural differences between functional or professional groups within the organization.[65] Different cultures may co-exist, sometimes with one of the subcultures being dominant.[66] This co-existence of different subcultures in an organization emphasizes the complexity of the cultural impact for a paradigm shift. Therefore, firms or parts of them are not always consistent in the culture they are rooted in. The Swiss Re example illustrates this: different business units at Swiss Re in 2003 clearly had different cultures. These cultural differences could be explained at least in part by the different stakeholders that were strategically relevant for the respective business unit.[67]

We see a promising field of research concerning the importance of culture for paradigm change in mutual value creation between firms and stakeholders.

Role of leaders

Changes in firms, in stakeholder networks, as well as in stakeholder organizations can be strongly influenced by leaders and their understanding of their role. Jones *et al.* created several types of stakeholder culture that comprise beliefs, values and practices that leaders in firms use to manage stakeholder relations.[68] They are based on different ethical frameworks as foundations for decision-making.

Freeman *et al.* take a similar course by discussing different kinds of narratives of capitalism.[69] In the different narratives, they analyzed the dominance of one specific leading group such as the government, investors or managers. And they conclude, "The wishful thinking behind this view goes something like, 'If only we were all to just follow the right leading group and align our interests with theirs, the ills of capitalism would be solved, and we would become more prosperous'."[70] The Stakeholder Capitalism concept is a proposition on how to overcome the shortcomings of this thinking due to the jointness of the different leaders in value creation. We consider the argumentations of Freeman *et al.*[71] and Jones *et al.*[72] in the following to characterize the leaders' role. We distinguish four specific leadership types in firms, influencing cultures differently and having different views of stakeholders (Table 9.1, p. 168).

The self-performer is not promoted or grounded by any economic or strategy theory. These business leaders are regarded as stars, not only by the attention they get but also by their remuneration. Their

Table 9.1 *Different leadership types in firms*

	Types of leaders			
	Self-performer	Shareholder value performer	Instrumentalist	Mutual value creator
Narratives of capitalism	Managerial capitalism	Shareholder capitalism	Stakeholder Capitalism from the instrumental perspective	Stakeholder Capitalism as an integration of ethics and capitalism
Normative core	Egoism, self-interest	Utilitarianism, enlightened self-interest	Utilitarianism, enlightened self-interest, extended property rights	Extended property rights; Kantian claim; Fromm's understanding of motivation
Theoretical foundations	Not theory based	Strategy theory RbV/ISV	Stakeholder theory of the firm	Stakeholder Capitalism; stakeholder paradigm
Stakeholder orientation; focus on:	Managers in the firm, others as means for personal goals of managers	Shareholders (and managers in the firms) stakeholder contribution to profit accepted	All stakeholders that contribute to value creation are considered	Firms and stakeholders as owners of different kind of resources
Environment	Constraints of market and society to be excluded/repressed	Constraints of market and society accepted; failures exploited	Acceptance of constraints by market and society; constant search of business opportunities within these constraints	Firm as integral part of society; embeddedness in stakeholder networks

attitude impacts the way they interact with stakeholders, such as the shareholders, employees or customers. They consider these stakeholders only in terms of enhancing their personal value creation. They gamble with the interests of speculative shareholders, exploit employees for personal gain and try to satisfy customers from a short-term perspective, all in order to push profits for the period they are at the helm.

The shareholder value performers are focused on the maximization of a firm's value, which is ultimately expressed in purely financial terms. They accept and appreciate the basic assumptions of the economic paradigm. They are achievement oriented and want to measure this achievement. Thereby, they follow a one-dimensional value function by creating value for the shareholders, which they assume also maximizes their own value. All other interactions with stakeholders are seen as a nexus of complete contracts serving to increase the shareholders' and their own value.

In the empirical cases we examined, we observed that most leaders belong to the category of instrumentalists. These leaders acknowledge the indispensable value creation potential of stakeholders. Whenever possible, they seek to tap these potentials to develop innovative solutions. Those leaders are constantly looking for win-win situations to improve their competitive advantage by including stakeholders. But they have a purely instrumental perspective in interacting with stakeholders.

However, these leaders are often confronted with the challenge that the capability for innovation is limited, when certain stakeholders are not acknowledged as human beings and owners, but only as a source of indispensable resources. Accepting stakeholders as owners also implies that the leaders have to be willing to give up the idea of always being able to manage stakeholder interactions, by being part of mutual value creation with other stakeholders in a network structure. This mindset leads to the fourth type of leadership, the mutual value creator.

In one of our research projects we could observe the following situation: a corporation was seeking innovative product solutions. They had experienced that the current research and development process was no longer successful. As a result, they broadened the cast of stakeholders and deepened their involvement. They decided to initiate a multi-stakeholder dialogue, by bringing in all the experience and knowledge of a broad cast of stakeholders. The manager of this company initiated a core team that was in charge of developing the overall concept for this truly multi-stakeholder dialogue. This core team consisted of a manager of the company, representatives of a public relations agency of the corporation, technical experts for the type of products, plus a moderator who was in charge of facilitating the multi-stakeholder dialogue. At the first meeting with the stakeholders, the core team realized that it was not appropriate for them to manage the dialogue alone. They sought a format in which all the stakeholders could take part as partners. During the second workshop, the representatives of the different stakeholder organizations began to realize that as partners in this process, they were confronted with similar challenges as the corporation and the core team. It took time to find common ground on how an innovative solution could be found for the product focused on. Some of the stakeholders began to accept that they should all submit to a paradigm shift, in which they would contribute as partners, independently of whether they were suppliers or NGOs.

In this example we can already observe a struggle for a paradigm shift, and that it is important that the leaders in firms and stakeholder organizations and groups are able to change their mindset. Interestingly, not only the purpose and the culture of the organization were dominant in this case, in which the leaders started to question the current process, but also their personalities. The leaders' personality traits obviously influence how paradigmatic change takes place.

Personal traits of leaders can be assessed by the widely accepted and empirically based five factor model of psychology:[73] the five factors are openness to experience, conscientiousness with respect to achievements, extroversion and introversion as a continuum, agreeableness to cooperate and neuroticism.[74] For instance with respect to the factor neuroticism, Fahr and Irlenbusch showed in their empirical research that individuals with low scores in anxiety are especially capable of stimulating trust between organizations.[75] Such an insight could also be relevant in the realm of mutual value creation where trust is basic. Post *et al.* have already emphasized that "The development of a culture of learning within an organization requires having in place a network of reciprocal trusting and trustworthy relationships based on mutual understanding and widely distributed benefits."[76] Such cultural effects in the network also influence the implementation of the stakeholder paradigm. The personal traits of leaders, and more specifically of founders of a corporation but also of the leaders of stakeholder organizations interacting with the corporation, might be an important factor to explain why and how a specific stakeholder culture stimulated or hindered a paradigmatic change to emerge.[77] The choice of leaders and their development in executive programs are important for the implementation of a paradigmatic change. We see here an interesting field for further interdisciplinary research, enhancing the foundation and the implementation of the new stakeholder paradigm.

Structural and legal impacts

Our understanding of the stakeholder paradigm also influences the structure of firms, stakeholder groups and organizations; primarily the interaction and network structures, the governance systems and the corresponding legal regulations. As we have seen in the previous chapters, the economic paradigm focuses on hierarchical, top-down processes.[78] This structural orientation is in contrast to the actual challenges for innovative solutions, where in a network view firms and stakeholders are engaged mostly in bottom-up processes.[79]

Structures and processes of firms and stakeholders

The readiness and ability of firms and stakeholders to contribute to value creation depends also on their structures and procedures. For this reason firms and recently also stakeholders have at times created specific departments to interact professionally with their stakeholders. Other structural elements that we could see in our empirical case studies are common group experience and training institutions, discussion forums, multi-stakeholder initiatives, etc. As to the interaction between firm and stakeholder, different patterns of intensity can take place. As we observed in our case research, the range extends from an occasional exchange of information to a constant collaboration. This is also discussed in the stakeholder engagement literature.[80]

Distinctiveness and complexity of network structures

Compared to most firms that are professionally organized, stakeholders have a variety of forms, ranging from the activities of individuals to highly professionalized organizations:

- Stakeholders sometimes act as individuals or as only weakly linked stakeholder groups, when the interest or purpose of individual human beings is in the foreground in contributing to value creation. There may even be occasions where individuals are highly recognized as a stakeholder in their own right. This is the case for people like the Dalai Lama representing a stake. Sometimes individuals are acting as respected advocates of so-called silent voices (e.g. a speaker for an indigenous group) (see part A in Figure 9.2).
- Another structured position is groups of similar stakeholders (e.g. customers or investors). The members of these groups may have individual interests and identities but also common characteristics as a group (see part B in Figure 9.2).[81]
- Furthermore, individuals can have multiple roles and memberships in different firms, stakeholder groups or organizations. This can result in multiple identities and the conflicting, complementary or cooperative interests of stakeholders (see part C in Figure 9.2).[82]
- Additionally, firms and stakeholder organizations are quite often not homogenous units but are composed of sub-groups. There can even be a distinction between internal (e.g. owners, employees) and external stakeholders and stakeholder groups (e.g. customer, NGOs, etc.) (see part D in Figure 9.2).[83]

Such structural differentiations of stakeholder networks and their subunits lead to the distinctiveness and complexity of mutual value creation.

To enhance the understanding of network interactions, it seems necessary to visualize the complexity of such networks.[84] In our case study research, we used topic maps to visualize the embeddedness of firms in their stakeholder networks, which was highly appreciated by the participants.[85] One of the interview partners concluded:

I already knew somehow that I am doing business in a complex world, but now I can see how it is structured.

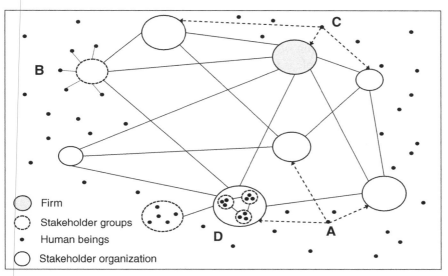

Figure 9.2 Structural differentiation in a stakeholder network

Concerning future research, we suggest exploring the differentiated structures of stakeholder networks and their subunits, in order to improve the understanding of mutual value creation in a network view.[86] Such studies can draw on social network theory.[87]

Governance systems and legal impacts

Already Blair and Stout claimed, "Scholarly and popular debates about corporate governance need to recognize that corporations mediate among the competing interests of various groups and individuals that risk firm-specific investments in a joint enterprise."[88] Several scholars similarly call for fundamental changes with respect to the governance systems in a comprehensive sense.[89] Stout made a strong statement for such a change at the firm level from an economic and legal perspective: "In contrast (i.e. to the shareholder primacy), once directors understand that shareholders do not in fact own the corporation and that they need not respond to shareholders' every whim, they can focus instead on getting the best possible corporate performance – on behalf of all stakeholders."[90] Also Winkler, in the ongoing legal debate in connection with corporate law, supports protection of stakeholders over shareholder primacy.[91] These statements suggest, from a structural as well as legal perspective, a shift in the direction of our understanding of the stakeholder paradigm. Stakeholder governance as a principle is focused, as this understanding of governance affects not only firms but three different levels of governance:

- Corporate governance
  As developed in Chapter 4 (pp. 50–52), Blair and Stout call the traditional understanding of corporate governance the "Grand Design of the Principal Agent Model," which relies on shareholder primacy.[92] Additionally to the principle of shareholder primacy, the key determining factors of corporate governance in the economic paradigm are the market forces and the legal regulations, sometimes additionally disciplined by soft laws. The traditional owners of corporations suggest that self-regulation is the best supplement to free competition in the markets, complemented by several kinds of codes of conduct, created by the firms themselves or by business associations.[93] With such codes of self-regulation, corporations also try to solve governance problems on their own, without involving actors from other sectors, especially the state. But mostly these codes neglect sanction mechanisms and therefore have a limited impact.[94] As the financial crisis demonstrated, the private sector alone could not guarantee a prudent system of financial services. In the perspective of the stakeholder paradigm, aside from new self-regulations, corporate law needs substantial changes. The OECD principle as an example offers the following framework at a corporate level: "The corporate governance framework should recognize the rights of stakeholders established by law or through mutual agreements and encourage active co-operation between corporations and stakeholders in creating wealth, jobs, and the sustainability of financially sound enterprises."[95]
- State governance[96]
  In a democracy, the political system is hierarchical with executive power attributed to state actors, which also have the possibility to sanction due to regulations. Two important roles of Western democracies are, first, the protection of the rights of the individual, to which also property rights belong, through neutral judgement and threat of sanctions. Second, the provision of public goods that goes beyond the protection of these individual rights, such as the welfare

state or the infrastructure that serves society as a whole.[97] Most approaches in political sciences are state-centric in that state actors and institutions, such as government, parliament, public authorities or the military, are the hub of interest.[98] This understanding no longer corresponds to the stakeholder paradigm, because it does not make consistent use of the advantages of mutuality, in which public as well as private organizations are part of network structures. It also does little to acknowledge the fact that governments of nation states as well as other state-actors can have multiple roles in such networks (see Chapter 6, pp. 99–100).

• Global governance[99]

Rigorous state-centrism has been given up in light of a new and modern political science view of international relations, as exemplified by the concept of global governance.[100] Thanks to scholars, who question the strong dominance of the governments of nation states and intergovernmental organizations (IGO) as the sole relevant political actors in inter- and transnational policy fields, we now have a better understanding of a system of cooperative global governance.[101] "The two main characteristics of the concept are first, the relevance of different actors in international relations, namely state *and* non-state actors; and second, systems of rule from the local to the global level."[102]

All relevant actors who are related to an issue – including state actors, MNCs and civil society – can now be seen as stakeholders by taking this global governance approach.[103] The policy agenda has lengthened and the issues have become more complex on a global level in recent years.[104] Therefore, distinct global issue networks (GINs) that address a specific urgent policy problem (e.g. world health, global economic regulation, energy) have been proposed by Held to bring together different stakeholders.[105] All relevant stakeholders would thus have a say in how a global public good that is important to them is provided, or how a specific issue is solved.[106]

In an empirical study, Fransen and Kolk compare what they call multi-stakeholder standards to other collaborative standards, according to membership, governance and implementation.[107] These other standards are drawn from single actors such as NGOs or IGOs like the UN, WTO or by business associations. The authors conclude, "Multi-stakeholder standards appear to have qualities that make them preferable over other collaborative standards."[108]

The existence of diffuse and complex transnational webs of governance today has been emphasized by Cerny.[109] He makes the point that the formation of transnational interest groups and the development of trans-governmental coalitions could bring different actors together in regular networks, thereby cutting across splintered nation states with their established political and economic borders.[110] Farer and Sisk also advise, "Global governance [has to] evolve in ways that enable key actors [to] collectively address ... international challenges."[111] In their opinion it is the only way to prevent a "neo-Malthusian catastrophe" manifested for example in deepening poverty, internal conflicts and the devastating effects of climate change.[112]

- Stakeholder governance[113]

In Table 9.2 we give an overview of these three levels of governance and describe how the stakeholder paradigm embraces these three levels, leading to stakeholder governance.

As we have seen throughout this book, in the perspective of the stakeholder paradigm, mutual value creation takes place within stakeholder networks. Therefore the stakeholder network view seems the appropriate perspective, at all three levels of governance (corporate, state and global).[114]

The global financial crisis created additional common issues that ask for stakeholder governance at different levels in a network perspective. Calls for more coordination, regulation and control in the financial sector were moderate as long as the globally interdependent financial markets were running well. With such substantial value creation in the financial sector, there was little demand for changes in governance by virtually all stakeholders, including investors, regulators (e.g. governments), mortgage takers, financial corporations (e.g. banks, hedge funds) and their employees, normal bank clients, as well as the public at large. It was only after the dotcom bubble burst that some measures were established, especially in the field of corporate governance. Examples include the codes of conduct or the Sarbanes-Oxley Act. These measures were in large part from a narrow perspective and their impact was moderated by this narrow understanding of governance. The claim for more sophisticated governance expanded rapidly after the financial crisis broke out and the network perspective became apparent. As an example in 2010, the EU established three new authorities for

Table 9.2 *The stakeholder paradigm and different levels of governance*

Governance level	Stakeholders (examples)	Coordination mechanism	Traditional view, economic paradigm	Stakeholder paradigm: stakeholder governance
Corporate	• Owners (shareholders, investors) • Management • Employees	• Market forces • Corporate law, self-regulation and soft laws	• Firms competing in market contexts	• Firms embedded in stakeholder networks
State	• Government • Citizens • Parties • National interest groups and advocacies	• Democratic participation • State has monopoly of power (including sanctions)	• State as regulator • Society as context factor	• State interactivity with stakeholders in different, sometimes multiple roles
Global[a]	• Government • Intergovernmental organizations (IGOs, e.g. UN, WTO) • Global NGOs, CSOs • MNCs	• International and transnational principles of cooperation • Power (hegemony) • Interdependence (economic)	• Cooperation of states may lead to treaties/IGOs • Global non-state actors should follow these rules • If no cooperation between states then often no regulation of non-state actors at all	• Multinational stakeholder networks complementing international cooperation across borders (e.g. in Multi-Stakeholder Initiatives (MSI))

[a] Global here means exclusively the highest level of human activity, not the collectivity of all levels from local to global (see Dingwerth & Pattberg, 2006).

supervising banks (EU Banking Authority, EBA), insurances (EU Insurance and Occupational Pensions Authority, EIOPA) and stock exchanges and markets (EU Securities and Markets Authority, ESMA).[115] It seems that the necessity for better governance is recognized, but it remains to be seen if these types of governance correspond to a stakeholder perspective and take into consideration mutuality and network interactions.

Regarding the structural and legal impacts, we can recognize the following areas for future development and research:

- One of the main challenges of governance systems is to develop mutuality and network interactions. Thereby it is important not only to bring in all relevant groups to be effective, but also to have legitimacy in the eyes of the stakeholders involved.[116]
- Stakeholders' perspectives should be incorporated in an appropriate way at the level of corporate governance (see Chapter 4, pp. 48–53).[117] Internal structure and process must be aligned to support mutual value creation with and for stakeholders.[118] In a recent empirical investigation, Spitzeck and Hansen showed different forms of stakeholder participation in the decision-making of firms.[119]
- The governance system rooted in a stakeholder perspective will require adaptations of the current legal bases in areas such as property rights, responsibilities of actors of firms *and* stakeholders, competition law, bankruptcy law, tax law and in corporate law.[120]
- Governance at the international and mostly at the state level can be developed further in a stakeholder perspective. The corresponding steps in the political sciences merit more attention and support.[121]

Epilogue

In our book we offered an analysis of the assumptions underpinning the current approaches. This analysis emphasizes that the basic assumptions of the neoclassical economic theory, i.e. self-interest and market efficient hypothesis, are at the present time still predominant in strategy theory, and even partly in the stakeholder theory of the firm. In proposing a paradigm shift, we aim to contribute to Stiglitz's call to reflect and revise the assumptions of the current theories, and to adapt them to the actual challenges. We suggest a shift to a stakeholder paradigm, where mutuality enhances benefits and reduces risks for the firm and its stakeholders embedded in networks, thereby leading to superior value. Superior value focuses on a continuous search by the firm and its engaged stakeholders to improve the quality of life of human beings and the sustainability of the natural world. This understanding of mutual value creation can be operationalized according to the three licenses, namely the license to operate, to innovate and to compete.

The overall basic assumption of our understanding of the stakeholder paradigm, and its operationalization in the three licenses, is that in a knowledge-based, networked society the purpose of the firm is mutual value creation with and for stakeholders. Figure E.1 shows this journey from the theory of the firm to a theory of value creation in networks, applying the principle of mutuality between firms and stakeholders in networks. In this new paradigm, it is not the *invisible* hand of the market that leads to an overall increase in the welfare of society, but the *visible* hand of the firm and the stakeholders. In other words: people work for people.[1]

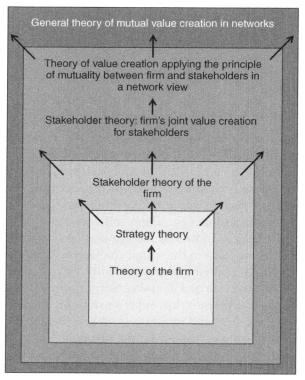

Figure E.1 Towards mutual value creation in networks

With regard to the proposed paradigm shift, we are pleased to be a part of it, and we hope that we can stimulate firms and a broad cast of stakeholders to join this path to contribute to the quality of life and the sustainability of the future.

Appendix: Methodological considerations

In our text and especially in the five chapters that focus on the licenses (Chapters 5–9), we refer to findings and observations gained from our empirical research. It is therefore appropriate to clarify here some basic aspects of how this research was conducted. In the following section the basic features of the methodology are discussed.

The researcher's choice and responsibility

All researchers make specific choices regarding theories and empirical methods.[1] Even though the arguments for these choices are made in accordance with scientific standards, the research questions, the literature and mainstream research, these choices are primarily based on the researcher's values, experience, education and socialization within the scientific community.[2] Furthermore, while working with and on theories and conducting empirical investigations, one is relying on the basic assumptions of these theories that either allow or limit insights. No matter what the field or object of research, it is never value neutral or totally objective. The choice of specific theories, and the thereby chosen or constructed basic assumptions, relate to the person doing the research. Economic theory and therefore also strategic management is shaped by those assumptions.[3]

Given this situation, it is the researcher's responsibility to make clear on what his or her assumptions are based, when theorizing or conducting empirical studies.[4] Furthermore, he or she has to reflect on whether or not these assumptions are appropriate when the model or framework is applied to real life situations.[5] This is especially true in the social sciences, as all the topics are socially constructed.[6] This also applies to research in strategic and stakeholder management which is to a large extent context-linked. Applying models or frameworks to these topics always affects the social construct and may lead to positive but also to negative developments. In the following we would like to make transparent how we worked methodologically and why.

Need for empirical research

The stakeholder paradigm and its implementation in practice are still relatively unexplored.[7] Only a few empirical studies about a firm's stakeholder orientation – a central construct of the stakeholder view – have emerged so far.[8] We therefore saw the need to improve the empirical foundation of the stakeholder paradigm and to discuss the appropriate methodology for gaining further empirically founded insights on stakeholder theory and practice.

Our author team comes from different theoretical perspectives, from different special fields of interest as well as from different backgrounds regarding scientific positioning. Different means of approaching the same topic challenged us at a meta-level. Inconsistencies in the interpretation can thus unveil "different real world nuances," which in turn lead to deeper insights in the analyzed areas.[9] The overall purpose, as well as the motivation for our research, is the continuous search for improving the quality of life, which makes the understanding of social science (and more specifically of the stakeholder paradigm) dynamic, and requires continual openness and willingness to learn from others.

The author team has been complemented by colleagues, who again represent different scientific positions and have thereby enriched the basic values and methodologies of our research.

Case study analysis

All our empirical studies are based on case study analysis. When we extended our empirical research, after finishing the SLOAN Foundation project "Redefining the Corporation"[10] in 2003, our aim was threefold: first, to analyze examples that illustrate the development and implementation of the stakeholder paradigm in practice; second, to further develop the stakeholder paradigm and to operationalize it through the framework of the three licenses; and, third, to identify "good practices" for the management.[11]

According to Eisenhardt[12] case studies are a well-established means of contributing to the development of theories.[13] Multiple data sources such as interviews or documents can be combined. In addition, case studies are well established as qualitative methods in various disciplines.[14] Case studies are particularly appropriate when "how" and "why" questions need to be answered, as Yin stresses: "The essence of a case study, the central tendency among all types of case study, is that it tries to illuminate a decision or set of decisions: why they were taken, how they were implemented, and with what result."[15] The questions that can be answered with case studies are exploratory, and can therefore contribute to our purpose of theory development. Moreover, case studies allow an in-depth analysis of complex real-life situations when the researcher cannot control the events. For this reason, case studies also contribute to knowledge creation, as the results are context-dependent and therefore conducive to rule-based learning.[16]

We are aware of the fact that case research in general can be criticized, especially with respect to the question of significance. In our case research, we were not aiming at significance in the statistical sense but rather at findings that reflect the perceptions of firms and stakeholders, concerning value creation in the economic and social reality.[17] All data (interviews and documents) were analyzed both quantitatively and qualitatively.[18] The quantitative analysis provided insights regarding the relative frequencies of the codes and how well grounded the findings in the data were. For example, the frequencies indicate what stakeholders or benefit potentials were most important in the perception of the management or the stakeholders. The rankings that were created on the basis of these frequencies turned out to be very valuable, not only for the further analysis of the data but also for the subsequent dialogue with the companies and the stakeholders. Complementary to this, a qualitative analysis provided deeper insight into the quality of the perceptions of the stakeholders, the issues and the benefit and risk potentials they perceived.

We distinguished three types of case study analysis that we rely on:

- The case studies "Good Practices of Stakeholder View" (2003–2007)

To uncover good practices and examples of how the stakeholder view is implemented in practice, we chose positive cases. These cases considered firms that have already implemented a certain degree of stakeholder oriented strategic management.[19] We analyzed six national and international firms all based in Switzerland or with a daughter company in the country. In order to be able to describe the conditions necessary for good practices, we analyzed similarities and dissimilarities among the cases. In order to compare the cases, only large firms from the telecom and the financial services sectors were selected. Thus, the environments of the firms, as well as their strategic stakeholders, and partly also specific events (characteristic for the whole industry) could be compared. We started the examination of the cases by a qualitative content analysis of documents. We analyzed those documents that described the firms' strategy, structure and culture. Two sources were used: on the one hand, public documents, i.e. from the firms' homepages. These included annual reports, company brochures, press releases, environmental and sustainability reports, codes of conduct, etc. On the other hand, we asked the firms for specific internal documents such as employee and customer surveys, internal strategy documents, presentations, etc.

The interviews we conducted were semi-structured. The interview questions were related to the main research questions, but were also based on the results gained from the document analysis. The main advantage of this type of interview is its flexibility, which makes it well suited for qualitative research.[20] The interviewer prepared a specific set of questions to be asked in order to answer the research questions. Yet the main aim was to understand the interviewee's perspective. Semi-structured interviews gave the interview partner ample space to express his/her opinion on the topics to be discussed, as well as to deviate and to introduce new issues he/she considered equally important. Thus, interview partners could prioritize certain topics, while the interviewer simultaneously had the opportunity to pose all of the prepared questions. The interviews consequently were comparable and yet genuine.

We conducted these empirical studies in a way that allowed for the recognition and understanding of the interactions and the perceptions of the different stakeholders, while applying a sound methodology to compare their similarities and their differences.[21] We conducted semi-structured interviews with managers as well as stakeholders.[22] We created a database comprising over 100 in-depth interviews, with the possibility of significant differences between the empirical contexts of the different cases. But as all our studies were based on the same specific methodological principles, we were nonetheless able to compare the different cases.[23]

In qualitative content analysis, a network system of categories and corresponding codes needed to be developed in order to analyze the documents and interviews.[24] The categories and codes were developed in several steps. The first codes were derived from the existing stakeholder theory. Next, we used these categories to code the firm documents. Where necessary, we extended the code list and included codes that emerged inductively. With the new code list, we then coded the interviews. Again, where necessary we included new codes that were gained inductively from the available material. Inductive and deductive category building are described as two possible approaches in qualitative content analysis.[25] We combined them as this proved more suitable and allowed us to develop categories and codes based on a constant comparison between theory and practice. As we used this system of codes for all case studies, the results were comparable. Moreover, such code categories also facilitated the enhancing and building of the framework of the three licenses.

The coding and analysis process was done with Atlas.ti, a specific software for qualitative data analysis, and set up as follows:[26] in the case of the interviews, they were first transcribed in order to code them. In the next step, the documents and interviews were interpreted and coded, based on the coding system that was developed inductively and deductively. During the coding phase, the researchers worked in pairs. They first coded the text on their own and then compared the results in order to validate the results. This corresponds to what is called inter-rater reliability.

The analysis that ensued from the coding phase was basically a qualitative interpretation but was supported by quantitative elements. The used codes were counted and a frequency table was established. These frequencies served as indicators as to which topics were the most important in the documents and interviews. In addition, co-occurrences of codes were analyzed as well, in order to identify patterns or clusters in the data, which could later be used to compare the different firms and to further develop the stakeholder view.[27]

After finishing the analysis of the single firms, an intra-industry and later an inter-industry comparison were made. Figure A.1 (see p. 186) gives an overview of our approach.

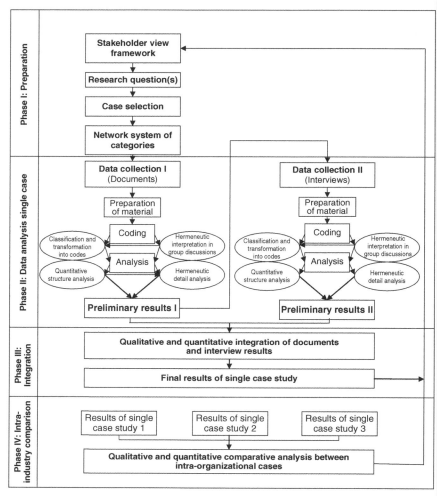

Figure A.1 Overview of the research process

- Action research based on case study (2006 to 2011)[28]

In addition, we partly applied action research in the case research.[29] The method is suited to simultaneously attempting to solve practical problems that firms face, while gathering scientific knowledge in a specific field (in our case stakeholder management). In each step of the research process, the results were analyzed and if necessary further action was discussed.[30] Action research can have different forms and degrees of intensity.[31] Based on this, the firm organized workshops with us and developed internal processes to handle areas of conflict.

We developed the following questions and steps for the action research process, based on the same methodological tools as described above (qualitative content analysis, semi-structured interviews, code system):

Step 1: Who are the relevant strategic stakeholders, and with what issues are they engaged, as perceived by the firm? How are the stakeholders linked to each other? As a starting point, we always identify stakeholders and issues with a selected team of the corporation.

Step 2a: What are the benefit and risk potentials of the relationships identified, as perceived by the management team of the corporation? This step was important in terms of first creating common ground in the firm, before contacting the stakeholders. In the cases we conducted, firm–stakeholder relationships were not without some tension. Therefore it was vital for the firm to first consider the consequences of a truly mutual value creation approach of identifying risk and benefit potentials, not only from a firm perspective but also in concert with stakeholders.

Step 2b: What is the meaning of the identified risk and benefit potentials to the strategic stakeholders involved? Each of the stakeholders involved was first interviewed independently to identify risk and benefit potentials. Because we interviewed several representatives of each stakeholder group, to each of the groups their own internal views were first presented. As we dealt with "real" relationships, we had to take care through confidentiality agreements that none of the information collected would be passed on without the prior consent of the parties interviewed. These confidentiality agreements had a trust building effect for the following workshops, bringing stakeholders and the corporations together.

Step 3: What are the similarities and differences of perceptions? This step was now truly interactive. According to conflict resolution or mediation methods, one started with the perceived similarities to create common ground first, and then worked out the differences or the more controversial aspects among the corporations and their stakeholders. The process was facilitated by a neutral third party, in our cases the research team.

Step 4: How do identified benefit and risk potentials affect corporate strategy? Risk and benefit potentials, as well as the concept of value creation identified in Step 3, had to be taken up by the corporation. If there were a sustainable effect on the relationships and the respective risk and benefit potentials involved, the corporation needed to integrate the insights gained in dialogue into its strategic planning process.

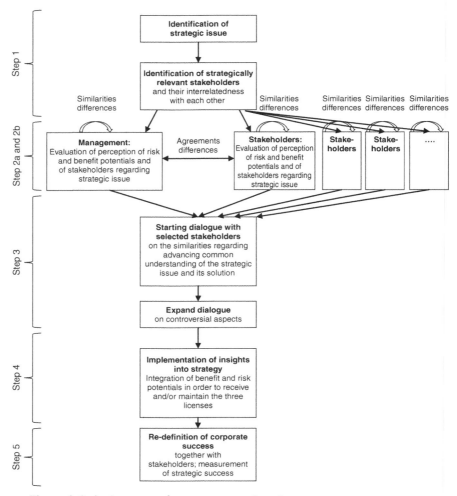

Figure A.2 Action research process: steps 1 to 5

Step 5: What is the concept of strategic success and how should it be measured? The value of the stakeholder management system lies in the fact that benefit and risk potentials have been identified and discussed together with the stakeholders. Therefore, a common understanding can be developed of what corporate success means, not only to the corporation itself but also to the strategically relevant or involved stakeholders. This step has been developed further to an evaluation concept that is now part of the next research project (see Chapter 5, pp. 91–93), based on case study and action research.

- Illustrative case studies[32]

The third category of case research was based on extensive document analysis, and was either already analyzed empirical cases for other purposes (e.g. Novo Nordisk) or was current illustrative cases (e.g. UBS financial crisis, BP oil spill, etc.).

The cases

In-depth studies[33]

The firms are either of Swiss origin or are Swiss subsidiaries of international corporations. The focus on Switzerland was given as we are from Swiss universities, and the research resources did not permit a global project. When corporations are mentioned in the text, the name always refers to the Swiss subsidiary. In this section, we will briefly describe them.

- Orange
  Orange Switzerland Inc. is a subsidiary completely owned by France Télécom and a leading telecommunication firm in Switzerland with mobile and internet services. In 1999 it entered the Swiss market, and with 1,145 employees in 2009 reported a turnover of CHF 1,296 million, thereby establishing itself among the top three telecommunications firms in the country.
  Homepage: www1.orange.ch/index.html
- Pfizer
  Pfizer Switzerland is a subsidiary completely owned by traded Pfizer Inc. and a leading pharmaceutical firm in Switzerland. In 1959 it entered the Swiss market, and with 310 employees in 2010 and an expected turnover of CHF 400 million, established itself as the top pharmaceutical firm in terms of market share in the country.
  Homepage: www.pfizer.ch
- Sunrise
  Sunrise Switzerland Inc. is a subsidiary completely owned by CVC Capital Partners and a leading telecommunication firm in Switzerland with a mix of fixed, mobile and internet services. In 2000

it established itself in the Swiss market, and with 1,600 employees in 2010 and a turnover of CHF 2,001 million, it is among the top three telecommunications firms in the country. It resulted from a merger of two earlier firms, founded in the context of the 1998 liberalization of the telecommunication industry in Switzerland.
Homepage: www1.sunrise.ch/

- Suva
  Suva (Swiss Accident Insurance Fund) is an independent company under public law and 100 percent owned by the companies insured and their employees. It is the largest obligatory accident insurance in Switzerland, insuring employees against illnesses and occupational and non-occupational accidents. It was established in 1912, has roughly 3,000 employees and enjoys a partial monopoly, and in 2009 reported an operating turnover of CHF 2,505 million.
  Homepage: www.suva.ch/

- Swisscom
  Swisscom Inc. is a telecommunication firm with 56.94 percent of the shares owned by the Swiss Federal Government, and offering a mix of fixed, mobile and internet services. It was founded in 1998 on the basis of its forerunner PTT (founded in 1852), and which, until the liberalization of the Swiss telecommunication industry in 1998, was the state monopoly for all post and telecommunication services. With 19,511 employees in 2009 and a turnover of CHF 12,001 million, it is the leading telecommunications firm in the country.
  Homepage: http://en.swisscom.ch/aboutswisscom

- Swiss Re
  Swiss Re (Swiss Reinsurance Corporation), founded in 1863, is a publicly traded firm and a market leader in the reinsurance business including life, health, property and liability coverage. In 2009 Swiss Re had 10,552 employees and reported total revenues of CHF 33,383 million.
  Homepage: www.swissre.com/

- ZKB (Zürcher Kantonalbank)
  ZKB (Zurich Cantonal Bank), founded in 1870, is an independent institution under public law owned 100 percent by the canton of Zurich. It is the third largest bank in Switzerland, and in 2009 it had 4,800 employees and a turnover of CHF 2,234 million.
  Homepage: www.zkb.ch/

Desk research

Apart from the in-depth studies, the book contains further examples of firms that were used to illustrate specific points. The examples resulted from desk research and are either based on scientific papers and books, or general publications.

The following are examples based on scientific papers and books:[34]

- Shell
  Shell may serve as a main case to illustrate how a wake-up call strengthens stakeholder management (events around Brent Spar and Nigeria).[35] Shell also serves as an example that a firm cannot always control its stakeholder network and the stakeholder interaction. This was illustrated by Shell's Camisea project.

- Greenpeace
  This case shows that firms not only have a responsibility toward their stakeholders but also vice versa. When Shell wanted to sink the Brent Spar oil rig in the North Sea, Greenpeace stepped in and successfully attacked Shell. This resulted in negative media coverage and boycotts for Shell. Later on, Greenpeace had to admit that it had operated with partly incorrect figures.

- Zurich Airport
  This case illustrates that sustainable value creation can only be achieved if it is based on conditions that are acceptable for all involved stakeholders. Zurich Airport had to adapt its landing corridors, as it failed to find a mutual solution with the citizens in Germany along the border. As the landing corridor extends into Germany, the German government forced Switzerland and Zurich Airport to protect German citizens from more air traffic, pollution and noise.

- Monsanto
  Different stakeholders can confront firms with social and political expectations. In the case of Monsanto, shareholders and institutional investors demanded that the corporation handle the "gene technology" issue in a responsible manner. These stakeholders also contributed to mutual value creation by contributing their knowledge and experience to developing innovative and sustainable solutions.

The following are examples based on general publications:[36]

- Apple

  The license to operate extends beyond the firm's borders. In 2010 Apple was held responsible for intolerable working conditions in its supplier firms in China.

- BP

  Firms need the acceptance and legitimation of a broad cast of stakeholders, including social and political stakeholders, as illustrated by the example of BP. The oil spill in the Gulf of Mexico in 2010 triggered a broad discussion on the moral and ethical standards that BP had to comply with, and a debate on regulation and self-regulation in the industry.

- Foxconn and Honda

  Outsourcing may cause problems in the firm's home country (loss of jobs), but also in the country to which jobs are transferred. This can be illustrated by the example of Foxconn and Honda employees in China. In 2010 they protested for higher wages and decent working conditions.

- GM/Opel

  Sometimes social and political stakeholders pressure a firm to maintain jobs and production locations despite losses in the current business. This can be seen in the example of General Motors, which wanted to close down Opel plants in Germany based exclusively on financial criteria and neglecting other stakeholders' expectations (e.g. German political parties and government).

- Lehman Brothers

  As firms are an integral part of society, social stakeholders are important to them. The example of Lehman Brothers illustrates that the failure of a bank affects not only its customers, but also an extended stakeholder network. Other banks depended on these stakeholders (including social and political stakeholders) in order to be bailed out.

- McDonald's

  This example illustrates the influence that customers can exert. As a major customer of meat suppliers, McDonald's has a great influence on animal husbandry.

- Novo Nordisk

  The firm's credo is that customers and society should be included in the value distribution process and that this should occur in a transparent way. Therefore, the firm set up an "economic stake-holder model" in which it reports the total sum of salaries paid to employees, the sum paid to suppliers for their services and products, the taxes paid to the government, the dividend attributed to the shareholders, etc.

- UBS

  UBS is Switzerland's largest bank acting at a global level. Customers sometimes challenge even such a large firm's license to operate, and this was the case with UBS. During the financial crisis, many clients withdrew their money from the bank.

Glossary

The purpose of this glossary is not to define specific terms but to make clear to the reader how these terms are used in this book. In our understanding of the stakeholder paradigm, some terms are attributed a different meaning than that generally used in the economic paradigm. The glossary serves to explain these meanings.

- Above-the-norm contribution
  Above-the-norm refers to any kind of resource contributions exceeding contractual obligations or expectations by the network members due to active motivation for value creation.
- Basic assumption
  The basic assumptions of a paradigm according to Kuhn are the "entire constellation of beliefs, values, techniques and so on shared by the members of a given community."[1] Thus, the overall basic assumption of the stakeholder paradigm is that in a knowledge-based, networked society the purpose of the firm is mutual economic and social value creation with and for stakeholders.
- Benefit and risk potentials
  Benefit and risk potentials emerge, are influenced or become accessible through interactions in stakeholder networks. We assume that firms and stakeholders can contribute in various roles in the value creation processes and thus impact the firm, any other stakeholders or the whole network. We can distinguish the following roles of contributors in networks:
  - Benefit providers: participants in value creation can contribute in a variety of ways, from emotional engagement to sharing resources.
  - Benefit receivers: participants in value creation can benefit due to gaining or enhancing their resources of any kind.
  - Risk bearers: by making specific contributions, the participants in value creation take specific risks. It may be difficult for them,

for example, to apply and evaluate specific knowledge outside the network.

- Risk providers: participants of value creation can pose potential threats to interactions in the network and can even destroy value.

- Common purposes

In a knowledge-based, networked society, human beings are more frequently voicing their interests and purposes in groups or organizations (firms and stakeholders), or are even combining such interests and purposes in new different organizational forms. Firms and their stakeholders contribute on a mutual basis to innovative solutions for issues, projects, products and services.

- Competition

Competition is understood as the benchmarking between similar kinds of value creation processes. The goal of benchmarking is to stimulate motivation for improving the value creation of the networks; rent reaping should not be the center of attention. Benchmarking is not focused only on monetary value, but rather includes all the benefits and risks of the participants. In this way a high degree of transparency is achieved regarding the quality of value creation for the participating members of networks.

- Cooperation

The processes of cooperation in various forms by the firm and the stakeholders in a network are as important as those of competition between such networks. Cooperation can lead to better solutions than pure competition.

- Economic paradigm

Standard economic theories model the firm as a purely economic institution, and its actors as driven by self-interest, with society as the constraining factor. The firm's total economic value creation is realized through combining and allocating factors of production in a competitive environment. Value creation is expressed through a utility function that focuses on one objective, namely value maximization for the owners of capital (e.g. shareholder value). The value-creating activities of the firm are first and primarily controlled by state laws and regulations or by voluntary self-regulation.

- Embeddedness
  In contrast to the economic paradigm, the stakeholder paradigm is not focused on the definition of a firm's boundaries, and therefore the distinction between internal and external stakeholders, but on the firm's and stakeholder's embeddedness in the dynamic stakeholder network. Thereby the firm and the stakeholders are contributors to value creation, which also implies that stakeholders themselves are embedded in stakeholder networks.
- Evaluation
  To evaluate the process of mutual value creation as well as the outcomes requires an assessment of how the benefits and risks differ, according to the perspective of the three licenses. In concrete situations, the firm together with its stakeholders will need to develop indicators for the evaluation of mutual processes and outcomes. Based on this broad assessment of indicators, benchmarking between different stakeholder networks and their value creation capacity can be made.
- Extended property rights
  In our understanding of the stakeholder paradigm, we intend to take a further step in the extension of property rights, away from an exclusively firm focused understanding of value creation to a network perspective. The firm and the stakeholders are understood as owners of different kinds of resources, bringing them into action in networks of value creation. Contributions can be in the form of transferring, exchanging or even enhancing resources that are owned by firms or stakeholders. The value created should be distributed between the firm and its stakeholders based on the participants' contributions of resources. Value distribution includes different forms of financial, material or immaterial compensation or any form of recognition.
- Firm
  The purpose of the firm is mutual economic and social value creation with and for stakeholders. The firm as an economic and social entity is embedded in stakeholder networks; sometimes it takes the lead in the stakeholder interactions, sometimes it is a contributing constituent. Firms can build on the constructive contribution of a broad cast of stakeholders and can fuel value creation for the whole network to enhance the quality of life.

- Human beings
  In a globalized world, human beings more frequently voice their interests and purposes in groups or organizations, or even combine such interests and purposes in new different organizational forms. Based on the Kantian claim, all human beings are ends and never means, which implies that stakeholders are not resource bearers but owners in the exchange of resources (e.g. knowledge, experience, values, education, personal and family profiles, and group affiliations) and in creating mutual value. All human beings deserve respect for similar and different perceptions on common issues, projects, products or services.
- Innovation
  Innovation is based on the pooling and development of the resources owned by the firm and all engaged stakeholders. Thus, innovation is the result of enhancing benefit potentials and reducing risk potentials in mutual value creation. Innovation in this sense means superior value creation of firms, interacting with stakeholders as resource contributors in a network view.
- Leadership
  We distinguish four specific leadership types in firms influencing cultures differently and having different views of stakeholders (self-performer, shareholder value performer, instrumentalist and mutual value creator).
- License
  License is not primarily a legal term here, but rather a comprehensive entitlement, granted to the firm by its stakeholders that includes a descriptive, instrumental and normative dimension. With respect to the license to operate, the firm and the stakeholders are achieving value creation in accordance with society; with respect to the license to innovate, they are improving mutual value creation by pooling and developing resources for innovative solutions; and with respect to the license to compete, motivation for mutual value creation is based on positioning and benchmarking in and between stakeholder networks.
- Motivation (active, passive)
  Since all human beings are ends according to Kant, they need to interact with other human beings primarily in an active and not only in a passive "motivation" according to Fromm. The passive

motivation focuses on controlling the interaction only to protect, for instance, property. The output of these interactions can be described as "having." In contrast, active motivation considers "being" as "process, activity and movement."

- Mutuality
  Mutuality implies that firm and stakeholders are contributing to value creation and are included in value distribution. Thereby, firms and stakeholders are seen as owners of their contributions. Mutuality induces superior forms of innovation, competition and the operation of firms and stakeholders, striving for solutions to complex projects, difficult issues or innovative products and services. Mutuality enhances benefits and reduces risks for the firm and its stakeholders embedded in the network, and therefore leads to superior value. This understanding of mutual value creation can be operationalized according to the three licenses.

- Network view/stakeholder network
  The stakeholder network comprises all contributors to a value creation process. The firm is perceived as one element within the network of stakeholders. The firm's and the stakeholders' positions within the network are constantly changing. Sometimes the firm is able to manage the stakeholder relations; sometimes the leadership goes to others in the network.

- Operationalization
  The operationalization of the stakeholder paradigm as we understand it is developed by the three licenses: to operate, to innovate and to compete. These licenses are not exclusively the legal authorization for corporate activity, but rather a comprehensive entitlement for a mutual value creation process between firm and the stakeholders. The operationalizations are supported by our empirical case research.

- Organization
  Organizations (e.g. corporations, non-governmental organizations, etc.), unlike living organisms, do not have a right to exist and survival per se. Their justification is to make a useful contribution to the needs of the society through their coordinated activities. In this way, they are transmitters of intention and purposes.

- Paradigm
  Paradigms are the basic assumptions on which a theory or a framework is built. Kuhn describes them as follows, "On the one hand,

it stands for the entire constellation of beliefs, values, techniques, and so on shared by the members of a given community. On the other, it denotes one sort of element in that constellation, the concrete puzzle-solutions which, employed as models of examples, can replace explicit rules as a basis for the solution of the remaining puzzles of normal science."[2]

- Positioning
  A firm's or stakeholder's positioning occurs in two different ways: first, it needs to position itself in its stakeholder network (e.g. vis-à-vis its different stakeholders) to enhance value creation and, secondly, some stakeholders are common to two or more firms and thus positioning occurs also vis-à-vis those common stakeholders.

- Quality of life
  According to the most widely acknowledged standards (see e.g. Human Development indices, Human Poverty indices, Satisfaction with Life indices, etc.), quality of life comprises wealth that includes primarily sustainable access to resources, education and health.

- Resources
  Innovation in the perspective of the license to innovate is based on the pooling and development of the resources owned by the firm and all engaged stakeholders. Doing business is not merely a fight for limited resources among rivals, but much more a constant striving for the discovery, development and improvement of non-limited resources such as knowledge and experience among firms and stakeholders.

- Stakeholder governance
  The stakeholder paradigm embraces three levels of governance, the corporate governance level, the state governance level and the global governance, leading to an overall concept of stakeholder governance.

- Stakeholder paradigm
  The stakeholder paradigm focuses on mutuality as a basic assumption and thereby advocates a network view to create value between firms and stakeholders, and to enhance the quality of life for human beings and the sustainability of the natural world.

- Stakeholders (cast of stakeholders)
  The cast of stakeholders are individuals, groups or organizations contributing to and participating in mutual value creation in the perspective of the three licenses. In identifying the cast of relevant

stakeholders of a firm, we first of all identify stakeholders as owners of limited or unlimited resources, which they contribute to the value creation process. This is based on an extended view of property rights (see especially Chapter 7). Second, the cast of stakeholders is also influenced by the fact that the firm can have different and changing positions in its environment and is always embedded in evolving stakeholder networks (see especially Chapter 8). As these stakeholders are interrelated with other stakeholders, sometimes they contribute not only directly to the value creation process but also indirectly. Third, some of the stakeholders, e.g. employees, contribute voluntarily to value creation. Some do not (e.g. neighbors) but are forced to or cannot abstain from contributing involuntarily. This occurs quite often for social and political stakeholders (see especially Chapter 6). In response, these involuntary stakeholders have specific expectations of a firm's value creation process and sometimes even have the power to influence it.

- Strategy
  In the stakeholder paradigm, strategies consider common actions of firms and stakeholders in a network view. Mutual value creation and distribution challenge the firms and their stakeholders to engage in specific kinds of strategic activities. The three licenses emphasize different aspects for firm and stakeholder strategies.

- Superior value
  We understand superior value as a continuous search by the firm and its engaged stakeholders to improve the quality of life of human beings and the sustainability of the natural world.

- Value creation (mutual)
  The underlying principle of mutual value creation is that the firm and stakeholders are indispensable contributors. The value arises from these contributions, which constitute the focus for the firm's but also for the stakeholders' strategy. The contribution of firms and stakeholders to value creation leads to appropriate participation in the value distribution.

Notes

1 Challenges for a new paradigm in strategic management

1. Barbera, 2010.
2. Stiglitz, 2010a.
3. Beck, 2010.
4. Reich, 2007: 7.
5. Habermas, 1998.
6. Giddens, 2007: 104.
7. BBC, 2009.
8. Freeman, Harrison, Wicks, Parmar & de Colle, 2010: 276.
9. Habermas, 1984.
10. Kuhn, 1996.
11. Kuhn, 1996: 175.
12. E.g. Ferraro, Pfeffer & Sutton, 2005; Musgrave, 1981; Stiglitz, 2009b; Thommen, 1983; Tsang, 2006.
13. Putnam, 2003.
14. Putnam, 2003: 31.
15. Sen, 1987.
16. Putnam, 2003: 50.
17. Popper, 1972.
18. Smith, 1852: 184.
19. E.g. Becerra, 2009; Foss & Foss, 2005; Ghoshal, 2005; Hahn, Kolk & Winn, 2010.
20. E.g. Asher, Mahoney & Mahoney, 2005; Becerra, 2009; Blair & Stout, 1999.
21. E.g. Beck, 2008, 2010; Freeman *et al.*, 2010; Reich, 2007.
22. Lenssen, 2009.
23. Khurana, 2007; Werhane, 2008.
24. Stiglitz, 2009a: 329.
25. Stiglitz, 2009a: 338.
26. Phelps, 2009: 13.
27. E.g. Freeman, Harrison & Wicks, 2007; Wood & Logsdon, 2001.
28. Vidal, 2009: 25.
29. E.g. Giddens, 1984; Gioia & Pitre, 1990; Okhuysen & Bonardi, 2011.

30. Scherer & Dowling, 1995: 11.
31. Gioia & Pitre, 1990: 596.
32. Gioia & Pitre, 1990.
33. Giddens, 1984.
34. Sachs, 2000.
35. Post, Preston & Sachs, 2002b.
36. Sachs, Groth & Schmitt, 2010.
37. Suddaby, Hardy & Huy, 2011.

2 The economic paradigm and its basic assumptions

1. E.g. Sen, 1987; Stiglitz, 2010b; Stiglitz, Sen & Fitoussi, 2010, for an overview see also Becerra, 2009.
2. For an overview see e.g. Cyert & March, 1992; Foss, 2008; Freeman, 2008; Moss Kanter, 1984.
3. E.g. Eisenhardt & Zbaracki, 1992; Ellsberg, 1961; Simon, 1955; Tversky & Kahneman, 1986.
4. Simon, 1955, 1956.
5. Foss, 2008.
6. E.g. Cyert & March, 1992; Foss, 2008; Picot, Dietl & Franck, 2008.
7. Foss, 2008.
8. E.g. Fama & Jensen, 1983; Jensen & Meckling, 1976.
9. E.g. Coase, 1991; Williamson, 1989.
10. E.g. Alchian & Demsetz, 1972; Grossman & Hart, 1986; Hart & Moore, 1990.
11. For an overview see e.g. Cyert & March, 1992; Milgrom & Roberts, 1992.
12. Freeman *et al.*, 2010.
13. Friedman, 1962: 133.
14. Jensen, 2002.
15. E.g. Fama & Jensen, 1983; Jensen & Meckling, 1976.
16. E.g. Alchian & Demsetz, 1972; Grossman & Hart, 1986; Hart & Moore, 1990.
17. E.g. Foss, 2000; Williamson, 1989.
18. For an overview see e.g. Foss, 2008.
19. E.g. Fehr & Tyran, 2005.
20. Fehr & Tyran, 2008.
21. Simon, 1947.
22. Foss, 2003.
23. Foss, 2003: 6.
24. Foss, 2003.
25. E.g. Stiglitz, 2009a.
26. Coase, 1991.

27. Hart, 2000: 131.
28. Hart, 2000.
29. See for an overview Becerra, 2009.
30. Hult, Ketchen & Slater, 2005.
31. Rumelt, Schendel & Teece, 1994.
32. Mahoney & Pandian, 1992: 364.
33. Becerra, 2009.
34. This approach is sometimes also labeled as "Market-based View of Strategy, MbV." In the literature, MbV is sometimes used synonymously for ISV. As the following text shows, we prefer the label ISV.
35. E.g. Barney, 1996b; Foss, 1996; Oster, 1994; Porter, 1985, 1991.
36. Bain, 1959.
37. Bain, quoted in Foss, 1996: 10.
38. E.g. Caves, 1980; Caves & Porter, 1977, 1978; Tirole, 1988.
39. E.g. Porter, 1980, 1985, 1986, 1991, 1996.
40. Barney, 1996a: ix.
41. Porter, 1991: 99.
42. Porter, 1991: 99.
43. Mahoney & Pandian, 1992: 364.
44. Freeman *et al.*, 2010: 136.
45. Porter, 2008: 89.
46. E.g. Hult & Ketchen, 2001; Hult *et al.*, 2005; Porter & Siggelkow, 2008.
47. Porter, 1996.
48. Porter, 1991; Porter & Teisberg, 2004.
49. Porter, 1991: 105.
50. Porter & Kramer, 2002, 2006, 2011; Porter & Reinhardt, 2007; Porter & van der Linde, 1995.
51. Porter & Kramer, 2011: 77.
52. Porter, 1991: 115.
53. Caves, 1984; Porter, 1991.
54. Caves, 1984: 128.
55. Porter & Kramer, 2011: 77.
56. Porter & Kramer, 2006.
57. Porter, 1991.
58. Porter, 1991: 109.
59. Porter, 1998.
60. Porter, 2008.
61. Porter, 1991: 111.
62. Porter, 1990, 1991.
63. Porter & Kramer, 2006, 2011.
64. E.g. Barney, 1996b; Foss, 1996; Ghemawat, 1986; Oster, 1994.

65. For an overview see Mauri & Michaels, 1998.
66. Barney, 1991: 115–116.
67. Porter & Kramer, 2006, 2011.
68. Porter & Kramer, 2011: 75.
69. Porter & Kramer, 2011: 77.
70. Foss, 1996.
71. E.g. Porter, 1980.
72. Porter, 1991.
73. Foss, 1996.
74. Porter & Kramer, 2011.
75. Foss, 1996: 11.
76. D'Aveni, 1994, 1995.
77. D'Aveni, 1994.
78. Porter, 1996.
79. Penrose, 1959.
80. Wernerfelt, 1984.
81. Grant, 1996: 110; Grant, 2010a.
82. Barney, 1991, 1996b.
83. Hall, 1992, 1993; see also Longo & Mura, 2008.
84. E.g. Coff, 2003; Grant, 1996; Herremans, Isaac, Kline & Nazari, 2010.
85. Kogut & Zander, 1996: 503.
86. Hansen & Wernerfelt, 1989.
87. E.g. Gruber, Heinemann, Brettel & Hungeling, 2010; Mauri & Michaels, 1998; McGahan & Porter, 2003; Newbert, 2007, 2008; Sirmon, Hitt, Arregle & Tochman Campbell, 2010; Trott, Maddocks & Wheeler, 2009.
88. E.g. Amit & Schoemaker, 1993; Barney, 1991, 1992; Conner, 1991; Dierickx & Cool, 1989; Grant, 1991; Hall, 1992, 1993; Leonard-Barton, 1992; Mahoney & Pandian, 1992; Peteraf, 1993; Rumelt, 1982; Teece, Pisano & Shuen, 1997; Wernerfelt, 1989, 1995.
89. Barney, 1996a, 2001.
90. Barney, 2001: 54.
91. Foss & Foss, 2005: 545.
92. Mahoney & Pandian, 1992: 369.
93. E.g. Hamel & Prahalad, 1996; Prahalad & Hamel, 1990.
94. E.g. Barney, 1991, 1996a, 1996b; Barney & Hesterly, 2010.
95. E.g. Dierickx & Cool, 1989; Ghemawat, 1991; Hamel & Heene, 1994; Hamel & Prahalad, 1993; Heene & Sanchez, 1997; Peteraf, 1993; Powell, Lovallo & Carnigal, 2006; Wernerfelt, 1984; Wilcox King, 2007.
96. The aspects of heterogeneity are discussed in detail in a special issue of the *Strategic Management Journal*; see Hoopes, Madsen & Walker, 2003.
97. Barney, 1991: 102.
98. Barney, 1991: 103.

99. Barney, 2001.
100. Barney, 2001: 47.
101. E.g. Conner & Prahalad, 1996; Foss & Foss, 2005; Kogut & Zander, 1992; Mahoney & Pandian, 1992; Peteraf, 1993.
102. Barney, 2001: 48.
103. Barney, 2001: 53.
104. Coff, 1999.
105. Mahoney & Pandian, 1992: 370.
106. E.g. Asher *et al.*, 2005; Foss & Foss, 2005.
107. Amit & Schoemaker, 1993: 33.
108. Barney & Hesterly, 1996.
109. Sirmon, Hitt & Ireland, 2007.
110. Foss & Foss, 2005.
111. E.g. Holcomb, Holmes & Connelly, 2009; Sirmon *et al.*, 2007.
112. Conner & Prahalad, 1996.
113. Simon, 1957: XXIV.
114. E.g. Aragon-Correa & Sharma, 2003; Blyler & Coff, 2003; Conner & Prahalad, 1996; Danneels, 2011; Grant, 1996; Kim & Mahoney, 2010; Kogut & Zander, 1996; Nonaka & Takeuchi, 1995; Spender, 1996; Teece, 2009; Teece *et al.*, 1997.
115. Hamel & Prahalad, 1994.
116. Hamel & Prahalad, 1994.
117. E.g. Chatain, 2011; Inkpen & Tsang, 2005; Lavie, 2006.
118. E.g. Barney, 1995, 2001; D'Aveni, 1994; Ghemawat, 1991; Lado, Boyd & Wright, 1992; Leonard-Barton, 1992; Sirmon *et al.*, 2007.
119. Porter, 1996.
120. Porter, 1996: 73.
121. Priem & Butler, 2001.
122. Barney, 1991; for further critical remarks see Lado *et al.*, 1992.
123. Barney, 2001.
124. Barney, 2001: 49.
125. Foss, 1996.
126. Foss, 1996.
127. Barney, 1996a.
128. For a more comprehensive view see Rühli & Sachs, 2005.
129. E.g. Barney, 2005; Blyler & Coff, 2003; Coff, 1999.
130. Stiglitz *et al.*, 2010.
131. See Stiglitz *et al.*, 2010.
132. Ghoshal, 2005; Rocha & Ghoshal, 2006.
133. Ghoshal & Moran, 1996.
134. Osterloh & Frey, 2003.
135. Bosse, Phillips & Harrison, 2009.
136. Nag, Hambrick & Chen, 2005.

137. Nag *et al.*, 2005: 21; emphasis added.
138. Mahoney, 2008: 21.
139. Henriques, 2008: 37.
140. Margolis, 2008: 29. The original quotation is as follows: "What is our North Star?
     - Accuracy?
     - Adherence to economic theory?
     - Logical elegance and concision?
     - Equipping future managers?
     - For the practical reality they will face
     - To understand causally what is not clear to the naked eye
     - To aspire to meet the responsibilities incumbent upon all in business to all parties with whom they interact."

3 Contribution of stakeholder theory to our understanding of the stakeholder paradigm

1. For a state of the art description of stakeholder theory we refer to Freeman *et al.*, 2010; Friedman & Miles, 2006; Phillips, 2003b.
2. Donaldson & Preston, 1995.
3. Donaldson & Preston, 1995.
4. Post *et al.*, 2002b.
5. All the following tables, where another source is not given, are based on our own empirical studies (see Appendix for more information).
6. Sachs, Rühli & Kern, 2009.
7. E.g. Freeman, 1984; Freeman *et al.*, 2010; Friedman & Miles, 2006; Frooman, 1999; Frooman & Murrell, 2005; Mitchell, Agle & Wood, 1997; Phillips, 2003b; Post *et al.*, 2002b.
8. Clarkson, 1998: 2.
9. Goodpaster, 1991.
10. Freeman, 1984.
11. Freeman, 1984: 46.
12. E.g. Clarkson, 1998; Freeman *et al.*, 2010; Gray, Owen & Adams, 1996; Jones & Wicks, 1999; Phillips, 2003b; Wood & Jones, 1993.
13. Frooman, 1999.
14. Friedman & Miles, 2006: 11.
15. E.g. Clarkson, 1998; Freeman & Gilbert, 1987; Freeman *et al.*, 2010; Frooman, 1999; Gray *et al.*, 1996; Jones & Wicks, 1999; Rowley & Moldoveanu, 2003; Wood & Jones, 1993.
16. E.g. Brenner, 1993; Calton & Lad, 1995; Clement, 2005; Deephouse & Suchman, 2008; Driscoll & Crombie, 2001; Hill & Jones, 1992; Phillips, 2003a; Waddock, 2008.

17. E.g. Bishop, 2000; Friedman & Miles, 2006; Gilmartin & Freeman, 2002; Hendry, 2001.
18. E.g. Goodpaster, 1991; Werhane, 2002, 2008; Willke & Willke, 2008.
19. E.g. Calton, 2004; Carroll & Hannan, 1989; Donaldson & Preston, 1995; Freeman *et al.*, 2010; Freeman & Phillips, 2002; Gibson, 2000; Weiss, 2009.
20. E.g. Blair, 1995; Boatright, 2002; Clarkson, 1995.
21. E.g. Boatright, 2002; Hill & Jones, 1992.
22. Mitchell *et al.*, 1997.
23. Deephouse & Suchman, 2008.
24. E.g. Asher *et al.*, 2005; Bosse *et al.*, 2009; Clarkson, 1995; Freeman, Martin & Parmar, 2007; Freeman *et al.*, 2010; Jones & Wicks, 1999; Kochan & Rubinstein, 2000.
25. E.g. Burchell & Cook, 2006b, 2008; Friedman & Miles, 2006; Mena *et al.*, 2010; Morsing & Schultz, 2006; Payne & Calton, 2002, 2004.
26. Rowley & Moldoveanu, 2003.
27. Brickson, 2007.
28. E.g. Brickson, 2007; Holzer, 2008; Jones, Felps & Bigley, 2007; Scott & Lane, 2000.
29. Turcotte, 1995.
30. Butterfield, Reed & Lemak, 2004.
31. Savage, Bunn, Gray, Xiao & Wang, 2008: 1.
32. Friedman & Miles, 2006: 161–162 according to Arnstein, 1969; in a similar way Bendell, 2003.
33. Burchell & Cook, 2008.
34. E.g. Bosse *et al.*, 2009; Frances-Gomez & del Rio, 2008; Payne & Calton, 2002; Sacconi, 2007.
35. Waddock, 2001.
36. Rowley, 1997a.
37. Freeman, 1984.
38. E.g. Boutilier, 2009; Calton & Payne, 2003; Frankforter & Hill, 2009; Frooman, 1999; Frooman & Murrell, 2005; Garriga, 2009; Gray, 1989; Habish, 2001; Roloff, 2008a; Rowley, 1997a; Savage *et al.*, 2008; Svendsen & Laberge, 2006; Windsor, 2008.
39. E.g. Granovetter, 1985; Kilduff, Tsai & Hanke, 2006; Uzzi, 1996.
40. Roloff, 2008a; Roloff & Assländer, 2010.
41. Post *et al.*, 2002b.
42. Post *et al.*, 2002b: 19.
43. Donaldson & Preston, 1995.
44. Post *et al.*, 2002b: 26.
45. Freeman, 1984.

46. E.g. Berman, Wicks, Kotha & Jones, 1999; Cennamo, Berrone & Gomez-Mejia, 2009; Donaldson & Preston, 1995; Hillman & Keim, 2001; Jones 1995; Margolis & Walsh, 2003; O'Higgins, 2010.
47. E.g. Rodgers & Gago, 2004; Sharma & Henriques, 2005; Wright, Smith & Wright, 2007.
48. E.g. Harrison & St. John, 1996; Steadman, Zimmerer & Green, 1995.
49. E.g. Barney & Clark, 2007; Bosse *et al.*, 2009; Harrison, Bosse & Phillips, 2007, 2010; Jones, 1995; Kim & Mahoney, 2010.
50. E.g. Greenwood & van Buren, 2010; Post, 1978; Post *et al.*, 2002b; Sachs, Rühli & Kern, 2009.
51. E.g. Asher *et al.*, 2005; Blair, 2005; Blair & Stout, 1999; Foss & Foss, 2005; Harrison *et al.*, 2007.
52. Blair & Stout, 1999: 265.
53. E.g. Berman *et al.*, 1999; Carroll, 2000; Margolis & Walsh, 2003; Rowley & Berman, 2000; Wood, 2010.
54. Margolis & Walsh, 2003.
55. Banks & Vera, 2007.
56. Banks & Vera, 2007.
57. Sachs, Rühli & Kern, 2009.
58. Donaldson & Preston, 1995.
59. For overviews see Agle *et al.*, 2008; Freeman *et al.*, 2010; Friedman & Miles, 2006; Nicolodi, 2007.
60. E.g. Boatright, 1994; Bosse *et al.*, 2009; Donaldson & Preston, 1995; Etzioni, 1998; Goodpaster, 1991; Hendry, 2001; Hill & Jones, 1992.
61. Goodpaster, 1991.
62. Goodpaster, 1991; see also Werhane, 2009.
63. Hendry, 2001: 225.
64. Hendry, 2001.
65. E.g. Asher *et al.*, 2005; Blair & Stout, 1999.
66. Kim & Mahoney, 2005.
67. Donaldson & Preston, 1995: 83.
68. Phillips, Freeman & Wicks, 2003.
69. Bosse *et al.*, 2009.
70. Bosse *et al.*, 2009.
71. Cropanzano, Bowen & Guilliland, 2007.
72. E.g. Burton & Dunn, 1996; Calton & Payne, 2003; Evan & Freeman, 1987; Freeman *et al.*, 2010; Friedman & Miles, 2006; Phillips *et al.*, 2003.
73. Evan & Freeman, 1987.
74. Evan & Freeman, 1987: 103.
75. Burton & Dunn, 1996.
76. E.g. Agle *et al.*, 2008; Freeman *et al.*, 2010.

77. Goodpaster, 1991; Hendry, 2001.
78. Sachs & Maurer, 2009.
79. Evan & Freeman, 1987.
80. Fromm, 1956: 15.
81. Fromm, 1997.
82. Fromm, 1997: 21.
83. Fromm, 1956: 24.
84. Fromm, 1997: 33; emphasis in the original.
85. Donaldson & Preston, 1995: 67.

4 The stakeholder paradigm

1. E.g. Asher *et al.*, 2005; Blair, 2005; Blair & Stout, 1999; Coff, 1999; Foss & Foss, 2005; Kim & Mahoney, 2006; Mahoney, McGahan & Pitelis, 2009; Stout, 2008.
2. Blair, 2005.
3. Mahoney, 2008.
4. E.g. Asher *et al.*, 2005; Blair, 2005; Blair & Stout, 1999; Kim & Mahoney, 2006.
5. Kim & Mahoney, 2010.
6. E.g. Blair & Stout, 1999; Coff, 1999.
7. E.g. Foss & Foss, 2005; Kim & Mahoney, 2010.
8. E.g. Asher *et al.*, 2005; Blair, 1995; Donaldson & Preston, 1995; Kim & Mahoney, 2007.
9. Asher *et al.*, 2005.
10. Asher *et al.*, 2005: 6.
11. Grandori, 2005.
12. Blair, 2005.
13. Asher *et al.*, 2005; see also Boatright, 2002, for a similar discussion on the nexus of contracts view.
14. Coff, 1999.
15. Asher *et al.*, 2005: 10.
16. Blair, 1995: 21.
17. Stout, 2008: 173.
18. Blair, 2005.
19. Stout, 2002: 1192.
20. Asher *et al.*, 2005.
21. Blair & Stout, 1999.
22. Blair, 1995.
23. Blair & Stout, 1999: 261.
24. Blair & Stout, 1999, 2005.
25. Stout, 2002.
26. van Buren, 2010.

27. Blair, 1995; Mahoney *et al.*, 2009.
28. Blair, 1995: 326; emphasis in the original.
29. Blair, 1995: 18.
30. Blair, 1995.
31. Freeman *et al.*, 2010.
32. See also Freeman, 1984; Freeman, Harrison & Wicks, 2007.
33. See also Freeman & Phillips, 2002.
34. See also Freeman, 2004; Freeman & McVea, 2001.
35. Freeman *et al.*, 2010.
36. Freeman *et al.*, 2010; Freeman & Liedtka, 1997; Freeman, Martin & Parmar, 2007.
37. Freeman *et al.*, 2010; Freeman, Martin & Parmar, 2007.
38. See also Freeman, 1984; Freeman & Phillips, 2002; McVea & Freeman, 2005.
39. Freeman *et al.*, 2010.
40. See also Freeman, 2008; Freeman, Harrison & Wicks, 2007; McVea & Freeman, 2005.
41. Freeman *et al.*, 2010: 7.
42. Freeman *et al.*, 2010: 412.
43. Freeman *et al.*, 2010: 50.
44. Freeman, Martin & Parmar, 2007; Freeman, Wicks & Parmar, 2004.
45. See also Harrison & Freeman, 2004.
46. Freeman *et al.*, 2010: 414.
47. For an overview, see Chapter 7 of Freeman *et al.*, 2010.
48. See also Werhane & Freeman, 1999.
49. Freeman *et al.*, 2010.
50. Freeman *et al.*, 2010; see also Freeman, Martin & Parmar, 2007.
51. Freeman *et al.*, 2010: 412.
52. Freeman *et al.*, 2010; Freeman, Martin & Parmar, 2007.
53. Freeman *et al.*, 2010: 410.
54. Freeman *et al.*, 2010: 48; see also Freeman, 2008; Freeman, Martin & Parmar, 2007.
55. Freeman *et al.*, 2010: 413
56. Freeman *et al.*, 2010: 285.
57. Freeman *et al.*, 2010: 415; see also Freeman, 2000; Freeman & Phillips, 2002.
58. See also Freeman, 1984; Freeman, Martin & Parmar, 2007; Freeman & Phillips, 2002.
59. Freeman *et al.*, 2010.
60. Freeman *et al.*, 2010: 111.
61. Giddens, 1984.
62. See Matten & Crane, 2005; Post *et al.*, 2002b; Sachs, 2000.
63. Freeman *et al.*, 2010.

64. See Post *et al.*, 2002b; Sachs, Rühli & Kern, 2009.
65. E.g.Freeman *et al.*, 2010; Post *et al.*, 2002b; Sachs, Rühli & Kern, 2009; Savage *et al.*, 2008; Waddock, Bodwell & Graves, 2002.
66. See Freeman, 2008; Maturana & Varela, 1987.
67. Freeman *et al.*, 2010; Giddens, 1984.
68. E.g. Lenssen, Perrini, Tencati & Lacy, 2007; Phillips & Caldwell, 2005; Post *et al.*, 2002b; Sveiby, 1997.
69. Sachs *et al.*, 2009.
70. Akerlof & Kranton, 2010; Rowley & Moldoveanu, 2003; Sachs, Rühli, Moser, Krishnan & Lakshman, 2010.
71. Sachs, Groth & Schmitt, 2010; Sachs, Schmitt & Perrin, 2008.
72. Freeman, Harrison & Wicks, 2007; Post *et al.*, 2002b; Winn, 2001.
73. Sen, 1987; Stiglitz, 2006; both interpreting Adam Smith's often cited invisible hand in a globalized world.
74. Stiglitz, 2010b: 276.
75. Freeman *et al.*, 2010.
76. Dawkins, 1986.

5 Our understanding of the stakeholder paradigm operationalized in the three licenses

1. Gabel, 2009.
2. Ferraro *et al.*, 2005; Grant, 2010a, 2010b.
3. E.g. Barbera, 2010; Grant, 2010b; Stiglitz, 2010b.
4. E.g. Matten & Crane, 2005; Post *et al.*, 2002b; Sachs, Rühli & Kern, 2009; Sachs, Rühli & Meier, in press; Scherer & Palazzo, 2007; Zadek, 2001.
5. E.g. Fehr & Fischbacher, 2004; Sen, 1987, 2002; Stiglitz, 2010b; Stiglitz *et al.*, 2010.
6. E.g. Wilson, 1998.
7. E.g. Bowles, Choi & Hopfensitz, 2003.
8. E.g. Nowak, Tarnita & Wilson, 2010; Williams, 1966.
9. Bowles *et al.*, 2003.
10. E.g. Bowles *et al.*, 2003; Fehr & Fischbacher, 2004; Gintis, 2003.
11. Prins *et al.*, 2010.
12. Human Development Index (HDI), online: www.hdr.undp.org/en/; Human Poverty Index (HPI), online: www.hdr.undp.org/en/statistics/indices/hpi/; Happy Planet Index (HPI), online: www.happyplanetindex.org/
13. Stiglitz *et al.*, 2010.
14. Stiglitz *et al.*, 2010.
15. Stiglitz *et al.*, 2010: 64.
16. Putnam, 2003.

17. Putnam, 2003: 64.
18. Reich, 2009.
19. Donaldson & Preston, 1995.
20. Freeman, 2009; Pirson & Lawrence, 2010; Stiglitz *et al.*, 2010.
21. Putnam, 2003; Stiglitz *et al.*, 2010; we thank Ed Freeman for bringing Hilary Putnam to our attention.
22. Sachs *et al.*, 2007a; Sachs *et al.*, 2009.
23. Donaldson & Preston, 1995.
24. See also Post *et al.*, 2002b; Sachs, Rühli & Kern, 2009.
25. Post *et al.*, 2002b.
26. Preston & Post, 1975: 39.
27. E.g. Freeman *et al.*, 2010; Freeman, Martin & Parmar, 2007; Pirson & Lawrence, 2010; Roloff, 2008a, 2008b; Sachs, Schmitt & Perrin, 2010; Wilson, Bunn & Savage, 2010.
28. E.g. Bäckstrand, 2006; Macdonald & Macdonald, 2010; Macdonald, 2008; Matten & Crane, 2005; O'Dwyer, 2005; Sachs, Rühli & Kern, 2009.
29. E.g. Foss & Foss, 2005; Foss, Klein, Kor & Mahoney, 2008; Post *et al.*, 2002b; Sachs, Rühli & Kern, 2009; Wang, He & Mahoney, 2009.
30. E.g. Davenport & Prusak, 2000; Leana & Rousseau, 2000; von Krogh, Nonaka & Aben, 2001.
31. Eklöf & Selivanova, 2008; Wallsten & Kosec, 2008.
32. E.g. Granovetter, 1985; Kilduff *et al.*, 2006; Uzzi, 1996.
33. When we mention Pfizer in the text we always refer to the Swiss subsidiary.
34. Sachs, Groth & Schmitt, 2010.
35. Santoro & Strauss, 2010.
36. Kern, Sachs & Rühli, 2007.
37. Boutilier, 2009.
38. Sachs, Groth & Schmitt, 2010.
39. E.g. Crane, Driver, Kaler, Parker & Parkinson, 2005; Freeman, 2004; Goodstein & Wicks, 2007; Sachs & Maurer, 2009; Schepers, 2006; Weidenbaum, 2009.
40. Ferri & Sandino, 2009; Logsdon & van Buren III, 2008; Monks, 2001; Nicolodi, 2007; Rehbein, Waddock & Graves, 2004.
41. E.g. Sachs, Rühli & Kern, 2009.
42. Post *et al.*, 2002b; Sachs, Rühli & Kern, 2009.
43. Post *et al.*, 2002b; Sachs, Rühli & Kern, 2009.
44. E.g. Herstatt, Lettl & Gemünden, 2006; Herstatt & von Hippel, 1992; Lüthje & Herstatt, 2004; Skiba & Herstatt, 2009.
45. E.g. Carroll & Ratner, 1996; Freeman *et al.*, 2010; Rowley & Moldoveanu, 2003; Sachs, Rühli & Kern, 2009.
46. E.g. Hardy, Lawrence & Grant, 2005.

47. E.g. Freeman, Harrison & Wicks, 2007; Freeman *et al.*, 2010; Freeman, Martin & Parmar 2007; Freeman *et al.*, 2004; Savage, Dunkin & Ford, 2004.
48. E.g. Asher *et al.*, 2005; Grandori, 2005; Kim & Mahoney, 2006, 2010.
49. E.g. Post *et al.*, 2002b; Roloff, 2008b; Sachs, Rühli & Kern, 2009; Savage *et al.*, 2008; Svendsen & Laberge, 2006.
50. E.g. Frooman, 1999; Frooman & Murrell, 2005; Post *et al.*, 2002b; Rowley, 1997a.
51. Friedman & Miles, 2006; Post *et al.*, 2002b.
52. E.g. Bosse *et al.*, 2009; Dawkins & Lewis, 2003; Sachs, Groth & Schmitt, 2010; Sachs, Schmitt & Perrin, 2010.
53. Coff, 1999.
54. E.g. Bowman & Ambrosini, 2000; Lepak, Smith & Taylor, 2007; Sachs, Groth & Schmitt, 2010.
55. Fromm, 1997.
56. Cooper & Owen, 2007; Paul, 2008; Pfeffer, 2010.
57. E.g. Roloff, 2008b; Roloff & Assländer, 2010; Savage *et al.*, 2008.
58. Sachs, Groth & Schmitt, 2010.
59. E.g. Austin, 2000; Basu & Palazzo, 2008; Burchell & Cook, 2006b; Crane & Livesey, 2003; Maclagan, 1999.
60. Accountability, UNEP & SRAC, 2005a: 80.

6 License to operate

1. E.g. Freeman *et al.*, 2010; Mahoney *et al.*, 2009; Post *et al.*, 2002b; Sachs, Rühli & Kern, 2009.
2. When Orange is mentioned in the text, we are always referring to the Swiss subsidiary.
3. Sachs, Rühli & Kern, 2009.
4. Yaziji & Doh, 2009.
5. Bengtsson, 2008; Starr, 2008.
6. Yaziji & Doh, 2009.
7. See criteria list Social Investment Forum, 2010: www.socialinvest.org/resources/mfpc/screening.cfm.
8. E.g. Bhimani & Soonawalla, 2005; Boesso & Kumar, 2007; Campbell, Moore & Shrives, 2006; Wood & Ross, 2006.
9. UBS, 2010.
10. Page, 2010.
11. E.g. Beck, 2000; Lad & Caldwell, 2009; Mark-Ungericht, 2001; Rifkin, 2004; Spar & La Mure, 2003; Wood & Logsdon, 2001; Yaziji & Doh, 2009.
12. Preston & Post, 1975: 11; italics in original.

13. Porter & Kramer, 2006: 81–82.
14. E.g. Elms & Phillips, 2009; Freeman, 2004; Hund, Engel-Cox, Fowler & Klee, 2002; Sachs & Maurer, 2009.
15. Reich, 2010: 148.
16. Mattingly & Greening, 2002.
17. E.g. Grunig & Hunt, 1984; Johnson & Meznar, 2005.
18. E.g. Hess, Rogovsky & Dunfee, 2002; Kemp, Boele & Brereton, 2006.
19. E.g. Buchholz & Rosenthal, 2004; Freeman *et al.*, 2007; Freeman *et al.*, 2010; Friedman & Miles, 2006; Matten & Crane, 2005.
20. E.g. Buchholz & Rosenthal, 2004; Fischer, Leydesdorff & Schophaus, 2004; Haas, 2004.
21. Perrin, 2010.
22. Mitchell *et al.*, 1997: 877.
23. Whereas the terms CSO and NGO are often used synonymously (Crane & Matten, 2007, 2010; Doh, 2008: Yaziji & Doh, 2009). In this book, we use the term NGO.
24. Yaziji & Doh, 2009.
25. Crane & Matten, 2007: 404.
26. Yaziji & Doh, 2009.
27. E.g. Clarkson, 1995; Freeman, 1984.
28. Galang, 2009.
29. Galang, 2009.
30. Crane & Matten, 2010; Fassin, 2009b.
31. Culpan & Trussel, 2005.
32. Dingwerth & Pattberg, 2006; Held, 2004.
33. See already Preston & Post, 1975.
34. Wilson *et al.*, 2010: 76.
35. E.g. Easton, 1965; Held, 1996; Terchek & Conte, 2001.
36. Crane & Matten, 2007.
37. McGrath, 2007; McGrath & Thomas, 2006; Vining, Shapiro & Borges, 2005.
38. Crane & Matten, 2007.
39. Reid, 2010.
40. E.g. Capriotti, 2009; Freeman, 1984; Freeman *et al.*, 2007; Hund *et al.*, 2002; Logsdon & Wood, 2002; Porter & Kramer, 2006; Post *et al.*, 2002b; Puncheva, 2008; Spar & La Mure, 2003; Zadek, 2004.
41. E.g. Perrin, 2010.
42. Post *et al.*, 2002b.
43. Perrin, 2010.
44. Perrin, 2010.
45. Kern *et al.*, 2007.
46. Kern *et al.*, 2007; Sachs, Rühli & Kern, 2009.

47. Post, Preston & Sachs, 2002a.
48. E.g. Monks, 2001; Nicolodi, 2007; Rehbein *et al.*, 2004.
49. E.g. Park-Poaps & Rees, 2010; Phillips & Caldwell, 2005; Tate, Ellram & Kirchoff, 2010.
50. Shell, 2005: 7.
51. Plaza-Ubeda, de Burgos-Jiménez & Carmona-Moreno, 2010.
52. E.g. Freeman *et al.*, 2010; Mahoney *et al.*, 2009; Reed & Reed, 2009; Savage *et al.*, 2008; Sloan, 2009.
53. Sloan, 2009.
54. Savage *et al.*, 2008.
55. Sloan, 2009.
56. Park-Poaps & Rees, 2010: 308, *sic.*
57. E.g. Kourula & Laasonen, 2010; Le Ber & Branzei, 2010; Wilson *et al.*, 2010.
58. Friedman & Miles, 2006.
59. E.g. den Hond & de Bakker, 2007; King, 2008.
60. E.g. Mattingly & Greening, 2002; Savage *et al.*, 2008.
61. E.g. Boutilier, 2009; King, 2008; Vallentin, 2009.
62. E.g. King, 2008; Vallentin, 2009.
63. Vallentin, 2009.
64. King, 2008; Vallentin, 2009.
65. Fassin, 2009a.
66. Post *et al.*, 2002a, 2002b; Sachs, Rühli & Kern, 2009.
67. Shell 2001: 43.
68. Kern *et al.*, 2007.
69. Kern *et al.*, 2007.
70. Hille, 2010.
71. ZKB, 2009
72. Novo Nordisk, 2007.
73. Frank, 2010.
74. Sachs, Groth & Schmitt, 2010; Sachs, Schmitt & Perrin, 2010.
75. E.g. Ramiller, 2005; Waddock, 2001.
76. E.g. Wheeler, Fabig & Boele, 2002; Yaziji & Doh, 2009.
77. Schmitt, 2007.
78. E.g. Sloan, 2009; Zollo & Winter, 2002.
79. Schmitt, 2007.
80. E.g. Banks & Vera, 2008; Margolis & Walsh, 2003; Waddock 2009; Wood, 2010
81. Carroll, 2000.
82. Rowley & Berman, 2000.
83. E.g. Eccles & Krzus, 2010; Fransen & Kolk, 2007; Paine, Deshpandé, Margolis & Bettcher, 2005; Scalet & Kelly, 2010.
84. E.g. Cheney, Roper & May, 2007; Waddock, 2008.

85. E.g. Garcia-Castro, Ariño & Canela, 2010; Margolis & Walsh, 2003; Marquis, Glynn & Davis, 2007.
86. Freeman *et al.*, 2010: 23.
87. E.g. Bies, Bartunek, Fort & Zald, 2007; Gainet, 2008; Marquis *et al.*, 2007.
88. Marquis *et al.*, 2007.
89. Marquis *et al.*, 2007: 939.
90. Waddock, 2008.
91. Lund-Thomsen & Reed, 2009.
92. Austin, 2000.
93. For a list of such indicators see Sachs, Rühli & Kern, 2009; see also Sachs, Groth & Schmitt, 2010; Sachs, Schmitt & Perrin, 2010.

7 License to innovate

1. E.g. Cooperrider & Fry, 2009; Hart & Milstein, 2003; Laugel & Laszlo, 2009; Sloan, 2009.
2. E.g. Asher *et al.*, 2005; Blair, 2005; Blair & Stout, 1999; Foss & Foss, 2005; Kim & Mahoney, 2006; Stout, 2010.
3. See also Asher *et al.*, 2005; Freeman *et al.*, 2010; Kim & Mahoney, 2006.
4. Tidd, Bessant & Pavitt, 2005.
5. Post *et al.*, 2002b: 53.
6. Sachs, Groth & Schmitt, 2010.
7. Sachs, Groth & Schmitt, 2010.
8. E.g. Davenport & Prusak, 2000; Leana & Rousseau, 2000; von Krogh *et al.*, 2001.
9. E.g. Herstatt *et al.*, 2006; Lüthje & Herstatt, 2004; Skiba & Herstatt, 2009.
10. Sachs, Rühli & Kern, 2009.
11. Drucker, 1993: 8; emphasis in the original.
12. Sachs, Groth & Schmitt, 2010.
13. Nahapiet & Ghoshal, 1998: 245, 248.
14. Dussauge, Garrette & Mitchell, 2004: 707.
15. Sachs, Groth & Schmitt, 2010; Sachs, Schmitt & Perrin, 2010.
16. ZKB, 2010.
17. Nidumolu, Prahalad & Rangaswami, 2009.
18. Sachs & Munshi, 2003.
19. Asher *et al.*, 2005: 14.
20. Moran & Ghoshal, 1996.
21. Wong, 2010.
22. Locher, 2006; see also the homepage of Swissmedic: www.swissmedic.ch/org/00063/index.html?lang=de&download.

23. E.g. Kochan & Rubinstein, 2000; Sachs & Maurer, 2009; Sachs & Rühli, 2001a; Wilson *et al.*, 2010.
24. Sachs, Rühli & Kern, 2009.
25. E.g. Brown & Eisenhardt, 1997; Leonard-Barton, 1992; March, 1991.
26. *The Economist*, 2010.
27. Post *et al.*, 2002b; Sachs, Rühli & Kern, 2009.
28. Sachs, Rühli & Kern, 2007a: 15.
29. E.g. Kay & Shelton, 2000; Marks & Mirvis, 1992.
30. Schmitt, 2007.
31. Schmitt, 2007: 230.
32. E.g. Helfat *et al.*, 2007; Teece, 2007, 2009; Teece *et al.*, 1997; Zollo & Winter, 2002.
33. Sachs, Rühli & Kern, 2009.
34. Wang & Barney, 2006: 466.
35. Asher *et al.*, 2005; Sachs & Maurer, 2009.
36. Kim & Mahoney, 2010.
37. Sachs, Rühli & Peter, 2003.
38. Novo Nordisk, 2007.
39. Post *et al.*, 2002b; Sachs, Rühli & Kern, 2009; Schmitt, 2007.
40. Sachs, Groth & Schmitt, 2010.
41. Department of Health, 2009; Gittelman, 2008.

8 License to compete

1. Freeman *et al.*, 2010.
2. Porter & Kramer, 2006, 2011.
3. E.g. Powell, Koput & Smith-Doerr, 1996; Stuart, 2000.
4. E.g. Beckman, Haunschild & Phillips, 2004; Gulati, Nohria & Zaheer, 2000; Moody & White, 2003; Powell, White, Koput & Owen-Smith, 2005; Rowley, 1997a; Rowley & Moldoveanu, 2003; Savage *et al.*, 2008; Schilling & Phelps, 2007; Schmitt, 2007; Uzzi, 1997; Uzzi & Spiro, 2005; Venkatraman & Lee, 2004.
5. Kern *et al.*, 2007.
6. Sachs, Groth & Schmitt, 2010.
7. E.g. Gulati & Gargiulo, 1999; Podolny & Page, 1998.
8. Sachs, Rühli & Kern, 2009.
9. AccountAbility, UNEP & SRAC, 2005a.
10. E.g. Fritsch & Kauffeld-Monz, 2010; Mitsuhashi & Greve, 2009.
11. Rowley, 1997a.
12. Uzzi, 1997.
13. Tsai & Wen, 2009.

14. E.g. Rowley, 1997b; Rowley & Moldoveanu, 2003; Savage *et al.*, 2008; Schilling & Phelps, 2007; Uzzi, 1997; Uzzi & Spiro, 2005.
15. Uzzi, 1996.
16. E.g. Greve, Baum, Mitsuhashi & Rowley, 2010; Rowley, Greve, Rao, Baum & Shipilov, 2005.
17. Granovetter, 2005; Gudmundsson & Lechner, 2006.
18. Schmitt, 2007: 43.
19. E.g. Chatterjee, 2009; Hayward, 2002; Hitt, Harrison, Ireland & Best, 1998; Spitzeck, 2008.
20. Roloff, 2008a; Roloff & Assländer, 2010.
21. Butterfield *et al.*, 2004; for similar argumentations regarding stakeholders' motivation for collaboration see also den Hond & de Bakker, 2007; Goodstein & Wicks, 2007.
22. Savage *et al.*, 2008.
23. UBS, 2010.
24. Sachs, Groth & Schmitt, 2010.
25. Post *et al.*, 2002b; Sachs, Rühli & Kern, 2009.
26. Gudmundsson & Lechner, 2006.
27. Sachs, Rühli & Kern, 2009.
28. Ashforth & Johnson, 2001.
29. Uzzi, 1997.
30. Brandenburger & Nalebuff, 1996.
31. Porter & Kramer, 2006, 2011.
32. Porter & Kramer, 2006, 2011.
33. Sachs, Rühli & Kern, 2009.
34. Rowley *et al.*, 2005.
35. Porter & Kramer, 2006: 89.
36. Kern *et al.*, 2007.
37. Sachs *et al.*, 2007a.
38. Sachs, Rühli, Moser, Krishnan & Lakshman, 2010.
39. Porter, 2008: 86.
40. Reuters, 2010; Spiegel-Online, 2010. For events later in the year of 2010 see also www.welt.de/wirtschaft/article9662117/Stellenabbau-Opel-faehrt-Produktion-wieder-hoch.html.

9 Challenges resulting from a paradigm shift

1. Karnani, 2010
2. E.g. Baum & Singh, 1994; Hannan & Freeman, 1977; Lovas & Ghoshal, 2000; Maurer & Sachs, 2005; Sachs, 2000; Sachs & Rühli, 2001b; Winter, Cattani & Dorsch, 2007.
3. Dawkins, 1989; Sachs & Rühli, 2001b.
4. E.g. Mayr, 1991; Smith, 1989; Williams, 1992.
5. E.g. Eldredge, 1995; Vrba, 1985.

6. E.g. Aldrich, 2000; Brown & Eisenhardt, 1997; Romanelli & Tushman, 1994; Tushman, Newman & Romanelli, 1986; Tushman & Romanelli, 1985.

7. Hannan & Freeman, 1977.

8. E.g. Allen, Strathern & Baldwin, 2006; Barnett & Burgelman, 1996; Baum & Singh, 1994; Hannan & Freeman, 1977.

9. Dobrev, Kim & Carroll, 2003.

10. E.g. Bouncken, Teichert & Koch, 2006; Sydow, Schreyögg & Koch, 2009.

11. E.g. Brown & Eisenhardt, 1997; Koch, Eisend & Petermann, 2009.

12. E.g. Brown & Eisenhardt, 1997; Gersick, 1991.

13. Quinn, 1980.

14. Global Reporting Initiative: www.globalreporting.org/Home.

15. UN Global Compact: www.unglobalcompact.org/.

16. Corporation 20/20: www.corporation2020.org/.

17. Waddock, 2009.

18. E.g. Freeman *et al.*, 2010; Matten & Moon, 2008; van Oosterhout & Heugens, 2006; Windsor, 2001, 2006.

19. Karnani, 2010; Lin, 2010.

20. Gersick, 1991.

21. E.g. Haveman, Russo & Meyer, 2001; Romanelli & Tushman, 1994.

22. Hannan & Freeman 1977, 1984.

23. Tushman *et al.*, 1986.

24. E.g. Miner, 1994; Shapira, 1994.

25. Johnson, Scholes & Whittington, 2008: 179.

26. Leonard-Barton, 1992.

27. Schreyögg & Kliesch-Eberl, 2007.

28. Reich, 2007.

29. E.g. Becker, 1976; Becker & Murphy, 2001; Buchanan & Tullock, 1962.

30. Cameron, 2000; Ewert, 2009.

31. Lenssen, Bevan & Fontrodona, 2010.

32. E.g. Barbera, 2010; Sen, 1987; Stiglitz, 2010b; Stiglitz *et al.*, 2010.

33. See also Post *et al.*, 2002b; Sachs, Rühli & Kern, 2009; Sachs, Rühli & Maurer, 2006a.

34. Santoro & Strauss, 2010.

35. Argyris & Schön, 1978.

36. Sachs, Groth & Schmitt, 2010.

37. Sachs, Groth & Schmitt, 2010.

38. Post *et al.*, 2002b; Sachs, Rühli & Kern, 2009.

39. Fiol & Lyles, 1985.

40. Senge, 1990.

41. Post *et al.*, 2002b; Sachs, Rühli & Kern, 2009; Schmitt, 2007.

42. Lenssen *et al.*, 2010: 340.

43. Stiglitz, 2010b: 296.
44. We thank James Post for his contribution to strengthening our main messages.
45. Freeman *et al.*, 2010.
46. In the Corporation 20/20 project, some of our requirements are reflected in "New principles for Corporate Design" (see www.corporation2020.org).
47. Corley & Gioia, 2011: 29.
48. For an overview, see Kim & Mahoney, 2005.
49. Kim & Mahoney, 2005.
50. Stiglitz, 2010b.
51. Pirson & Lawrence, 2010.
52. Hofstede, 1998.
53. Calori & Sarnin, 1991.
54. Sachs, Rühli & Mittnacht, 2005.
55. Witt & Redding, 2009.
56. Veser, 2005.
57. Sachs, Rühli, Moser, Krishnan & Lakshman, 2010.
58. Christensen & Gordon, 1999.
59. Lee & Yu, 2004.
60. E.g. Fisher, 2010; Jones *et al.*, 2007; Lee & Yu, 2004; Posner, 2010.
61. Hall, 1992, 1993.
62. E.g. Crane, Matten & Spence, 2008; Crane, McWilliams, Matten, Moon & Siegel, 2008; Visser, Matten, Pohl & Tolhurst, 2007; Waddock & Bodwell, 2007.
63. Sachs, Rühli & Kern, 2009.
64. E.g. Allen *et al.*, 2006; Baum & Singh, 1994; Hannan & Freeman, 1977.
65. Calori & Sarnin, 1991.
66. Deshpandé & Parasuraman, 1986.
67. Sachs *et al.*, 2005
68. Jones *et al.*, 2007.
69. Freeman *et al.*, 2007.
70. Freeman *et al.*, 2007: 309.
71. Freeman *et al.*, 2007.
72. Jones *et al.*, 2007.
73. Nadkarni & Herrmann, 2010.
74. McCrae *et al.*, 2000; McCrae & John, 1992.
75. Fahr & Irlenbusch, 2008.
76. Post *et al.*, 2002b: 46.
77. Fisher, 2010.
78. Pirson & Lawrence, 2010.
79. Svendsen & Laberge, 2006.

80. E.g. AccountAbility, UNEP & SRAC, 2005a, 2005b; Friedman & Miles, 2006; Payne & Calton, 2002.
81. E.g. Harrison & Freeman, 1999; Rowley & Moldoveanu, 2003.
82. E.g. den Hond & de Bakker, 2007; Neville & Menguc, 2006.
83. E.g. Harrison & St. John, 1996; Kern, 2009.
84. E.g. L. C. Freeman, 2009; Werhane, 2008.
85. Kern, 2009.
86. E.g. Phillips & Caldwell, 2005; Roloff, 2008a; Rowley, 1997a; Svendsen & Laberge, 2006.
87. E.g. Granovetter, 1985; Kilduff *et al.*, 2006; Uzzi, 1996.
88. Blair & Stout, 1999: 323.
89. E.g. Bäckstrand, 2006; Bendell, 2005; Harrison & Freeman, 2004; Huse, 2007; Kaler, 2002; Lenssen *et al.*, 2010; Mahoney *et al.*, 2009; Matten & Crane, 2005.
90. Stout, 2010: 64.
91. Winkler, 2004.
92. Blair & Stout, 1999.
93. E.g. Fransen & Kolk, 2007; King & Lenox, 2000; Sethi, 2003.
94. E.g. Christmann & Taylor, 2006; Howard, Nash & Ehrenfeld, 2000; King & Lenox, 2000; Kolk & van Tuldere, 2002; Lenox & Nash, 2003.
95. OECD, 2004: 21.
96. Parts of this section are to be published in an article by Sachs, Rühli & Meier in the *Journal of Business Ethics* (in press).
97. E.g. Diamond & Mirrlees, 1971; Kaul & Mendoza, 2003; Kramer, 2004; Oguh, 2009.
98. E.g. Immergut, 1992; Keohane & Nye, 1977; Morgenthau, 1948; Waltz, 1979.
99. Parts of this section are to be published in an article by Sachs *et al.* in the *Journal of Business Ethics* (in press).
100. Abbott & Snidal, 2009; Dingwerth & Pattberg, 2006; Messner & Nuscheler, 2003; Rasche, 2008; Reinicke, 1997.
101. E.g. Abbott & Snidal, 2009; Benner, Reinicke & Witte, 2004; Brütsch & Lehmkuhl, 2007; Dingwerth & Pattberg, 2006; Held, 2004; Reinicke, 1997; Rosenau & Czempiel, 1992. International generally means relations between nation-state actors (in some cases non-state actors such as firms or NGOs are involved), whereas transnational generally means relations between non-state actors (e.g. NGOs, firms); e.g. Keck & Sikkink, 1999.
102. Sachs *et al.*, in press. See also Dingwerth & Pattberg, 2006; Rosenau, 1995.
103. See e.g. Benedek, 2006, 2008; Benner *et al.*, 2004.

104. Kaul, Conceição, Le Goulven & Mendoza, 2003.
105. E.g. Dingwerth & Pattberg, 2006; Held, 2004.
106. E.g. Held, 2004; Rondinelli, 2002; Wolf, 2000, 2003.
107. Fransen & Kolk, 2007.
108. Fransen & Kolk, 2007: 678.
109. Cerny, 2000.
110. E.g. Benner *et al.*, 2004; Midttun, 2007; Rasche, 2009.
111. Farer & Sisk, 2010: 2.
112. Farer & Sisk, 2010.
113. Parts of this section are to be published in an article by Sachs *et al.* in the *Journal of Business Ethics* (in press).
114. Zadek, 2001.
115. See www.cep.eu/en/analyses-of-eu-policy/financial-services/eba/
116. Rasche, 2010.
117. E.g. Asher *et al.*, 2005; Chatterjee & Harrison, 2001; Freeman *et al.*, 2010; Matten & Crane, 2005.
118. Pirson & Lawrence, 2010.
119. Spitzeck & Hansen, 2010.
120. E.g. Blair, 2005; Hemphill, 2004; Reich, 2009; Stout, 2010; Takala & Pallab, 2000.
121. Reich, 2009.

Epilogue

1. See also Chandler, 2007, for the visible hands of managers.

Appendix: Methodological considerations

1. E.g. Bryman & Bell, 2007; Putnam, 2003; Reyes, 2005; Thommen, 1983.
2. Freeman *et al.*, 2010.
3. E.g. Khurana, 2007; Leedy & Ormrod, 2010; Sen, 1987; Stiglitz, 2010b.
4. E.g. Becker & Niehaves, 2007; Hanrahan, 2003; Höijer, 2008.
5. E.g. Barbera, 2010; Pirson & Lawrence, 2010; Stiglitz, 2010b.
6. Freeman *et al.*, 2010.
7. Caldwell, 2004; Freeman *et al.*, 2010; Lamont, 2004; Mattingly, 2004; Post *et al.*, 2002b.
8. E.g. Agle, Mitchell & Sonnenfeld, 1999; Berman *et al.*, 1999; Coombs & Gilley, 2005; Greenley & Foxall, 1997; Hazlett & McKee, 2008; Hillman & Keim, 2001; Post *et al.*, 2002b; Shropshire & Hillman, 2007; Yang, Shen, Ho, Drew & Xue, in press.
9. Patton, 1999: 1193.

10. Post *et al.*, 2002b.
11. See especially our former publications, Sachs & Maurer, 2009; Sachs, Rühli & Kern, 2007b, 2009; Sachs, Rühli & Mittnacht, 2007.
12. Eisenhardt, 1989.
13. E.g. Eisenhardt & Graebner, 2007; Flyvbjerg, 2006; George & Bennett, 2005; Harrison & Freeman, 1999; Yin, 2009.
14. Creswell, 2009.
15. Yin, 2009: 17.
16. Flyvbjerg, 2006.
17. E.g. Bansel & Corley, 2011; Combs, 2010; Eisenhardt & Graebner, 2007; Siggelkow, 2007; Tushman, O'Reilly, Fenollosa, Kleinbaum & McGrath, 2007.
18. Creswell, 2009.
19. Ragin, 2000.
20. Bryman & Bell, 2007.
21. E.g. Creswell, 2007; Yin, 2009.
22. E.g. Bryman & Bell, 2007; Creswell, 2009; Flick, 2009.
23. E.g. Bryman & Bell, 2007; Eisenhardt, 1989; Stake, 2006; Yin, 2009.
24. Creswell, 2009; Flick, 2009.
25. Creswell, 2009; Leedy & Ormrod, 2010.
26. See homepage of Atlas.ti: www.atlasti.com/.
27. Miles & Huberman, 1994.
28. Sachs, Schmitt & Perrin, 2010.
29. E.g. Cho & Egan, 2010; Gustavsen, 2006; Heron & Reason, 2006; Sachs, Groth & Schmitt, 2010; Sachs, Schmitt & Perrin, 2010; Tsai, Pan & Chiang, 2004; Van de Ven, 2007.
30. E.g. Baskerville & Myers, 2004; Tsai *et al.*, 2004.
31. E.g. Gustavsen, 2006; Heron & Reason, 2006; Senge & Scharmer, 2006.
32. Yin, 2009.
33. These studies were conducted in the case studies "Good Practices of Stakeholder View" and the action research based on the case study described in the last paragraph. The reference is given in the text when the case is described.
34. The reference is given in the text when the case is described.
35. Post *et al.*, 2002b.
36. The reference is given in the text when the case is described.

Glossary

1. Kuhn, 1996: 175.
2. Kuhn, 1996: 175.

Bibliography

Abbott, K. W., & Snidal, D. (2009). The Governance Triangle: Regulatory Standards Institutions and the Shadow of the State. In W. Mattli & N. Woods (Eds.), *The Politics of Global Regulation* (44–88). Princeton University Press.

AccountAbility, UNEP & SRAC (2005a). The Stakeholder Engagement Manual. Volume 1: The Guide to Practitioners' Perspectives on Stakeholder Engagement. Retrieved from www.accountability21. net/uploadedFiles/publications/Stakeholder%20Engagement_ Practitioners%27%20Perspectives.pdf.

(2005b). The Stakeholder Engagement Manual. Volume 2: The Practitioner's Handbook on Stakeholder Engagement. Retrieved from www.accountability21.net/uploadedFiles/publications/Stakeholder% 20Engagement%20Handbook.pdf.

Agle, B. R., Donaldson, T., Freeman, R. E., Jensen, M. C., Mitchell, R. K., & Wood, D. J. (2008). Dialogue: Towards Superior Stakeholder Theory. *Business Ethics Quarterly*, **18**(2), 153–190.

Agle, B. R., Mitchell, R. K., & Sonnenfeld, J. A. (1999). Who Matters to CEOs? An Investigation of Stakeholder Attributes and Salience, Corporate Performance, and CEO Values. *Academy of Management Journal*, **42**(5), 507–525.

Akerlof, G. A., & Kranton, R. (2010). Identity Economics. *The Economists' Voice*, **7**(2). Retrieved from www.bepress.com/ev/vol7/iss2/art6/.

Alchian, A. A., & Demsetz, H. (1972). Production, Information Costs, and Economic Organization. *The American Economic Review*, **62**(5), 777–795.

Aldrich, H. E. (2000). *Organizations Evolving*. London: Sage.

Allen, P. M., Strathern, M., & Baldwin, J. S. (2006). Evolutionary Drive: New Understandings of Change in Socio-Economic Systems. *Emergence: Complexity & Organization*, **8**(2), 2–19.

Amit, R., & Schoemaker, P. J. H. (1993). Strategic Assets and Organizational Rent. *Strategic Management Journal*, **14**(1), 33–46.

Aragon-Correa, J. A., & Sharma, S. (2003). A Contingent Resource-Based View of Proactive Corporate Environmental Strategy. *Academy of Management Review*, **28**(1), 71–88.

Argyris, C., & Schön, D. A. (1978). *Organizational Learning: A Theory of Action Perspective*. Reading, MA: Addison-Wesley.

Arnstein, S. R. (1969). A Ladder of Citizen Participation. *American Institute of Planners Journal*, 35(July), 216–224.

Asher, C. C., Mahoney, J. M., & Mahoney, J. T. (2005). Towards a Property Rights Foundation for a Stakeholder Theory of the Firm. *Journal of Management and Governance*, 9(1), 5–32.

Ashforth, B. E., & Johnson, S. A. (2001). Which Hat to Wear? The Relative Salience of Multiple Identities in Organizational Contexts. In M. A. Hogg & D. J. Terry (Eds.), *Social Identity Processes in Organizational Contexts* (31–48). Philadelphia: Psychology Press.

Austin, J. E. (2000). *The Collaboration Challenge: How Nonprofits and Businesses Succeed Through Strategic Alliances*. Dorchester: Jossey-Bass.

Bäckstrand, K. (2006). Democratizing Global Environmental Governance? Stakeholder Democracy after the World Summit on Sustainable Development. *European Journal of International Relations*, 12(4), 467–498.

Bain, J. S. (1959). *Industrial Organization*. New York: John Wiley.

Banks, M., & Vera, D. (2007). *Towards a Typology of Stakeholder Management Strategies*. Paper presented at the Academy of Management, Philadelphia, PA.

(2008). *Stakeholder Management Strategies, Institutional Forces, and Firm Performance: An Empirical Examination of Strategy Content*. Paper presented at the Academy of Management (AoM) Annual Meeting, Anaheim, CA.

Bansal, P. T., & Corley, K. (2011). The Coming of Age for Qualitative Research: Embracing the Diversity of Qualitative Methods. *Academy of Management Journal*, 54(2), 233–237.

Barbera, R. J. (2010). If It Were a Fight, They Would Have Stopped It in December of 2008. *The Berkeley Electronic Press: The Economists' Voice*, April (May 4), 1–4. Retrieved from www.bepress.com/ev/.

Barnett, W. P., & Burgelman, R. A. (1996). Evolutionary Perspectives on Strategy. *Strategic Management Journal*, 17(S1), 5–19.

Barney, J. B. (1991). Firm Resources and Sustained Competitive Advantage. *Journal of Management*, 17(1), 99–120.

(1992). Integrating Organizational Behavior and Strategy Formulation Research: A Resource Based Analysis. In P. Shrivastava, A. Huff & J. E. Dutton (Eds.), *Advances in Strategic Management, Vol. 8* (39–61). Greenwich, CT: JAI Press.

(1995). Looking Inside for Competitive Advantage. *Academy of Management Executive*, 9(4), 49–61.

(1996a). *Gaining and Sustaining Competitive Advantage*. New York: Addison-Wesley.

(1996b). The Resource-Based Theory of the Firm. *Organization Science*, 7(5), 469.

(2001). Is the Resource-Based "View" a Useful Perspective for Strategic Management Research? Yes. *Academy of Management Review*, 26(1), 41–56.

(2005). Should Strategic Management Research Engage Public Policy Debates? *Academy of Management Journal*, 48(6), 945–948.

Barney, J. B., & Clark, D. N. (2007). *Resource-Based Theory: Creating and Sustaining Competitive Advantage*. New York: Oxford University Press.

Barney, J. B., & Hesterly, W. (1996). Organizational Economics: Understanding the Relationship between Organizations and Economic Analysis. In S. R. Clegg, C. Hardy & W. R. Nord (Eds.), *Handbook of Organization Studies* (115–147). London: Sage.

(2010). *Strategic Management and Competitive Advantage. Concepts and Cases* (3rd edn). Upper Saddle River: Pearson.

Baskerville, R., & Myers, M. D. (2004). Special Issue on Action Research in Information Systems: Making IS Research Relevant to Practice – Foreword. *MIS Quarterly*, 28(3), 329–335.

Basu, K., & Palazzo, G. (2008). Corporate Social Responsibility: A Process Model of Sensemaking. *Academy of Management Review*, 33(1), 122–136.

Baum, J. A. C., & Singh, J. V. (1994). Organizational Hierarchies and Evolutionary Processes: Some Reflections on a Theory of Organizational Evolution. In J. A. C. Baum & J. V. Singh (Eds.), *Evolutionary Dynamics of Organizations* (3–20). New York: Oxford University Press.

BBC (2009). Free Market Flawed, says Survey. *BBC* (November 9). Retrieved from http://news.bbc.co.uk/2/hi/8347409.stm.

Becerra, M. (2009). *Theory of the Firm for Strategic Management: Economic Value Analysis*. Cambridge University Press.

Beck, U. (2000). *What Is Globalization?* Malden: Blackwell.

(2008). Risikogesellschaften und die Transnationalisierung sozialer Ungleichheiten. In P. A. Berger & A. Weiss (Eds.), *Transnationalisierung sozialer Ungleichheit* (19–40). Wiesbaden: VS Verlag für Sozialwissenschaften.

(2010). Remapping Social Inequalities in an Age of Climate Change: For a Cosmopolitan Renewal of Sociology. *Global Networks*, 10(2), 165–181.

Becker, G. S. (1976). *The Economic Approach to Human Behavior*. University of Chicago Press.

Becker, G. S., & Murphy, K. M. (2001). *Social Economics: Market Behavior in a Social Environment*. Cambridge, MA: Harvard University Press.

Becker, J., & Niehaves, B. (2007). Epistemological Perspectives on IS Research: A Framework for Analysing and Systematizing Epistemological Assumptions. *Info Systems Journal*, 17, 197–214.

Beckman, C. M., Haunschild, P. R., & Phillips, D. J. (2004). Friends or Strangers? Firm-Specific Uncertainty, Market Uncertainty, and Network Partner Selection. *Organization Science*, 15(3), 259–275.

Bendell, J. (2003). Talking for Change? Reflections on Effective Stakeholder Dialogue. In J. Andriof, S. Waddock, B. Husted & S. S. Rahman (Eds.), *Unfolding Stakeholder Thinking* (Vol. 2, 53–69). Sheffield: Greenleaf Publishing Limited.

(2005). In Whose Name? The Accountability of Corporate Social Responsibility. *Development in Practice*, 15(3&4), 362–374.

Benedek, W. (2006). Global Governance der Weltwirtschaft. In P. Koller (Ed.), *Die globale Frage: Empirische Befunde und ethische Herausforderungen* (257–274). Vienna: Passagen Verlag.

(2008). The Emerging Global Civil Society: Achievements and Prospects. In V. Rittberger & M. Nettesheim (Eds.), *Authority in the Global Political Economy* (170–185). Houndmills: Palgrave Macmillan.

Bengtsson, E. (2008). Socially Responsible Investing in Scandinavia – a Comparative Analysis. *Sustainable Development*, 16, 155–168.

Benner, T., Reinicke, W. H., & Witte, J. M. (2004). Multisectoral Networks in Global Governance: Towards a Pluralistic System of Accountability. *Government and Opposition*, 39(2), 191–210.

Berman, S. L., Wicks, A. C., Kotha, S., & Jones, T. M. (1999). Does Stakeholder Orientation Matter? The Relationship between Stakeholder Management Models and Firm Financial Performance. *Academy of Management Journal*, 42(5), 488–506.

Bhimani, A., & Soonawalla, K. (2005). From Conformance to Performance: The Corporate Responsibilities Continuum. *Journal of Accounting and Public Policy*, 24(3), 165–174.

Bies, R. J., Bartunek, J. M., Fort, T. L., & Zald, M. N. (2007). Corporations as Social Change Agents: Individual, Interpersonal, Institutional, and Environmental Dynamics. *Academy of Management Review*, 32(3), 788–793.

Bishop, J. D. (2000). A Framework for Discussing Normative Theories of Business Ethics. *Business Ethics Quarterly*, 10(3), 563–591.

Blair, M. M. (1995). *Ownership and Control: Rethinking Corporate Governance for the Twenty-First Century*. Washington, DC: Brookings Institution.

(2005). Closing the Theory Gap: How the Economic Theory of Property Rights Can Help Bring "Stakeholders" Back into Theories of the Firm. *Journal of Management and Governance*, 9(1), 33–39.

Blair, M. M., & Stout, L. A. (1999). A Team Production Theory of Corporate Law. *Virginia Law Review*, **85**(2), 247–328.

Blyler, M., & Coff, R. W. (2003). Dynamic Capabilities, Social Capital, and Rent Appropriation: Ties that Split Pies. *Strategic Management Journal*, **24**(7), 677–686.

Boatright, J. R. (1994). Fiduciary Duties and the Shareholder-Management Relation: Or, What's so Special about Shareholders? *Business Ethics Quarterly*, **4**(4), 393–407.

   (2002). Contractors as Stakeholders: Reconciling Stakeholder Theory with the Nexus-of-Contracts Firm. *Journal of Banking and Finance*, **26**(9), 1837–1852.

Boesso, G., & Kumar, K. (2007). Drivers of Corporate Voluntary Disclosure: A Framework and Empirical Evidence from Italy and the United States. *Accounting, Auditing & Accountability Journal*, **20**(2), 269–296.

Bosse, D. A., Phillips, R. A., & Harrison, J. S. (2009). Stakeholders, Reciprocity, and Firm Performance. *Strategic Management Journal*, **30**(4), 447–456.

Bouncken, R. B., Teichert, T., & Koch, M. (2006). *Blending Management Styles for Learning Alliances*. Paper presented at the Academy of Management, Atlanta, GA. Academy of Management Best Conference.

Boutilier, R. G. (2009). *Stakeholder Politics: Social Capital, Sustainable Development and the Corporation*. Stanford: Greenleaf Publishing.

Bowles, S., Choi, J.-K., & Hopfensitz, A. (2003). The Co-Evolution of Individual Behaviors and Social Institutions. *Journal of Theoretical Biology*, **223**(2), 135–147.

Bowman, C., & Ambrosini, V. (2000). Value Creation Versus Value Capture: Towards a Coherent Definition of Value in Strategy. *British Journal of Management*, **11**(1), 1–15.

Brandenburger, A. M., & Nalebuff, B. J. (1996). *Co-Opetition*. New York: Doubleday.

Brenner, S. N. (1993). *The Stakeholder Theory of the Firm and Organizational Decision-Making: Some Propositions and a Model*. Paper presented at the International Association for Business and Society (IABS) Annual Meeting, San Diego, CA.

Brickson, S. L. (2007). Organizational Identity Orientation: The Genesis of the Role of the Firm and Distinct Forms of Social Value. *Academy of Management Review*, **32**(3), 864–888.

Brown, S. L., & Eisenhardt, K. M. (1997). The Art of Continuous Change: Linking Complexity Theory and Time-Paced Evolution in Relentlessly Shifting Organizations. *Administrative Science Quarterly*, **42**(1), 1–34.

(1998). *Competing on the Edge – Strategy as Structured Chaos.* Boston: Harvard Business School Press.

Brütsch, C., & Lehmkuhl, D. (2007). Complex Legalization and the Many Moves to Law. In C. Brütsch & D. Lehmkuhl (Eds.), *Law and Legalization in Transnational Relations* (9–32). London: Routledge.

Bryman, A., & Bell, E. (2007). *Business Research Methods* (2nd edn). Oxford University Press.

Buchanan, J. M., & Tullock, G. (1962). *The Calculus of Consent: Logical Foundations of Constitutional Democracy.* Ann Arbor: University of Michigan Press.

Buchholz, R. A., & Rosenthal, S. B. (2004). Stakeholder Theory and Public Policy: How Governments Matter. *Journal of Business Ethics*, 51(2), 143–153.

Burchell, J., & Cook, J. (2006a). Assessing the Impact of Stakeholder Dialogue: Changing Relationships between NGOs and Companies. *Journal of Public Affairs*, 6(3–4), 210–227.

(2006b). It's Good to Talk? Examining Attitudes towards Corporate Social Responsibility Dialogue and Engagement Processes. *Business Ethics: A European Review*, 15(2), 154–170.

(2008). Stakeholder Dialogue and Organisational Learning: Changing Relationships between Companies and NGOs. *Business Ethics: A European Review*, 17(1), 35–46.

Burton, B. K., & Dunn, C. P. (1996). Feminist Ethics as Moral Grounding for Stakeholder Theory. *Business Ethics Quarterly*, 6(2), 133–147.

Butterfield, K. D., Reed, R., & Lemak, D. J. (2004). An Inductive Model of Collaboration From the Stakeholder's Perspective. *Business & Society*, 43(2), 162–195.

Caldwell, C. (2004). Book Review Essay: Effective Governance in Managing Change – Common Perspective from two Lenses. *Academy of Management Review*, 29(2), 296–301.

Calori, R., & Sarnin, P. (1991). Corporate Culture and Economic Performance: A French Study. *Organization Studies*, 12(1), 49–74.

Calton, J. M. (2004). Social Contracting in a Pluralist Process of Moral Sense Making: A Dialogic Twist on the ISCT. *Journal of Business Ethics*, 68(3), 329–346.

Calton, J. M., & Lad, L. J. (1995). Social Contracting as a Trust-Building Process of Network Governance. *Business Ethics Quarterly*, 5(2), 271–295.

Calton, J. M., & Payne, S. L. (2003). Coping With Paradox: Multistakeholder Learning Dialogue as a Pluralist Sensemaking Process for Addressing Messy Problems. *Business & Society*, 42(1), 7–42.

Cameron, J. (2000). Development Economics, the New Institutional Economics and NGOS. *Third World Quarterly*, **21**(4), 627–635.

Campbell, D., Moore, G., & Shrives, P. (2006). Cross-Sectional Effects in Community Disclosure. *Accounting, Auditing & Accountability Journal*, **19**(1), 96–114.

Capriotti, P. (2009). Economic and Social Roles of Companies in the Mass Media: The Impact Media Visibility Has on Businesses' Being Recognized as Economic and Social Actors. *Business & Society*, **48**(2), 225–242.

Carroll, A. B. (2000). A Commentary and an Overview of Key Questions on Corporate Social Performance Measurement. *Business & Society*, **39**(4), 466–478.

Carroll, G. R., & Hannan, M. T. (1989). Density Delay in the Evolution of Organizational Populations: A Model and Five Empirical Tests. *Administrative Science Quarterly*, **34**(3), 411–430.

Carroll, W. K., & Ratner, R. S. (1996). Master Framing and Cross-Movement Networking in Contemporary Social Movements. *The Sociological Quarterly*, **37**(4), 601–625.

Caves, R. E. (1980). Industrial Organization, Corporate Strategy and Structure. *Journal of Economic Literature*, **18**(1), 64–92.

(1984). Economic Analysis and the Quest for Competitive Advantage. *The American Economic Review*, **74**(2), 127–132.

Caves, R. E., & Porter, M. E. (1977). From Entry Barriers to Mobility Barriers: Conjectural Decisions and Contrived Deterrence to New Competition. *Quarterly Journal of Economics*, **91**(2), 241–262.

(1978). Market Structure, Oligopoly, and Stability of Market Shares. *The Journal of Industrial Economics*, **26**(4), 289–313.

Cennamo, C., Berrone, P., & Gomez-Mejia, L. R. (2009). Does Stakeholder Management have a Dark Side? *Journal of Business Ethics*, **89**(4), 491–507.

Cerny, P. G. (2000). Globalization and the Disarticulation of Political Power: Towards a New Middle Ages? In H. Goverde, P. G. Cerny, M. Haugaard & H. H. Lentner (Eds.), *Power in Contemporary Politics: Theories, Practices, Globalizations* (170–186). London: Sage.

Chandler, A. (1977). *The Visible Hand: A Managerial Revolution in American Business*. Cambridge, MA: Belknap Press.

Chatain, O. (2011). Value Creation, Competition, and Performance in Buyer-Supplier Relationships. *Strategic Management Journal*, **32**(1), 76–102.

Chatterjee, S. (2009). The Keys to Successful Acquisition Programmes. *Long Range Planning*, **42**(2), 137–163.

Chatterjee, S., & Harrison, J. S. (2001). Corporate Governance. In M. A. Hitt, R. E. Freeman & J. S. Harrison (Eds.), *The Blackwell Handbook of Strategic Management* (543–563). Oxford: Blackwell.

Cheney, G., Roper, J., & May, S. K. (2007). Overview. In S. K. May, G. Cheney & J. Roper (Eds.), *The Debate over Corporate Social Responsibility* (3–12). Oxford University Press.

Chi, T. (1994). Trading in Strategic Resources: Necessary Conditions, Transaction Cost Problems, and Choice of Exchange Structure. *Strategic Management Journal*, 15(4), 271–290.

Cho, Y., & Egan, T. M. (2010). The State of the Art of Action Learning Research. *Advances in Developing Human Resources*, 12(2), 163–180.

Christensen, E. W., & Gordon, G. G. (1999). An Exploration of Industry, Culture and Revenue Growth. *Organization Studies*, 20(3), 397–422.

Christmann, P., & Taylor, G. (2006). Firm Self-Regulation through International Certifiable Standards: Determinants of Symbolic versus Substantive Implementation. *Journal of International Business Studies*, 37(6), 863–878.

Clarkson, M. B. E. (1995). A Stakeholder Framework for Analyzing and Evaluating Corporate Social Performance. *Academy of Management Review*, 20(1), 92–117.

(1998). *The Corporation and its Stakeholders: Classic and Contemporary Readings*. University of Toronto Press.

Clement, R. W. (2005). The Lessons from Stakeholder Theory for U.S. Business Leaders. *Business Horizons*, 48(3), 255–264.

Coase, R. H. (1960). The Problem of Social Cost. *Journal of Law and Economics*, 3, 1–44.

(1991). The Nature of the Firm. In O. E. Williamson & S. G. Winter (Eds.), *The Nature of the Firm: Origins, Evolution, and Development* (18–33). New York: Oxford University Press.

Coff, R. W. (1999). When Competitive Advantage Doesn't Lead to Performance: The Resource-Based View and Stakeholder Bargaining Power. *Organization Science*, 10(2), 119–133.

(2003). The Emergent Knowledge-Based Theory of Competitive Advantage: An Evolutionary Approach to Integrating Economics and Management. *Managerial and Decision Economics*, 24(4), 245–251.

Combs, J. G. (2010). From the Editors: Big Samples and Small Effects: Let's Not Trade Relevance and Rigor for Power. *Academy of Management Journal*, 53(1), 9–13.

Conner, K. R. (1991). A Historical Comparison of Resource-Based Theory and Five Schools of Thought Within Industrial Organization

Economics: Do We Have a New Theory of the Firm? *Journal of Management*, 17(1), 121–154.

Conner, K. R., & Prahalad, C. K. (1996). A Resource-Based Theory of the Firm: Knowledge versus Opportunism. *Organization Science*, 7(5), 477–501.

Coombs, J. E., & Gilley, K. M. (2005). Stakeholder Management as a Predictor of CEO Compensation: Main Effects and Interactions with Financial Performance. *Strategic Management Journal*, 26(9), 827–840.

Cooper, S. M., & Owen, D. L. (2007). Corporate Social Reporting and Stakeholder Accountability: The Missing Link. *Accounting, Organizations and Society*, 32(7–8), 649–667.

Cooperrider, D., & Fry, R. (2009). A Peter Drucker Moment: Harnessing the Innovation-Generating Potential of a Shareholder and Stakeholder Theory of the Firm. *Journal of Corporate Citizenship*, 36(Winter), 3–6.

Corley, K. G., & Gioia, D. A. (2011). Building Theory about Theory Building: What Constitutes a Theoretical Contribution? *Academy of Management Review*, 38(1), 12–32.

Crane, A., Driver, C., Kaler, J., Parker, M., & Parkinson, J. (2005). Stakeholder Democracy: Towards a Multi-Disciplinary View. *Business Ethics: A European Review*, 14(1), 67–75.

Crane, A., & Livesey, S. (2003). Are You Talking to Me? Stakeholder Communication and the Risks and Rewards of Dialogue. In J. Andriof, S. Waddock, B. Husted & S. S. Rahman (Eds.), *Unfolding Stakeholder Thinking 2. Relationships, Communication, Reporting and Performance* (Vol. 2, 39–52). Sheffield: Greenleaf Publishing.

Crane, A., McWilliams, A., Matten, D., Moon, J., & Siegel, D. S. (Eds.). (2008). *The Oxford Handbook of Corporate Social Responsibility*. Oxford University Press.

Crane, A., & Matten, D. (2007). *Business Ethics: Managing Corporate Citizenship and Sustainability in the Age of Globalization* (2nd edn). Oxford University Press.

(2010). *Business Ethics: Managing Corporate Citizenship and Sustainability in the Age of Globalization* (3rd edn). Oxford University Press.

Crane, A., Matten, D., & Spence, L. J. (Eds.). (2008). *Corporate Social Responsibility: Readings and Cases in a Global Context*. Abingdon: Routledge.

Creswell, J. W. (2007). *Inquiry and Research Design: Choosing Among Five Approaches* (2nd edn). Thousand Oaks: Sage.

(2009). *Research Design: Qualitative, Quantitative, and Mixed Method Approaches* (3rd edn). Thousand Oaks: Sage.

Cropanzano, R., Bowen, D. E., & Guilliland, S. W. (2007). The Management of Organizational Justice. *Academy of Management Perspectives*, **21**(4), 34–48.

Culpan, R., & Trussel, J. (2005). Applying the Agency and Stakeholder Theories to the Enron Debacle: An Ethical Perspective. *Business & Society Review*, **110**(1), 59–76.

Cyert, R. M., & March, J. G. (1992). *A Behavioral Theory of the Firm*. Oxford: Blackwell.

D'Aveni, R. A. (1994). *Hypercompetition: Managing the Dynamics of Strategic Maneuvering*. New York: Free Press.

(1995). *Hypercompetitive Rivalries: Competing in Highly Dynamic Environments*. New York: Free Press.

Danneels, E. (2011). Trying to Become a Different Type of Company: Dynamic Capability at Smith Corona. *Strategic Management Journal*, **32**(1), 1–31.

Davenport, T. H., & Prusak, L. (2000). *Working Knowledge. How Organizations Manage what They Know*. Boston: Harvard Business School Press.

Dawkins, J., & Lewis, S. (2003). CSR in Stakeholder Expectations: And Their Implication for Company Strategy. *Journal of Business Ethics*, **44**(2–3), 185–193.

Dawkins, R. (1986). *The Blind Watchmaker: Why the Evidence of Evolution Reveals a Universe Without Design*. Bath: Norton Press.

(1989). *The Selfish Gene*. Oxford University Press.

Deephouse, D. L., & Suchman, M. C. (2008). Legitimacy in Organizational Insitutionalism. In R. Greenwood, C. Oliver, K. Sahlin & R. Suddaby (Eds.), *The SAGE Handbook of Organizational Institutionalism* (49–77). Thousand Oaks: Sage.

Demsetz, H. (1967). Toward a Theory of Property Rights. *American Economic Review*, **57**, 347–359.

den Hond, F., & de Bakker, F. G. A. (2007). Ideologically Motivated Activism: How Activist Groups Influence Corporate Social Change Activities. *Academy of Management Review*, **32**(3), 901–924.

Department of Health. (2009). *Ministerial Industry Strategy Group: Pharmaceutical Industry: Competitiveness and Performance Indicators* 2009. London: Department of Health. Retrieved from www.dh.gov.uk/prod_consum_dh/groups/dh_digitalassets/@dh/@en/@ps/documents/digitalasset/dh_113133.pdf.

Deshpandé, R., & Parasuraman, A. (1986). Linking Corporate Culture to Strategic Planning. *Business Horizons*, **29**(3), 28–37.

Diamond, P. A., & Mirrlees, J. A. (1971). Optimal Taxation and Public Production I: Production Efficiency. *The American Economic Review*, 61(1), 8–27.

Dierickx, I., & Cool, K. (1989). Asset Stock Accumulation and Sustainability of Competitive Advantage. *Management Science*, 35(12), 1504–1511.

Dingwerth, K., & Pattberg, P. (2006). Global Governance as a Perspective on World Politics. *Global Governance*, 12(2), 185–203.

Dobrev, S. D., Kim, T.-Y., & Carroll, G. R. (2003). Shifting Gears, Shifting Niches: Organizational Inertia and Change in the Evolution of the U.S. Automobile Industry, 1885–1981. *Organization Science*, 14(3), 264–282.

Doh, J. P. (2008). Between Confrontation and Cooperation: Corporate Citizenship and NGOs. In A. G. Scherer & G. Palazzo (Eds.), *Handbook Of Research On Global Corporate Citizenship* (273–292). Cheltenham: Edward Elgar.

Donaldson, T., & Preston, L. E. (1995). The Stakeholder Theory of the Corporation: Concepts, Evidence, and Implications. *Academy of Management Review*, 20(1), 65–91.

Driscoll, K., & Crombie, A. (2001). Stakeholder Legitimacy Management and the Qualified Good Neighbor: The Case of Nova Nada and JDI. *Business & Society*, 40(4), 442–471.

Drucker, P. F. (1993). *Post-Capitalist Society*. New York: HarperCollins.

Dussauge, P., Garrette, B., & Mitchell, W. (2004). Asymmetric Performance: The Market Share Impact of Scale and Link Alliances in the Global Auto Industry. *Strategic Management Journal*, 25(7), 701–711.

Easton, D. (1965). *A Framework for Political Analysis*. Englewood Cliffs: Prentice Hall.

Eccles, R. G., & Krzus, M. P. (2010). *One Report: Integrated Reporting for a Sustainable Strategy*. Hoboken: Wiley.

The Economist (2010, July 24). After the Leak: BP and the Gulf, *The Economist*.

Eisenhardt, K. M. (1989). Building Theories from Case Study Research. *Academy of Management Review*, 14(4), 532–550.

Eisenhardt, K. M., & Graebner, M. E. (2007). Theory Building from Cases: Opportunities and Challenges. *Academy of Management Journal*, 50(1), 25–32.

Eisenhardt, K. M., & Zbaracki, M. J. (1992). Strategic Decision Making. *Strategic Management Journal*, 13(S2), 17–37.

Eklöf, J., & Selivanova, I. (2008). Human Aspect in Service Quality: EPSI Benchmark Studies. *Total Quality Management*, 19(7–8), 827–841.

Eldredge, N. (1995). *Reinventing Darwin – The Great Evolutionary Debate*. London: Weidenfeld & Nicolson.

Ellsberg, D. (1961). Risk, Ambiguity and the Savage Axioms. *Quarterly Journal of Economics*, 75(4), 643–669.

Elms, H., & Phillips, R. A. (2009). Private Security Companies and Institutional Legitimacy: Corporate and Stakeholder Responsibility. *Business Ethics Quarterly*, 19(3), 403–432.

Etzioni, A. (1998). A Communitarian Note on Stakeholder Theory. *Business Ethics Quarterly*, 8(4), 679–691.

Evan, W. M., & Freeman, R. E. (1987). A Stakeholder Theory of the Modern Corporation: Kantian Capitalism. In T. L. Beauchamp & N. E. Bowie (Eds.), *Ethical Theory and Business* (97–106). Englewood Cliffs: Prentice Hall.

Ewert, B. (2009). Economization and Marketization in the German Healthcare System: How Do Users Respond? *German Policy Studies*, 5(1), 21–44.

Fahr, R., & Irlenbusch, B. (2008). Identifying Personality Traits to Enhance Trust between Organisations: An Experimental Approach. *Managerial and Decision Economics*, 29(6), 469–487.

Fama, E. F., & Jensen, M. C. (1983). Separation of Ownership and Control. *Journal of Law and Economics*, 26(2), 301–325.

Farer, T., & Sisk, T. D. (2010). Enhancing International Cooperation: Between History and Necessity. *Global Governance*, 16(1), 1–12.

Fassin, Y. (2009a). Inconsistencies in Activists' Behaviours and the Ethics of NGOs. *Journal of Business Ethics*, 90(4), 503–521.

(2009b). The Stakeholder Model Refined. *Journal of Business Ethics*, 84(1), 113–135.

Fehr, E., & Fischbacher, U. (2004). Social Norms and Human Cooperation. *Trends in Cognitive Sciences*, 8(4), 185–190.

Fehr, E., & Tyran, J.-R. (2005). Individual Irrationality and Aggregate Outcomes. *Journal of Economic Perspectives*, 19(4), 43–66.

(2008). Limited Rationality and Strategic Interaction: The Impact of the Strategic Environment on Nominal Inertia. *Econometrica*, 76(2), 353–394.

Ferraro, F., Pfeffer, J., & Sutton, R. I. (2005). Economic Language and Assumptions: How Theories can Become Self-Fulfilling. *Academy of Management Review*, 30(1), 8–24.

Ferri, F., & Sandino, T. (2009). The Impact of Shareholder Activism on Financial Reporting and Compensation: The Case of Employee Stock Options Expensing. *The Accounting Review*, 84(2), 433–466.

Fiol, C. M., & Lyles, M. A. (1985). Organizational Learning. *Academy of Management Review*, 10(4), 803–813.

Fischer, C., Leydesdorff, L., & Schophaus, M. (2004). Science Shops in Europe: The Public as Stakeholder. *Science and Public Policy*, 31(3), 199–211.

Fisher, G. (2010). *The Emergence of Stakeholder Culture: Founder and Early Stakeholder Imprinting Effects*. Paper presented at the Academy of Management Annual Meeting, Montreal, Canada.

Flick, U. (2009). *An Introduction to Qualitative Research* (4th edn). London: Sage.

Flyvbjerg, B. (2006). Five Misunderstandings About Case-Study Research. *Qualitative Inquiry*, 12(2), 219–245.

Foss, K., & Foss, N. J. (2005). Resources and Transaction Costs: How Property Rights Economics Furthers the Resource-Based View. *Strategic Management Journal*, 26(6), 541–553.

Foss, N. J. (1996). Research in Strategy, Economics, and Michael Porter. *Journal of Management Studies*, 33(1), 1–24.

(2000). The Theory of the Firm: An Introduction to Themes and Contributions. In N. J. Foss (Ed.), *The Theory of the Firm: Critical Perspectives on Business and Management, Vol. 1* (xv–lxi). London: Routledge.

(2003). The Rhetorical Dimensions of Bounded Rationality: Herbert A. Simon and Organizational Economics. In S. Rizzello (Ed.), *Cognitive Developments in Economics* (158–176). London: Routledge.

Foss, N. J. (Ed.). (2008). *The Theory of the Firm: Critical Perspectives on Business and Management* (Vol. I). London: Routledge.

Foss, N. J., Klein, P. G., Kor, Y. Y., & Mahoney, J. T. (2008). Entrepreneurship, Subjectivism, and the Resource-Based View: Toward a New Synthesis. *Strategic Entrepreneurship Journal*, 2(1), 73–94.

Frances-Gomez, P., & del Rio, A. (2008). Stakeholder's Preference and Rational Compliance: A Comment on Sacconi's "CSR as a Model for Extended Corporate Governance II: Compliance, Reputation and Reciprocity". *Journal of Business Ethics*, 82(1), 59–76.

Frank, T. (2010). Oil Fund Chief Promises Fast, Fair Payments. *USA Today* (June 21). Retrieved from www.usatoday.com/news/nation/2010–06 –20-gulf-oil_N.htm?csp=usat.me.

Frankforter, S. A., & Hill, V. (2009). *A Model of Stakeholder Networks: Qualities, Relationships and Structure*. Paper presented at the Academy of Management, Chicago, IL.

Fransen, L. W., & Kolk, A. (2007). Global Rule-Setting for Business: A Critical Analysis of Multi-Stakeholder Standards. *Organization*, 14(5), 667–684.

Freeman, L. C. (2009). Methods of Social Network Visualization. In R. A. Meyers (Ed.), *Encyclopedia of Complexity and Systems Science* (205). Berlin: Springer.

Freeman, R. E. (1984). *Strategic Management. A Stakeholder Approach.* Boston: Pitman.

(2000). Business Ethics at the Millennium. *Business Ethics Quarterly,* 10(1), 169–180.

(2004). The Stakeholder Approach Revisited. *Zeitschrift für Wirtschafts- und Unternehmensethik zfwu,* 5(3), 228–241.

(2008). *Managing for Stakeholders: Trade-offs or Value Creation.* Paper presented at the International Association for Business and Society (IABS) Annual Meeting, Tampere, Finland.

(2009). Turning Point: Can Stakeholder Theorists Seize the Moment? *Journal of Corporate Citizenship,* 36(December), 21–24.

Freeman, R. E., & Gilbert, D. R. J. (1987). Managing Stakeholder Relationships. In S. P. Sethi & C. M. Falbe (Eds.), *Business and Society: Dimensions of Conflict and Cooperation* (397–423). Lexington Books.

Freeman, R. E., Harrison, J. S., & Wicks, A. C. (2007). *Managing for Stakeholders: Survival, Reputation, and Success.* New Haven: Yale University Press.

Freeman, R. E., Harrison, J. S., Wicks, A. C., Parmar, B. L., & De Colle, S. (2010). *Stakeholder Theory: The State of the Art.* Cambridge University Press.

Freeman, R. E., & Liedtka, J. (1997). Stakeholder Capitalism and the Value Chain. *European Management Journal,* 15(3), 286–296.

Freeman, R. E., & McVea, J. F. (2001). A Stakeholder Approach To Strategic Management. In M. A. Hitt, R. E. Freeman & J. S. Harrison (Eds.), *The Blackwell Handbook of Strategic Management* (189–207). Oxford: Blackwell.

Freeman, R. E., Martin, K., & Parmar, B. (2007). Stakeholder Capitalism. *Journal of Business Ethics,* 74(4), 303–314.

Freeman, R. E., & Phillips, R. A. (2002). Stakeholder Theory: A Libertarian Defense. *Business Ethics Quarterly,* 12(3), 331–349.

Freeman, R. E., Wicks, A. C., & Parmar, B. (2004). Stakeholder Theory and "The Corporate Objective Revisited." *Organization Science,* 15(3), 364–369.

Friedman, A. L., & Miles, S. (2006). *Stakeholders: Theory and Practice.* Oxford University Press.

Friedman, M. (1962). *Capitalism and Freedom.* University of Chicago Press.

Fritsch, M., & Kauffeld-Monz, M. (2010). The Impact of Network Structure on Knowledge Transfer: An Application of Social Network Analysis in the Context of Regional Innovation Networks. *Annals of Regional Science,* 44(1), 21–38.

Fromm, E. (1956). *The Art of Loving.* New York: Harper & Row.

(1997). *To Have or to Be?* London: Continuum.

Frooman, J. S. (1999). Stakeholder Influence Strategies. *Academy of Management Review*, **24**(2), 191–205.

Frooman, J. S., & Murrell, A. J. (2005). Stakeholder Influence Strategies: The Roles of Structural and Demographic Determinants. *Business & Society*, **44**(1), 3–31.

Gabel, L. H. (2009). Corporate Responsibility in Economics. In C. Smith & G. Lenssen (Eds.), *Mainstreaming Corporate Responsibility: Cases and Text for Integrating Corporate Responsibility across the Business School Curriculum* (248–263). Chichester: Wiley.

Gainet, C. (2008). *Corporate Social Responsibility Barriers.* Paper presented at the International Association for Business and Society (IABS) Annual Meeting, Tampere, Finland.

Galang, R. N. (2009). *Sovereign Enforcer or Subordinate Enabler: The Government in the Management Literature.* Paper presented at the Academy of Management, Chicago, IL.

Garcia-Castro, R., Ariño, M. A., & Canela, M. A. (2010). Does Social Performance Really Lead to Financial Performance? Accounting for Endogeneity. *Journal of Business Ethics*, **92**(1), 107–126.

Garriga, E. (2009). Cooperation in Stakeholder Networks: Firms' "Tertius Iungens" Role. *Journal of Business Ethics*, **90**(4), 623–637.

George, A. L., & Bennett, A. (2005). *Case Studies and Theory Development in the Social Sciences.* Boston: MIT Press.

Gersick, C. J. G. (1991). Revolutionary Change Theories: A Multilevel Exploration of the Punctuated Equilibrium Paradigm. *Academy of Management Review*, **16**, 10–36.

Ghemawat, P. (1986). Sustainable Advantage. *Harvard Business Review*, **64**, 53–58.

(1991). *Commitment: The Dynamic of Strategy.* New York: Free Press.

Ghoshal, S. (2005). Bad Management Theories Are Destroying Good Management Practices. *Academy of Management Learning & Education*, **4**(1), 75–91.

Ghoshal, S., & Moran, P. (1996). Bad for Practice: A Critique of the Transaction Cost Theory. *Academy of Management Review*, **21**(1), 13–47.

Gibson, K. (2000). The Moral Basis of Stakeholder Theory. *Journal of Business Ethics*, **26**(3), 245–257.

Giddens, A. (1984). *The Constitution of Society: Outline of a Theory of Structuration.* Cambridge: Polity Press.

(2007). *Europe in the Global Age.* Cambridge: Polity Press.

Gilmartin, M. J., & Freeman, E. R. (2002). Business Ethics and Health Care: A Stakeholder Perspective. *Health Care Management Review*, **27**(2), 52–65.

Gintis, H. (2003). The Hitchhiker's Guide to Altruism: Gene-culture Coevolution, and the Internalization of Norms. *Journal of Theoretical Biology*, **220**(4), 407–418.

Gioia, D. A., & Pitre, E. (1990). Multiparadigm Perspectives on Theory Building. *Academy of Management Review*, **15**(4), 584–602.

Gittelman, M. (2008). A Note on the Value of Patents as Indicators of Innovation: Implications for Management Research. *Academy of Management Perspectives*, **22**(3), 21–27.

Goodpaster, K. E. (1991). Business Ethics and Stakeholder Analysis. *Business Ethics Quarterly*, **1**(1), 53–73.

Goodstein, J. D., & Wicks, A. C. (2007). Corporate and Stakeholder Responsibility: Making Business Ethics a Two-Way Conversation. *Business Ethics Quarterly*, **17**(3), 375–398.

Grandori, A. (2005). Neither Stakeholder Nor Shareholder "Theories": How Property Right and Contract Theory can Help in Getting Out of the Dilemma. *Journal of Management and Governance*, **9**(1), 41–46.

Granovetter, M. (1985). Economic Action and Social Structure: The Problem of Embeddedness. *American Journal of Sociology*, **91**(3), 481–510.

(2005). The Impact of Social Structure on Economic Outcomes. *Journal of Economic Perspectives*, **19**(1), 33–50.

Grant, R. M. (1991). The Resource-Based Theory of Competitive Advantage: Implications for Strategy Formulation. *California Management Review*, **33**(3), 114–135.

(1996). Toward a Knowledge-Based Theory of the Firm. *Strategic Management Journal*, **17**(Winter), 109–122.

(2010a). *Contemporary Strategy Analysis: Text & Cases* (7th edn). Chichester: John Wiley & Sons.

(2010b). *Shareholder Value Maximization: "Dumb Idea" or Cornerstone of Effective Management*. Paper presented at the The Academy of Business in Society (EABIS) Thought Leadership Symposium: "The Future of Economics and Management in a Post-Crisis World," Stresa, Italy.

Gray, B. (1989). *Collaborating: Finding Common Ground for Multiparty Problems*. San Francisco: Jossey-Bass.

Gray, R., Owen, D., & Adams, C. (1996). *Accounting and Accountability: Changes and Challenges in Corporate Social and Environmental Reporting*. London: Prentice Hall.

Greenley, G. E., & Foxall, G. R. (1997). Multiple Stakeholder Orientation in U.K. Companies and the Implications for Company Performance. *Journal of Management Studies*, **34**(2), 259–284.

Greenwood, M., & Van Buren III, H. J. (2010). Trust and Stakeholder Theory: Trustworthiness in the Organisation–Stakeholder Relationship. *Journal of Business Ethics*, 95(3), 425–438.

Greve, H. R., Baum, J. A. C., Mitsuhashi, H., & Rowley, T. J. (2010). Built to Last but Falling Apart: Cohesion, Friction, and Withdrawal from Interfirm Alliances. *Academy of Management Journal*, 53(2), 302–322.

Grossman, S. J., & Hart, O. D. (1986). The Costs and Benefits of Ownership: A Theory of Vertical and Lateral Integration. *Journal of Political Economy*, 94(4), 691–719.

Gruber, M., Heinemann, F., Brettel, M., & Hungeling, S. (2010). Configurations of Resources and Capabilities and Their Performance Implications: An Exploratory Study on Technology Ventures. *Strategic Management Journal*, 31(12), 1337–1356.

Grunig, J. E., & Hunt, T. T. (1984). *Managing Public Relations*. New York: Rinehart & Winston.

Gudmundsson, S. V., & Lechner, C. (2006). Multilateral Airline Alliances: Balancing Strategic Constraints and Opportunities. *Journal of Air Transport Management*, 12(3), 153–158.

Gulati, R., & Gargiulo, M. (1999). Where Do Interorganizational Networks Come From? *American Journal of Sociology*, 104(5), 1439–1493.

Gulati, R., Nohria, N., & Zaheer, A. (2000). Strategic Networks. *Strategic Management Journal*, 21(3), 203–215.

Gustavsen, B. (2006). Theory and Practice: The Mediating Discourse. In P. Reason & H. Bradbury (Eds.), *Handbook of Action Research* (17–26). London: Sage.

Haas, T. (2004). The Public Sphere as a Sphere of Publics: Rethinking Habermas's Theory of the Public Sphere. *Journal of Communication*, 54(1), 178–184.

Habermas, J. (1984). *The Theory of Communicative Action: Reason and the Rationalization of Society* (T. McCarthy, Trans. Vol. 1). Boston: Beacon Press.

(1998). Learning by Disaster? A Diagnostic Look Back on the Short 20th Century. *Constellations*, 5(3), 307–320.

Habish, A. (2001). Foreword. In J. Andriof & M. McIntosh (Eds.), *Perspectives on Corporate Citizenship* (11–12). Sheffield: Greenleaf Publishing.

Hahn, T., Kolk, A., & Winn, M. (2010). A New Future for Business? Rethinking Management Theory and Business Strategy. *Business & Society*, 49(3), 385–401.

Hall, R. (1992). The Strategic Analysis of Intangible Resources. *Strategic Management Journal*, 13(2), 135–144.

(1993). A Framework Linking Intangible Resources and Capabilities to Sustainable Competitive Advantage. *Strategic Management Journal*, **14**(8), 607–618.

Hamel, G., & Heene, A. (Eds.). (1994). *Competence-Based Competition.* Chichester: Wiley & Sons.

Hamel, G., & Prahalad, C. K. (1993). Strategy as Stretch and Leverage. *Harvard Business Review*, **71**, 75–84.

(1994). *Competing for the Future.* Boston: Harvard Business School Press.

(1996). Competing in the New Economy: Managing out of Bounds. *Strategic Management Journal*, **17**(3), 237–242.

Hannan, M. T., & Freeman, J. (1977). The Population Ecology of Organizations. *American Journal of Sociology*, **82**(5), 929–964.

(1984). Structural Inertia and Organizational Change. *American Sociological Review*, **49**(2), 149–164.

Hanrahan, M. (2003). Challenging the Dualistic Assumptions of Academic Writing: Representing Ph.D. Research as Embodied Practice. *Forum Qualitative Social Research*, **4**(2), 1–20.

Hansen, G. S., & Wernerfelt, B. (1989). Determinants of Firm Performance: The Relative Importance of Economic and Organizational Factors. *Strategic Management Journal*, **10**(5), 399–411.

Hardy, C., Lawrence, T. B., & Grant, D. (2005). Discourse and Collaboration: The Role of Conversations and Collective Identity. *Academy of Management Review*, **30**(1), 58–77.

Harrison, J. S., Bosse, D., & Phillips, R. A. (2007). *Stakeholder Theory and Competitive Advantage.* Paper presented at the Academy of Management, Philadelphia, PA.

(2010). Managing for Stakeholders, Stakeholder Utility Functions, and Competitive Advantage. *Strategic Management Journal*, **31**(1), 58–74.

Harrison, J. S., & Freeman, R. E. (1999). Stakeholders, Social Responsibility, and Performance: Empirical Evidence and Theoretical Perspectives. *Academy of Management Journal*, **42**(5), 479–485.

(2004). Special Topic: Democracy in and around Organizations. Is Organizational Democracy Worth the Effort? *Academy of Management Executive*, **18**(3), 49–53.

Harrison, J. S., & St. John, C. H. (1996). Managing and Partnering with External Stakeholders. *Academy of Management Executive*, **10**(2), 46–60.

Hart, O. (2000). An Economist's Perspective on the Theory of the Firm. In N. J. Foss (Ed.), *The Theory of the Firm: Critical Perspectives on Business and Management* (Vol. 1, 130–147). London: Routledge.

Hart, O., & Moore, J. (1990). Property Rights and the Nature of the Firm. *Journal of Political Economy*, **98**(6), 1119–1158.

Hart, S. L. (1995). A Natural-Resource-Based View of the Firm. *Academy of Management Review*, **20**(4), 986–1014.

Hart, S. L., & Milstein, M. B. (2003). Creating Sustainable Value. *Academy of Management Executive*, **17**(2), 56–69.

Haveman, H. A., Russo, M. V., & Meyer, A. D. (2001). Organizational Environments in Flux: The Impact of Regulatory Punctuations on Organizational Domains, CEO Succession, and Performance. *Organization Science*, **12**(3), 253–273.

Hayward, M. L. A. (2002). When do Firms Learn from their Acquisition Experience? Evidence from 1990–1995. *Strategic Management Journal*, **23**(1), 21–39.

Hazlett, S.-A., & McKee, L. (2008). *Achieving CSR through Stakeholder Management: An Empirical Investigation*. Paper presented at the Corporate Responsibility Research Conference (CRRC), Belfast.

Heene, A., & Sanchez, R. (1997). *Competence-Based Strategic Management*. Chichester: Wiley.

Held, D. (1996). *Models of Democracy* (2nd edn). Stanford University Press.

(2004). *Global Covenant: The Social Democratic Alternative to the Washington Consensus*. Cambridge: Polity Press.

Helfat, C. E., Finkelstein, S., Mitchell, W., Peteraf, M. A., Singh, H., Teece, D. J., & Winter, S. G. (2007). *Dynamic Capabilities: Understanding Strategic Change in Organizations*. Malden: Blackwell.

Hemphill, T. A. (2004). Antitrust, Dynamic Competition and Business Ethics. *Journal of Business Ethics*, **50**(2), 127–135.

Hendry, J. (2001). Economic Contracts Versus Social Relationships as a Foundation for Normative Stakeholder Theory. *Business Ethics: A European Review*, **10**(3), 223–232.

Henriques, I. (2008). *Stakeholder Theory and Environmental Sustainability*. Paper presented at the Academy of Management (AoM) Annual Meeting, Anaheim, CA.

Heron, J., & Reason, P. (2006). The Practice of Co-operative Inquiry: Research "with" rather than "on" People. In P. Reason & H. Bradbury (Eds.), *Handbook of Action Research* (144–154). London: Sage.

Herremans, I. M., Isaac, R. G., Kline, T. J. B., & Nazari, J. A. (2010). Intellectual Capital and Uncertainty of Knowledge: Control by Design of the Management System. *Journal of Business Ethics*, **98**, 627–640.

Herstatt, C., Lettl, C., & Gemünden, H.-G. (2006). Learning from Users for Radical Innovations. *International Journal of Technology Management*, **33**(1), 25–45.

Herstatt, C., & von Hippel, E. (1992). From Experience: Developing New Product Concepts Via the Lead User Method: A Case Study in a "Low-Tech" Field. *Journal of Product Innovation Management*, 9(3), 213–221.

Hess, D., Rogovsky, N., & Dunfee, T. W. (2002). The Next Wave of Corporate Community Involvement: Corporate Social Initiatives. *California Management Review*, 44(2), 110–125.

Hill, C. W. L., & Jones, T. M. (1992). Stakeholder–Agency Theory. *Journal of Management Studies*, 29(2), 131–154.

Hille, K. (2010). Foxconn to Raise Salaries 20% After Suicides. *Financial Times* (May 28). Retrieved from www.ft.com/cms/s/2/5e1ee750–6-a05–11df-a978–00144feab49a.html#axzz17Vkgbwro.

Hillman, A. J., & Keim, G. D. (2001). Shareholder Value, Stakeholder Management, and Social Issues: What's the Bottom Line? *Strategic Management Journal*, 22(2), 125–139.

Hitt, M. A., Harrison, J. S., Ireland, R. D., & Best, A. (1998). Attributes of Successful and Unsuccessful Acquisitions of US Firms. *British Journal of Management*, 9(2), 91–114.

Hofstede, G. (1998). Attitudes, Values and Organizational Culture: Disentangling the Concepts. *Organization Studies*, 19(3), 477–493.

Höijer, B. (2008). Ontological Assumptions and Generalizations in Qualitative (Audience) Research. *European Journal of Communication*, 23(3), 275–294.

Holcomb, T. R., Holmes Jr., R. M., & Connelly, B. L. (2009). Making the Most of what You Have: Managerial Ability as a Source of Resource Value Creation. *Strategic Management Journal*, 30(5), 457–485.

Holzer, B. (2008). Turning Stakeseekers Into Stakeholders: A Political Coalition Perspective on the Politics of Stakeholder Influence. *Business & Society*, 47(1), 50–67.

Hoopes, D. G., Madsen, T. L., & Walker, G. (2003). Guest Editors' Introduction to the Special Issue: Why is there a Resource-Based View? Toward a Theory of Competitive Heterogeneity. *Strategic Management Journal*, 24(10), 889–902.

Howard, J., Nash, J., & Ehrenfeld, J. (2000). Standard or Smokescreen? Implementation of a Voluntary Environmental Code. *California Management Review*, 42(2), 63–82.

Hult, G. T. M., & Ketchen, D. J. (2001). Does Market Orientation Matter? A Test of the Relationship Between Positional Advantage and Performance. *Strategic Management Journal*, 22(9), 899–906.

Hult, G. T. M., Ketchen, D. J., & Slater, S. F. (2005). Market Orientation and Performance: An Integration of Disparate Approaches. *Strategic Management Journal*, 26(12), 1173–1181.

Hund, G. E., Engel-Cox, J. A., Fowler, K. M., & Klee, H. (2002). Two-Way Responsibility. The Role of Industry and its Stakeholders in Working Towards Sustainable Development. In J. Andriof, S. Waddock, B. Husted & S. Sutherland Rahman (Eds.), *Unfolding Stakeholder Thinking: Theory, Responsibility and Engagement* (217–231). Sheffield: Greenleaf Publishing.

Huse, M. (2007). *Boards, Governance and Value Creation: The Human Side of Corporate Governance*. Cambridge University Press.

Immergut, E. M. (1992). The Rules of the Game: The Logic of Health Policy-Making in France, Switzerland and Sweden. In S. Steinmo, K. Thelen & F. Longstreth (Eds.), *Structuring Politics: Historical Institutionalism in Comparative Analysis* (57–89). Cambridge University Press.

Inkpen, A. C., & Tsang, E. W. (2005). Social Capital, Networks, and Knowledge Transfer. *Academy of Management Review*, **30**(1), 146–165.

Jensen, M. C. (2002). Value Maximization, Stakeholder Theory and the Corporate Objective Function. *Business Ethics Quarterly*, **12**(2), 235–256.

Jensen, M. C., & Meckling, W. H. (1976). Theory of the Firm: Managerial Behavior, Agency Costs, and Ownership Structure. *Journal of Financial Economics*, **3**(4), 305–360.

Johnson, G., Scholes, K., & Whittington, R. (2008). *Exploring Corporate Strategy: Text and Cases* (8th edn). Harlow: Prentice Hall.

Johnson Jr., J. H., & Meznar, M. B. (2005). Public Affairs Perceptions and Practices: A Ten-Year (1993–2003) Comparison. *Journal of Public Affairs*, **5**(1), 55–65.

Jones, T. M. (1995). Instrumental Stakeholder Theory: A Synthesis of Ethics and Economics. *Academy of Management Review*, **20**(2), 404–437.

Jones, T. M., Felps, W., & Bigley, G. A. (2007). Ethical Theory and Stakeholder-Related Decisions: The Role of Stakeholder Culture. *Academy of Management Review*, **32**(1), 137–155.

Jones, T. M., & Wicks, A. C. (1999). Convergent Stakeholder Theory. *Academy of Management Review*, **24**(2), 206–221.

Kaler, J. (2002). Responsibility, Accountability and Governance. *Business Ethics: A European Review*, **11**(4), 327–334.

Karnani, A. (2010). The Case Against Corporate Social Responsibility, *Wall Street Journal* (August 23). Retrieved from http://online.wsj.com/article/SB10001424052748703338004575230112664504890.html.

Kaul, I., Conceição, P., Le Goulven, K., & Mendoza, R. U. (2003). Overview: Why do Global Public Goods Matter Today? In I. Kaul, P. Conceição,

K. Le Goulven & R. U. Mendoza (Eds.), *Providing Global Public Goods: Managing Globalization* (2–58). Oxford University Press.

Kaul, I., & Mendoza, R. U. (2003). Advancing the Concept of Public Goods. In I. Kaul, P. Conceição, K. Le Goulven & R. U. Mendoza (Eds.), *Providing Global Public Goods: Managing Globalization* (78–111). Oxford University Press.

Kay, I. T., & Shelton, M. (2000). The People Problems in Mergers. *McKinsey Quarterly*, **4**, 27–37.

Keck, M. E., & Sikkink, K. (1999). Transnational Advocacy Networks in International and Regional Politics. *International Social Science Journal*, 51(159), 89–101.

Kemp, D., Boele, R., & Brereton, D. (2006). Community Relations Management Systems in the Minerals Industry: Combining Conventional and Stakeholder-Driven Approaches. *International Journal of Sustainable Development*, 9(4), 390–403.

Keohane, R. O., & Nye, J. S. (1977). *Power and Interdependence: World Politics in Transition*. Boston: Little, Brown and Company.

Kern, I. (2009). *The Suitability of Topic Maps Tools for Knowledge Creation With Stakeholders*. Bern: Haupt.

Kern, I., Sachs, S., & Rühli, E. (2007). Stakeholder Relations and Maintaining the License to Operate: A Comparative Case Study of the Swiss Telecommunications Industry. *Corporate Governance*, 7(4), 446–454.

Khurana, R. (2007). *From Higher Aims to Hired Hands: The Social Transformation of American Business Schools and the Unfulfilled Promise of Management as a Profession*. Princeton University Press.

Kilduff, M., Tsai, W., & Hanke, R. (2006). A Paradigm Too Far? A Dynamic Stability Reconsideration of the Social Network Research Program. *Academy of Management Review*, 31(4), 1031–1048.

Kim, J., & Mahoney, J. T. (2005). Property Rights Theory, Transaction Costs Theory, and Agency Theory: An Organizational Economics Approach to Strategic Management. *Managerial and Decision Economics*, 26(4), 223–242.

(2006). How Property Rights Economics Furthers the Resource-Based View: Resources, Transaction Costs and Entrepreneurial Discovery. *International Journal of Strategic Change Management*, 1(1–2), 40–52.

(2007). Appropriating Economic Rents from Resources: An Integrative Property Rights and Resource-Based Approach. *International Journal of Learning and Intellectual Capital*, 4(1), 11–28.

(2010). A Strategic Theory of the Firm as a Nexus of Incomplete Contracts: A Property Rights Approach. *Journal of Management*, 36(4), 806–826.

King, A. A., & Lenox, M. J. (2000). Industry Self-Regulation without Sanctions: The Chemical Industry's Responsible Care Program. *Academy of Management Journal*, 43(4), 698–716.

King, B. (2008). A Social Movement Perspective of Stakeholder Collective Action and Influence. *Business & Society*, 47(1), 21–49.

Koch, J., Eisend, M., & Petermann, A. (2009). Path Dependence in Decision-Making Processes: Exploring the Impact of Complexity under Increasing Returns. *BuR – Business Research*, 2(1), 67–84.

Kochan, T. A., & Rubinstein, S. A. (2000). Toward a Stakeholder Theory of the Firm: The Saturn Partnership. *Organization Science*, 11(4), 367–386.

Kogut, B., & Zander, U. (1992). Knowledge of the Firm, Combinative Capabilities, and the Replication of Technology. *Organization Science*, 3(3), 383–397.

(1996). What Firms Do? Coordination, Identity, and Learning. *Organization Science*, 7(5), 502–518.

Kolk, A., & van Tuldere, R. (2002). Child Labor and Multinational Conduct: A Comparison of International Business and Stakeholder Codes. *Journal of Business Ethics*, 36(3), 291–301.

Kourula, A., & Laasonen, S. (2010). Nongovernmental Organizations in Business and Society, Management, and International Business Research: Review and Implications from 1998 to 2007. *Business & Society*, 49(1), 35–67.

Kramer, M. H. (2004). *John Locke and the Origins of Private Property: Philosophical Explorations of Individualism, Community, and Equality*. Cambridge University Press.

Kuhn, T. S. (1962). *The Structure of Scientific Revolutions* (1st edn). University of Chicago Press.

(1970). *The Structure of Scientific Revolutions* (2nd edn). University of Chicago Press.

(1996). *The Structure of Scientific Revolutions* (3rd edn). University of Chicago Press.

Lad, L. J., & Caldwell, C. B. (2009). Collaborative Standards, Voluntary Codes and Industry Self-Regulation: The Role of Third-Party Organisations. *Journal of Corporate Citizenship*, 35(December), 67–80.

Lado, A. A., Boyd, N. G., & Wright, P. (1992). A Competency-Based Model of Sustainable Competitive Advantage: Toward a Conceptual Integration. *Journal of Management*, 18(1), 77–91.

Lamont, B. T. (2004). Book Review: Redefining the Corporation – Stakeholder Management and Organizational Wealth. *Administrative Science Quarterly*, **49**(1), 145–147.

Laugel, J.-F., & Laszlo, C. (2009). Financial Crisis: The Opportunity for Sustainable Value Creation in Banking and Insurance. *Journal of Corporate Citizenship*, **35**(December), 24–38.

Lavie, D. (2006). The Competitive Advantage of Interconnected Firms: An Extension of the Resource-Based View. *Academy of Management Review*, **31**(3), 638–658.

Le Ber, M. J., & Branzei, O. (2010). (Re)Forming Strategic Cross-Sector Partnerships: Relational Processes of Social Innovation. *Business & Society*, **49**(1), 140–172.

Leana, C. R., & Rousseau, D. M. (2000). Relational Wealth. The Advantages of Stability in a Changing Economy. In C. R. Leana & D. M. Rousseau (Eds.), *Relational Wealth: The Advantages of Stability in a Changing Economy* (3–24). New York: Oxford University Press.

Lee, S. K. J., & Yu, K. (2004). Corporate Culture and Organizational Performance. *Journal of Managerial Psychology*, **19**(4), 340–359.

Leedy, P. D., & Ormrod, J. E. (2010). *Practical Research: Planning and Design* (9th edn). Harlow: Pearson Education.

Lenox, M. J., & Nash, J. (2003). Industry Self-Regulation and Adverse Selection: A Comparison Across Four Trade Association Programs. *Business Strategy and the Environment*, **12**(6), 343–356.

Lenssen, G. (2009). *A Crisis of Governance? Questions on Turbulent Times*. Paper presented at the The Academy of Business in Society (EABIS) Annual Leaders Forum, Brussels.

Lenssen, G., Bevan, D., & Fontrodona, J. (2010). Guest Editorial: Corporate Responsibility and Governance: The Responsible Corporation in a Global Economy. *Corporate Governance*, **10**(4), 340–346.

Lenssen, G., Perrini, F., Tencati, A., & Lacy, P. (2007). Guest Editorial: Corporate Responsibility, Strategic Management and the Stakeholder View of the Firm. *Corporate Governance*, **7**(4), 344–354.

Leonard-Barton, D. (1992). Core Capabilities and Core Rigidities: A Paradox in Managing New Product Development. *Strategic Management Journal*, **13**(S1), 111–125.

Lepak, D. P., Smith, K. G., & Taylor, M. S. (2007). Value Creation and Value Capture: A Multilevel Perspective. *Academy of Management Review*, **32**(1), 180–194.

Liebeskind, J. P. (1996). Knowledge, Strategy, and the Theory of the Firm. *Strategic Management Journal*, **17**, 93–107.

Lin, L.-W. (2010). Corporate Social Responsibility in China: Window Dressing or Structural Change? *Berkeley Journal of International Law,* **28**(1), 64–100.

Locher, H. (2006). Prozess- und Organisationsanalyse Swissmedic. *Pharmajournal,* **23**, 13–18.

Logsdon, J. M., & van Buren III., H. J. (2008). Justice and Large Corporations: What Do Activist Shareholders Want? *Business & Society,* **47**(4), 523–548.

Logsdon, J. M., & Wood, D. J. (2002). Business Citizenship: From Domestic to Global Level of Analysis. *Business Ethics Quarterly,* **12**(2), 155–187.

Longo, M., & Mura, M. (2008). Stakeholder Management and Human Resources: Development and Implementation of a Performance Measurement System. *Corporate Governance,* **8**(2), 191–213.

Lovas, B., & Ghoshal, S. (2000). Strategy as Guided Evolution. *Strategic Management Journal,* **21**(9), 875–896.

Lund-Thomsen, P., & Reed, D. (2009). Introduction: Special Issue on Business Partnerships for Development. *Journal of Business Ethics,* **90**(1), 1–2.

Lüthje, C., & Herstatt, C. (2004). The Lead User Method: An Outline of Empirical Findings and Issues for Future Research. *R&D Management,* **34**(5), 553–568.

McCrae, R. R., Costa, P. T. J., Ostendorf, F. *et al.* (2000). Nature over Nurture: Temperament, Personality, and Lifespan Development. *Journal of Personality and Social Psychology,* **78**(1), 173–186.

McCrae, R. R., & John, O. P. (1992). An Introduction to the Five-Factor Model and Its Applications. *Journal of Personality,* **60**(2), 175–215.

Macdonald, K., & Macdonald, T. (2010). Democracy in a Pluralist Global Order: Corporate Power and Stakeholder Representation. *Ethics & International Affairs,* **24**(1), 19–43.

Macdonald, T. (2008). *Global Stakeholder Democracy: Power and Representation Beyond Liberal States.* Oxford University Press.

McGahan, A. M., & Porter, M. E. (2003). The Emergence and Sustainability of Abnormal Profits. *Strategic Organization,* **1**(1), 79–108.

McGrath, C. (2007). Framing Lobbying Messages: Defining and Communicating Political Issues Persuasively. *Journal of Public Affairs,* **7**(3), 269–280.

McGrath, C., & Thomas, C. S. (2006). *Poachers Turned Gamekeepers: British and American Legislators with Previous Professional Lobbying Experience.* Paper presented at the Annual Meeting of the American Political Science Association, Philadelphia, PA.

Maclagan, P. (1999). Corporate Social Responsibility as a Participative Process. *Business Ethics: A European Review*, 8(1), 43–49.

McVea, J. F., & Freeman, R. E. (2005). A Names-and-Faces Approach to Stakeholder Management: How focusing on Stakeholders as Individuals Can Bring Ethics and Enrepreneurial Strategy Together. *Journal of Management Inquiry*, 14(1), 57–69.

Mahoney, J. T. (2008). *Towards a Stakeholder Theory of Strategic Management*. Paper presented at the Academy of Management (AoM) Annual Meeting, Anaheim, CA.

Mahoney, J. T., McGahan, A. M., & Pitelis, C. N. (2009). The Interdependence of Private and Public Interests. *Organization Science*, 20(6), 1034–1052.

Mahoney, J. T., & Pandian, J. R. (1992). The Resource-Based View within the Conversation of Strategic Management. *Strategic Management Journal*, 13(5), 363–380.

March, J. G. (1991). Exploration and Exploitation in Organizational Learning. *Organization Science*, 2(1), 71–87.

Margolis, J. D. (2008). *The Logic of Stakeholder Theory*. Paper presented at the Academy of Management (AoM) Annual Meeting, Anaheim, CA.

Margolis, J. D., & Walsh, J. P. (2003). Misery Loves Companies: Rethinking Social Initiatives by Business. *Administrative Science Quarterly*, 48(2), 268–305.

Mark-Ungericht, B. (2001). Business and Newly Emerging Civil Society Actors: Between Conflict and New Forms of Social Dialogue. *Global Business Review*, 2(1), 55–69

Marks, M. L., & Mirvis, P. H. (1992). Rebuilding After the Merger: Dealing with "Survivor Sickness." *Organizational Dynamics*, 21(2), 18–32.

Marquis, C., Glynn, M. A., & Davis, G. F. (2007). Community Isomorphism and Corporate Social Action. *Academy of Management Review*, 32(3), 925–945.

Matten, D., & Crane, A. (2005). What is Stakeholder Democracy? Perspectives and Issues. *Business Ethics: A European Review*, 14(1), 6–13.

Matten, D., & Moon, J. (2008). "Implicit" and "Explicit" CSR: A Conceptual Framework For a Comparative Understanding of Corporate Social Responsibility. *Academy of Management Review*, 33(2), 404–424.

Mattingly, J. E. (2004). Book Review: "Redefining the Corporation: Stakeholder Management and Organizational Wealth." *Academy of Management Review*, 29(3), 520–523.

Mattingly, J. E., & Greening, D. W. (2002). Public-Interest Groups as Stakeholders. In J. Andriof, S. Waddock, B. Husted & S. Sutherland Rahman (Eds.), *Unfolding Stakeholder Thinking: Theory, Responsibility and Engagement* (267–279). Sheffield: Greenleaf Publishing.

Maturana, H. R., & Varela, F. J. (1987). *The Tree of Knowledge: Biological Roots of Human Understanding* (K. Ludewig, Trans.). Boston: Shambhala.

Maurer, M., & Sachs, S. (2005). Implementing the Stakeholder View: Learning Processes for a Changed Stakeholder Orientation. *Journal of Corporate Citizenship*, **17**, 93–107.

Mauri, A. J., & Michaels, M. P. (1998). Firm and Industry Effects within Strategic Management: An Empirical Examination. *Strategic Management Journal*, **19**(3), 211–219.

Mayer, K. J., & Argyres, N. S. (2004). Learning to Contract: Evidence from the Personal Computer Industry. *Organization Science*, **15**(4), 394–410.

Mayr, E. (1991). *One Long Argument*. Cambridge, MA: Harvard Business Press.

Mena, S., de Leede, M., Baumann, D., Black, N., Lindeman, S., & McShane, L. (2010). Advancing the Business and Human Rights Agenda: Dialogue, Empowerment, and Constructive Engagement. *Journal of Business Ethics*, **93**(1), 161–188.

Messner, D., & Nuscheler, F. (2003). Das Konzept Global Governance – Stand und Perspektiven. *INEF Report*, **67**, 1–52. Retrieved from http://inef.uni-due.de/cms/files/report67.pdf.

Midttun, A. (2007). *Corporate (Social) Responsibility as an Arena for Partnered Governance: From the Business to the Public Policy Case*. Paper presented at the Academy of Business in Society (EABIS) Annual Colloquium, Barcelona, Spain.

Miles, M. B., & Huberman, M. (1994). *Qualitative Data Analysis: An Expanded Sourcebook* (2nd edn). Thousand Oaks: Sage.

Milgrom, P., & Roberts, J. (1992). *Economics, Organization and Management*. Englewood Cliffs: Prentice Hall.

Miner, A. S. (1994). Seeking Adaptive Advantage: Evolutionary Theory and Managerial Action. In J. A. C. Baum & J. V. Singh (Eds.), *Evolutionary Dynamics of Organizations* (76–89). New York: Oxford University Press.

Mitchell, R. K., Agle, B. R., & Wood, D. J. (1997). Toward a Theory of Stakeholder Identification and Salience: Defining the Principle of Who and What Really Counts. *Academy of Management Review*, **22**(4), 853–886.

Mitsuhashi, H., & Greve, H. R. (2009). A Matching Theory of Alliance Formation and Organizational Success: Complementarity and Compatibility. *Academy of Management Journal*, 52(5), 975–995.

Monks, R. A. G. (2001). *The New Global Investors: How Shareowners Can Unlock Sustainable Prosperity Worldwide*. Oxford: Capstone.

Moody, J., & White, D. R. (2003). Structural Cohesion and Embeddedness: A Hierarchical Concept of Social Groups. *American Sociological Review*, 68(1), 103–127.

Moran, P., & Ghoshal, S. (1996). *Value Creation by Firms*. Paper presented at the Academy of Management (AoM) Best Paper Proceedings.

Morgenthau, H. J. (1948). *Politics among Nations*. Boston: McGraw-Hill.

Morsing, M., & Schultz, M. (2006). Corporate Social Responsibility Communication: Stakeholder Information, Response and Involvement Strategies. *Business Ethics: A European Review*, 15(4), 323–338.

Moss Kanter, R. (1984). *When Giants Learn to Dance: Mastering the Challenge of Strategy, Management, and Careers in the 1990s*. New York: Simon & Schuster.

Musgrave, A. (1981). "Unreal Assumptions" in Economic Theory: The F-Twist Untwisted. *Kyklos*, 34, 377–387.

Nadkarni, S., & Herrmann, P. (2010). CEO Personality, Strategic Flexibility, and Firm Performance: The Case of the Indian Business Process Outsourcing Industry. *Academy of Management Journal*, 53(5), 1050–1073.

Nag, R., Hambrick, D. C., & Chen, M.-J. (2005). *What Is Strategic Management, Really? Empirical Introduction of a Consensus Definition of the Field*. Paper presented at the Academy of Management (AoM) Annual Meeting, Hawaii, HI.

Nahapiet, J., & Ghoshal, S. (1998). Social Capital, Intellectual Capital, and the Organizational Advantage. *Academy of Management Review*, 23(2), 242–266.

Neville, B. A., & Menguc, B. (2006). Stakeholder Multiplicity: Toward an Understanding of the Interactions between Stakeholders. *Journal of Business Ethics*, 66(2006), 377–391.

Newbert, S. L. (2007). Empirical Research on the Resource-Based View of the Firm: An Assessment and Suggestions for Future Research. *Strategic Management Journal*, 28(2), 121–146.

(2008). Value, Rareness, Competitive Advantage, and Performance: A Conceptual-Level Empirical Investigation of the Resource-Based View of the Firm. *Strategic Management Journal*, 29(7), 745–768.

Nicolodi, R. (2007). *Pension Fund Engagement as a Sustainability Driver: A Stakeholder-Theory-Based Legitimation of Sustainable Pension Fund Engagement in a Swiss Context.* Bern: Haupt.

Nidumolu, R., Prahalad, C. K., & Rangaswami, M. R. (2009). Why Sustainability is Now the Key Driver of Innovation. *Harvard Business Review*, September, 57–64.

Nonaka, I., & Takeuchi, H. (1995). *The Knowledge-Creating Company: How Japanese Companies Create the Dynamics of Innovation.* New York: Oxford University Press.

Novo Nordisk. (2007). Economic Stakeholder Model. Retrieved from http://annualreport2007.novonordisk.com/images/annual_report/AR_07/PDF/AR07_p94.pdf.

Nowak, M. A., Tarnita, C. E., & Wilson, E. O. (2010). The Evolution of Eusociality. *Nature*, **466**(August), 1057–1062.

O'Dwyer, B. (2005). Stakeholder Democracy: Challenges and Contributions from Social Accounting. *Business Ethics: A European Review*, **14**(1), 28–41.

O'Higgins, E. R. E. (2010). Corporations, Civil Society, and Stakeholders: An Organizational Conceptualization. *Journal of Business Ethics*, **94**(2), 157–176.

OECD. (2004). *OECD Principles of Corporate Governance.* Paris: Organisation for Economic Co-operation and Development (OECD). Retrieved from www.oecd.org/dataoecd/32/18/31557724.pdf.

Oguh, E. (2009). *John Locke and Property as a Human Right Today: Towards a New Theory of Property Rights.* Saarbrücken: Lambert Academic Publishing.

Okhuysen, G., & Bonardi, J.-P. (2011). Editors' Comments: The Challenges of Building Theory by Combining Lenses. *Academy of Management Review*, **38**(1), 8–11.

Oster, S. M. (1994). *Modern Competitive Analysis* (2nd edn). New York: Oxford University Press.

Osterloh, M., & Frey, B. S. (2003). Corporate Governance for Crooks? The Case for Corporate Virtue. *ZEW Working Paper No. 164.* Zurich.

Oxley, J. E. (1999). Institutional Environment and the Mechanisms of Governance: The Impact of Intellectual Property. *Journal of Economic Behavior & Organization*, **38**(3), 283–310.

Page, S. (2010). Most Fear Lasting Damage in Gulf; Poll: Obama Needs to Take BP to Task, *USA Today* (June 15). Retrieved from www.usatoday.com/printedition/news/20100615/1apoll15_st.art.htm.

Paine, L., Deshpandé, R., Margolis, J. D., & Bettcher, K. E. (2005). Up to Code: Does Your Company's Conduct Meet World-Class Standards? *Harvard Business Review*, **83**, 122–133.

Park-Poaps, H., & Rees, K. (2010). Stakeholder Forces of Socially Responsible Supply Chain Management Orientation. *Journal of Business Ethics*, **92**(2), 305–322.

Patton, M. Q. (1999). Enhancing the Quality and Credibility of Qualitative Analysis. *Health Services Research*, **34**(5, Part II (December 1999)), 1189–1208.

Paul, K. (2008). Corporate Sustainability, Citizenship and Social Responsibility Reporting. A Website Study of 100 Model Corporations. *Journal of Corporate Citizenship*, **32**(Winter), 63–78.

Payne, S. L., & Calton, J. M. (2002). Towards a Managerial Practice of Stakeholder Engagement: Developing Multi-Stakeholder Learning Dialogues. In J. Andriof, S. Waddock, B. Husted & S. Sutherland Rahman (Eds.), *Unfolding Stakeholder Thinking: Theory, Responsibility and Engagement* (Vol. 1, 121–135). Sheffield: Greenleaf.

(2004). Exploring Research Potentials and Applications for Multi-Stakeholder Learning Dialogues. *Journal of Business Ethics*, **55**(1), 71–78.

Penrose, E. T. (1959). *The Theory of the Growth of the Firm* (Reprint 1968 edn). Oxford: Blackwell.

Perrin, I. (2010). *Medien als Chance und Risiko: Eine Untersuchung zum Verhältnis von Wirtschaftsunternehmen und Medienorganisationen*. Bern: Haupt.

Peteraf, M. A. (1993). The Cornerstones of Competitive Advantage: A Resource-Based View. *Strategic Management Journal*, **14**(3), 179–191.

Pfeffer, J. (2010). Building Sustainable Organizations: The Human Factor. *Academy of Management Perspectives*, February, 34–45.

Phelps, E. (2009). Uncertainty Bedevils the Best System, *The Financial Times* (April 15, p. 13). Retrieved from www.ft.com/cms/s/0/a0bc4628–2921–11de-bc5e-00144feabdc0.html?nclick_check=1.

Phillips, R. (2003a). Stakeholder Legitimacy. *Business Ethics Quarterly*, **13**(1), 25–41.

(2003b). *Stakeholder Theory and Organizational Ethics*. San Francisco: Berrett-Koehler Publishers.

Phillips, R., & Caldwell, C. B. (2005). Value Chain Responsibility: A Farewell to Arm's Length. *Business & Society Review*, **110**(4), 345–370.

Phillips, R., Freeman, R. E., & Wicks, A. C. (2003). What Stakeholder Theory is Not. *Business Ethics Quarterly*, **13**(4), 479–502.

Picot, A., Dietl, H., & Franck, E. (2008). *Organisation: Eine ökonomische Perspektive* (Vol. 5, aktualisierte und überarbeitete Auflage). Stuttgart: Schäffer-Poeschel.

Pirson, M. A., & Lawrence, P. R. (2010). Humanism in Business: Towards a Paradigm Shift? *Journal of Business Ethics*, **93**(4), 553–565.

Plaza-Ubeda, J. A., de Burgos-Jiménez, J., & Carmona-Moreno, E. (2010). Measuring Stakeholder Integration: Knowledge, Interaction and Adaptational Behavior Dimensions. *Journal of Business Ethics*, 93(3), 419–442.

Podolny, J. M., & Page, K. L. (1998). Network Forms of Organization. *Annual Review of Sociology*, 24, 57–76.

Popper, K. (1972). *Objective Knowledge: An Evolutionary Approach*. Oxford University Press.

Porter, M. E. (1980). *Competitive Strategy: Techniques for Analyzing Industries and Competitors*. New York: Free Press.

(1985). *Competitive Advantage: Creating and Sustaining Superior Performance*. New York: Free Press.

(1986). *Competition in Global Industries: A Conceptual Framework*. Boston: Harvard Business School Press.

(1990). *The Competitive Advantage of Nations*. New York: Free Press.

(1991). Towards a Dynamic Theory of Strategy. *Strategic Management Journal*, 12(S2), 95–117.

(1996). What is Strategy? *Harvard Business Review*, 74, 61–78.

(1998). Clusters and the New Economics of Competition. *Harvard Business Review*, November–December, 77–90.

(2008). The Five Competitive Forces That Shape Strategy. *Harvard Business Review*, 86, 78–93.

Porter, M. E., & Kramer, M. R. (2002). The Competitive Advantage of Corporate Philanthropy. *Harvard Business Review*, December, 57–68.

(2006). The Link Between Competitive Advantage and Corporate Social Responsibility. *Harvard Business Review*, 84, 78–92.

(2011). Creating Shared Value. *Harvard Business Review*, 89, 62–77.

Porter, M. E., & Reinhardt, F. L. (2007). A Strategic Approach to Climate. *Harvard Business Review*, October, 22–26.

Porter, M. E., & Siggelkow, N. (2008). Contextual Interactions within Activity Systems and Sustainability of Competitive Advantage. *Academy of Management Perspectives*, 22(2), 34–56.

Porter, M. E., & Teisberg, E. O. (2004). Redefining Competition in Health Care. *Harvard Business Review*, June, 65–76.

Porter, M. E., & van der Linde, C. (1995). Green and Competitive: Ending the Stalemate. *Harvard Business Review*, 73, 120–134.

Posner, B. Z. (2010). Another Look at the Impact of Personal and Organizational Values Congruency. *Journal of Business Ethics*, 97(4), 535–541.

Post, J. E. (1978). Research on Patterns of Corporate Response to Social Change. In L. E. Preston (Ed.), *Research in Corporate Social Performance and Policy* (Vol. 1, 55–77). Greenwich, CT: JAI Press.

Post, J. E., Preston, L. E., & Sachs, S. (2002a). Managing the Extended Enterprise: The New Stakeholder View. *California Management Review*, **45**(1), 6–28.

(2002b). *Redefining the Corporation: Stakeholder Management and Organizational Wealth.* Stanford University Press.

Powell, T. C., Lovallo, D., & Carnigal, C. (2006). Causal Ambiguity, Management Perception, and Firm Performance. *Academy of Management Review*, **31**(1), 175–196.

Powell, W. W., Koput, K. W., & Smith-Doerr, L. (1996). Interorganizational Collaboration and the Locus of Innovation: Networks of Learning in Biotechnology. *Administrative Science Quarterly*, **41**(1), 116–145.

Powell, W. W., White, D. R., Koput, K. W., & Owen-Smith, J. (2005). Network Dynamics and Field Evolution: The Growth of Interorganizational Collaboration in the Life Sciences. *American Journal of Sociology*, **110**(4), 1132–1205.

Prahalad, C. K., & Hamel, G. (1990). The Core Competence of the Corporation. *Harvard Business Review*, **68**, 79–91.

Preston, L. E., & Post, J. E. (1975). *Private Management and Public Policy: The Principle of Public Responsibility.* Englewood Cliffs: Prentice Hall.

Priem, R. L., & Butler, J. E. (2001). Is the Resource-Based "View" a Useful Perspective for Strategic Management Research? *Academy of Management Review*, **26**(1), 22–40.

Prins, G., Galiana, I., Green, C. *et al.* (2010). The Hartwell Paper. A new Direction for Climate Policy after the Crash of 2009. Retrieved from http://eprints.lse.ac.uk/27939/1/HartwellPaper_English_version.pdf.

Puncheva, P. (2008). The Role of Corporate Reputation in the Stakeholder Decision-Making Process. *Business & Society*, **47**(3), 272–290.

Putnam, H. (2003). *The Collapse of the Fact/Value Dichotomy and Other Essays.* Cambridge, MA: Harvard University Press.

Quinn, J. B. (1980). *Strategies for Change: Logical Incrementalism.* Homewood: Richard D. Irwin.

Ragin, C. C. (2000). *Fuzzy Set Social Science.* University of Chicago Press.

Ramiller, N. C. (2005). Applying the Sociology of Translation to a System Project in a Lagging Enterprise. *Journal of Information Technology Theory and Application*, **7**(1), 51–76.

Rasche, A. (2008). *In Search of Global Governance: The Contribution of the United Nations Global Compact.* Paper presented at the Academy of Management (AoM) Annual Meeting, Anaheim, CA.

(2009). "A Necessary Supplement": What the United Nations Global Compact Is and Is Not. *Business & Society*, **48**(4), 511–537.

(2010). Collaborative Governance 2.0. *Corporate Governance*, **10**(4), 500–511.

Reed, A. M., & Reed, D. (2009). Partnerships for Development: Four Models of Business Involvement. *Journal of Business Ethics*, **90**(Supplement 1), 3–37.

Rehbein, K., Waddock, S., & Graves, S. B. (2004). Understanding Shareholder Activism: Which Corporations are Targeted? *Business & Society*, **43**(3), 239–267.

Reich, R. B. (2007). *Supercapitalism: The Transformation of Business, Democracy, and Everyday Life*. New York: Alfred A. Knopf.

(2009). Government in Your Business. *Harvard Business Review*, July–August, 94–99.

(2010). *Aftershock: The Next Economy and America's Future*. New York: Alfred A. Knopf.

Reid, P. (2010). Goldman Sachs' Revolving Door, *CBS News Investigates* (April 7).

Reinicke, W. H. (1997). Global Public Policy. *Foreign Affairs*, **76**(6), 127–138.

Reuters. (2010). GM will Opel mit Stellenabbau und Steuergeld sanieren. *Reuters Deutschland* (February 9). Retrieved from http://de.reuters. com/article/companiesNews/idDEBEE6180EA20100209.

Reyes, X. A. (2005). *How the Language and Culture of Scholars Affects their Choice of Subjects and Methods of Research: Investigating the Researcher's Habits of Mind*. Lewiston: The Edwin Mellen Press.

Rifkin, J. (2004). *The European Dream: How Europe's Vision of the Future Is Quietly Eclipsing the American Dream*. New York: Tarcher/Penguin.

Rocha, H. O., & Ghoshal, S. (2006). Beyond Self-Interest Revisited. *Journal of Management Studies*, **43**(3), 585–619.

Rodgers, W., & Gago, S. (2004). Stakeholder Influence on Corporate Strategies Over Time. *Journal of Business Ethics*, **52**(4), 349–363.

Roloff, J. (2008a). Learning from Multi-Stakeholder Networks: Issue-Focused Stakeholder Management. *Journal of Business Ethics*, **82**(1), 233–250.

(2008b). A Life Cycle Model of Multi-Stakeholder Networks. *Business Ethics: A European Review*, **17**(3), 311–325.

Roloff, J., & Assländer, M. S. (2010). Corporate Autonomy and Buyer–Supplier Relationships: The Case of Unsafe Mattel Toys. *Journal of Business Ethics*, **97**(4), 517–534.

Romanelli, E., & Tushman, M. L. (1994). Organizational Transformation as Punctuated Equilibrium: An Empirical Test. *Academy of Management Journal*, **37**(5), 1141–1166.

Rondinelli, D. A. (2002). Transnational Corporations: International Citizens or New Sovereigns. *Business & Society Review*, 107(4), 391–413.

Rosenau, J. N. (1995). Governance in the Twenty-First Century. *Global Governance*, 1(1), 13–43.

Rosenau, J. N., & Czempiel, E.-O. (1992). Governance, Order, and Change in World Politics. In J. N. Rosenau & E.-O. Czempiel (Eds.), *Governance Without Government: Order and Change in World Politics* (1–30). Cambridge University Press.

Rowley, T. J. (1997a). Moving Beyond Dyadic Ties: A Network Theory of Stakeholder Influences. *Academy of Management Review*, 22(4), 887–910.

(1997b). *Where does Stakeholder Theory Fit? A Critique of Existing Theories of the Firm*. Paper presented at the International Association for Business and Society (IABS) Annual Meeting, 1997 Proceedings, Destin, FL.

Rowley, T. J., & Berman, S. L. (2000). A Brand New Brand of Corporate Social Performance. *Business and Society*, 39(4), 397–418.

Rowley, T. J., Greve, H. R., Rao, H., Baum, J. A. C., & Shipilov, A. V. (2005). Time to Break Up: The Social and Instrumental Antecedents of Exits from Interfirm Exchange Cliques. *Academy of Management Journal*, 48(3), 499–520.

Rowley, T. J., & Moldoveanu, M. (2003). When Will Stakeholder Groups Act? An Interest- and Identity-Based Model of Stakeholder Group Mobilization. *Academy of Management Review*, 28(2), 204–219.

Rühli, E., & Sachs, S. (2005). Practical Issues in Implementing the Stakeholder View as a Core Competence. In R. Sanchez & A. Heene (Eds.), *Competence Perspectives on Resources, Stakeholders and Renewal* (217–233). Oxford: Elsevier.

Rumelt, R. P. (1982). Diversification Strategy and Profitability. *Strategic Management Journal*, 3(4), 359–369.

Rumelt, R. P., Schendel, D. E., & Teece, D. J. (1994). Fundamental Issues in Strategy. In R. P. Rumelt, D. E. Schendel & D. J. Teece (Eds.), *Fundamental Issues in Strategy: A Research Agenda* (9–47). Boston: Harvard Business School Press.

Sacconi, L. (2007). A Social Contract Account for CSR as Extended Model of Corporate Governance (II): Compliance, Reputation and Reciprocity. *Journal of Business Ethics*, 75(1), 77–96.

Sachs, S. (2000). *Die Rolle der Unternehmung in ihrer Interaktion mit der Gesellschaft*. Bern: Haupt.

Sachs, S., Groth, H., & Schmitt, R. (2008). *Understanding the Stakeholders' Perception of a Common Strategic Issue to Manage a Stakeholder*

Network: A Single Case Study in the Pharmaceutical Industry. Paper presented at the International Association for Business and Society (IABS) Annual Meeting, Tampere, Finland.

(2010). The "Stakeholder View" Approach: An Untapped Opportunity to Manage Corporate Performance and Wealth. *Strategic Change,* **19**(3–4), 147–162.

Sachs, S., & Maurer, M. (2009). Toward Dynamic Corporate Stakeholder Responsibility: From Corporate Social Responsibility Toward a Comprehensive and Dynamic View of Corporate Stakeholder Responsibility. *Journal of Business Ethics,* **85**(3), 535–544.

Sachs, S., Maurer, M., Rühli, E., & Hoffmann, R. (2006). Corporate Social Responsibility from a "Stakeholder View" Perspective: CSR Implementation by a Swiss Mobile Telecommunication Provider. *Corporate Governance,* **6**(4), 506–515.

Sachs, S., & Munshi, N. (2003). *Interrelatedness and Value Creation in Firm-Stakeholder Networks.* Paper presented at the Academy of Management (AoM) Annual Meeting, Seattle, WA.

Sachs, S., & Rühli, E. (2001a). *The Contribution of Evolution Theory to a New Normative Core for Stakeholder Theory.* Paper presented at the International Association for Business and Society (IABS) Annual Meeting, Sedona, AZ.

(2001b). An Evolutionary Concept of Multilevel Strategic Change: The Shell Case. *Strategic Change,* **10**(8), 449–456.

(2007). *Global Governance as Challenge for the Strategic Management.* Paper presented at the Academy of Business in Society (EABIS) Annual Colloquium, Barcelona, Spain.

Sachs, S., Rühli, E., & Kern, I. (2007a). *Lizenz zum Managen. Mit Stakeholdern zum Erfolg: Herausforderungen und Good Practices.* Bern: Haupt.

(2007b). *Stakeholder Relations as a Corporate Core to Operate, Compete and Innovate.* Paper presented at the International Association for Business and Society (IABS) Annual Meeting, Florence, Italy.

(2007c). *Lizenz zum Managen.* Bern: Haupt.

(2008). *The Globalization as Challenge for the Stakeholder Management.* Paper presented at the Academy of Management (AoM) Annual Meeting, Anaheim, CA.

(2009). *Sustainable Success with Stakeholders: The Untapped Potential.* Houndmills: Palgrave Macmillan.

Sachs, S., & Rühli, E. & Maurer, M. (2006a). The Effects of Liberalization and Privatization on Former Monopolist's Stakeholder Interactions. *Politeia, XXII*(**82**), 60–74.

(2006b). *Strategic Management: A New Challenging Perspective.* Paper presented at the Academy of Management (AoM) Annual Meeting, Atlanta, GA.

Sachs, S., Rühli, E. & Meier, C. (2009). *Value Creation Through Stakeholder Governance*. Paper presented at the Academy of Management (AoM) Annual Meeting, Chicago, IL.

(2011). Stakeholder Governance as a Response to Wicked Issues. *Journal of Business Ethics*. Now available online at www.springerlink.com/content/u5234g63388356h8/.

Sachs, S., Rühli, E. & Mittnacht, V. (2005). A CSR Framework Due to Multiculturalism: The Swiss Re Case. *Corporate Governance*, 5(3), 52–60.

(2007). *How Stakeholder Relations Impact Corporate Strategy: An Empirical Investigation*. Paper presented at the International Association for Business and Society (IABS) Annual Meeting, Florence, Italy.

Sachs, S., Rühli, E., Moser, M., Krishnan, N., & Lakshman, G. (2010). *Microfinance in India: The Stakeholder Networks as Untapped Potential*. Paper presented at the Academy of Business in Society (EABIS) Annual Colloquium, St. Petersburg, Russia.

Sachs, S., Rühli, E., & Peter, D. (2003). *Implementing the Stakeholder View: Changing Managers' Values to Enhance Strategic Success*. Paper presented at the International Association for Business and Society (IABS) Annual Meeting, Rotterdam, Netherlands.

Sachs, S., Schmitt, R., & Perrin, I. (2008). *Stakeholder Value Management System*. Paper presented at the International Association for Business and Society (IABS) Annual Meeting, Tampere, Finland.

(2010). Stakeholder Value Creation System. *Notizie di Politeia*, XXVI(98), 31–49.

Sachs, S., & Veser, M. (2005). *Normative Foundation of Stakeholder View: An International Perspective*. Paper presented at the Society for Business Ethics (SBE) Annual Meeting, Honolulu, HI.

Santoro, M. A., & Strauss, R. (2010). *Too Big to Fail: Ethical Breakdown of the U.S. Financial System*. Paper presented at the Academy of Management (AoM) Annual Meeting, Montreal, Canada.

Savage, G. T., Bunn, M. D., Gray, B., Xiao, Q., & Wang, S. (2008). *Stakeholder Collaboration: Implications for Stakeholder Theory and Practice*. Paper presented at the International Association for Business and Society (IABS) Annual Meeting, Tampere, Finland.

Savage, G. T., Dunkin, J. W., & Ford, D. M. (2004). Responding to a Crisis: A Stakeholder Analysis of Community Health Organizations. *Journal of Health and Human Services Administration*, 26(4), 383–414.

Scalet, S., & Kelly, T. M. (2010). CSR Rating Agencies: What is Their Global Impact? *Journal of Business Ethics*, 94(1), 69–88.

Schepers, D. H. (2006). The Impact of NGO Network Conflict on the Corporate Social Responsibility Strategies of Multinational Corporations. *Business & Society*, 45(3), 282–299.

Scherer, A. G., & Dowling, M. J. (1995). Towards a Reconciliation of the Theory-Pluralism in Strategic Management – Incommensurability and the Constructivist Approach of the Erlangen School. *Advances in Strategic Management*, **12A**, 195–247.

Scherer, A. G., & Palazzo, G. (2007). Toward a Political Conception of Corporate Responsibility – Business and Society Seen From a Habermasian Perspective. *Academy of Management Review*, **32**(4), 1096–1120.

Schilling, M. A., & Phelps, C. C. (2007). Interfirm Collaboration Networks: The Impact of Large-Scale Network Structure on Firm Innovation. *Management Science*, **53**(7), 1113–1126.

Schmitt, R. (2007). *Dealing with an Open Stakeholder Society: An Investigation into the Camisea Project.* Bern: Haupt.

Schreyögg, G., & Kliesch-Eberl, M. (2007). How Dynamic can Organizational Capabilities be? Towards a Dual-Process Model of Capability Dynamization. *Strategic Management Journal*, **28**(9), 913–933.

Scott, S. G., & Lane, V. R. (2000). A Stakeholder Approach to Organizational Identity. *Academy of Management Review*, **25**(1), 43–62.

Sen, A. (1987). *On Ethics and Economics.* Oxford: Blackwell Publishing.

(2002). *Rationality and Freedom.* Cambridge, MA: Harvard University Press.

Senge, P. M. (1990). *The Fifth Discipline: The Art and Practice of the Learning Organization.* New York: Currency.

Senge, P. M., & Scharmer, K. O. (2006). Community Action Research: Learning as a Community of Practitioners, Consultants and Researchers. In P. Reason & H. Bradbury (Eds.), *Handbook of Action Research* (195–206). London: Sage.

Sethi, S. P. (2003). *Setting Global Standards: Guidelines for Creating Codes of Conduct in Multinational Corporations.* Hoboken: John Wiley & Sons.

Shapira, Z. (1994). Evolution, Externalities, and Managerial Action. In J. A. C. Baum & J. V. Singh (Eds.), *Evolutionary Dynamics of Organizations* (117–124). New York: Oxford University Press.

Sharma, S., & Henriques, I. (2005). Stakeholder Influences on Sustainability Practices in the Canadian Forest Products Industry. *Strategic Management Journal*, **26**(2), 159–180.

Shell (2001). *People, Planet and Profits.* The Hague: Royal Dutch Shell, plc.

(2005). Shell General Business Principles. Retrieved from www-static.shell.com/static/public/downloads/corporate_pkg/sgbp_english.pdf.

Shropshire, C., & Hillman, A. J. (2007). A Longitudinal Study of Significant Change in Stakeholder Management. *Business & Society*, **46**(1), 63–87.

Siggelkow, N. (2007). Persuasion with Case Studies. *Academy of Management Journal*, 50(1), 20–24.

Simon, H. A. (1947). *Administrative Behavior*. New York: Macmillan.

(1955). A Behavioral Model of Rational Choice. *Quarterly Journal of Economics*, 69(1), 99–118.

(1956). Rational Choice and the Structure of the Environment. *Psychological Review*, 63(2), 129–138.

(1957). *Administrative Behavior* (2nd edn). New York: Macmillan.

Sirmon, D. G., Hitt, M. A., Arregle, J.-L., & Tochman Campbell, J. (2010). The Dynamic Interplay of Capability Strengths and Weaknesses: Investigating the Bases of Temporary Competitive Advantage. *Strategic Management Journal*, 31(13), 1386–1409.

Sirmon, D. G., Hitt, M. A., & Ireland, R. D. (2007). Managing Firm Resources in Dynamic Environments to Create Value: Looking Inside the Black Box. *Academy of Management Review*, 32(1), 273–292.

Skiba, F., & Herstatt, C. (2009). Users as Sources for Radical Innovations: Opportunities from Collaborations with Service Lead Users. *International Journal of Services Technology and Management*, 12(3), 317–337.

Sloan, P. (2009). Redefining Stakeholder Engagement: From Control to Collaboration. *Journal of Corporate Citizenship*, 36(Winter), 25–40.

Smith, A. (1852). *Inquiry into the Nature and Causes of the Wealth of Nations*. London: T. Nelson & Sons.

Smith, J. M. (1989). *Evolutionary Genetics*. Oxford, New York, Tokyo: Oxford University Press.

Spar, D. L., & La Mure, L. T. (2003). The Power of Activism: Assessing the Impact of NGOs on Global Business. *California Management Review*, 45(3), 78–101.

Spender, J.-C. (1996). Making Knowledge the Basis of a Dynamic Theory of the Firm. *Strategic Management Journal*, 17(Winter), 45–62.

Spiegel-Online. (2010). Betriebsrat fürchtet deutlich größeren Stellenabbau (February 1). Retrieved from www.spiegel.de/wirtschaft/unternehmen/0,1518,675279,00.html.

Spitzeck, H. (2008). *Moralische Organisationsentwicklung: Was lernen Unternehmen durch Kritik von Nichtregierungsorganisationen?* Bern: Haupt.

Spitzeck, H., & Hansen, E. G. (2010). Stakeholder Governance: How Stakeholders Influence Corporate Decision Making. *Corporate Governance*, 10(4), 378–391.

Stake, R. E. (2006). *Multiple Case Study Analysis*. New York: The Guilford Press.

Starr, M. A. (2008). Socially Responsible Investment and Pro-Social Change. *Journal of Economic Issues*, XLII(1), 51–73.

Steadman, M. E., Zimmerer, T. W., & Green, R. F. (1995). Pressures from Stakeholders Hit Japanese Companies. *Long Range Planning*, **28**(6), 29–37.

Stiglitz, J. E. (2006). *Making Globalization Work: The Next Steps to Global Justice*. New York: Norton

   (2009a). The Anatomy of a Murder: Who Killed America's Economy? *Critical Review: A Journal of Politics and Society*, **21**(2 & 3), 329–339.

   (2009b). The Current Economic Crisis and Lessons for Economic Theory. *Eastern Economic Journal*, **35**, 281–296.

   (2010a). The Dangers of Deficit Reduction. *The Economists' Voice*, **7**(1), 1–3. Retrieved from www.bepress.com/ev/vol7/iss1/art6/.

   (2010b). *Freefall: America, Free Markets, and the Sinking of the World Economy*. New York: W. W. Norton & Co.

Stiglitz, J. E., Sen, A., & Fitoussi, J.-P. (2010). *Mismeasuring Our Lives: Why DGP Doesn't Add Up*. New York: Free Press.

Stout, L. A. (2002). Bad and Not-So-Bad Arguments for Shareholder Primacy. *Southern California Law Review*, **75**(5), 1189–1209.

   (2008). Why We Should Stop Teaching Dodge v. Ford. *Virginia Law & Business Review*, **3**(1), 163–176.

   (2010). Shareholders as Owners: Legal Reality Or Urban Legend? *NACD Directorship*, April/May, 62–64.

Stuart, T. E. (2000). Interorganizational Alliances and the Performance of Firms: A Study of Growth and Innovation Rates in a High-Technology Industry. *Strategic Management Journal*, **21**(8), 791–811.

Suddaby, R., Hardy, C., & Huy, Q. N. (2011). Where Are the New Theories of Organization? *Academy of Management Review*, **36**(2), 236–246.

Sveiby, K. E. (1997). *The New Organizational Wealth: Managing and Measuring Knowledge-Based Assets*. San Francisco: Berrett-Koehler.

Svendsen, A., & Laberge, M. (2006). A New Direction for CSR: Engaging Networks for Whole System Change. In J. Jonker & M. de Witte (Eds.), *The Challenge of Organizing and Implementing Corporate Social Responsibility* (131–147). Houndmills: Palgrave Macmillan.

Sydow, J., Schreyögg, G., & Koch, J. (2009). Organizational Path Dependence: Opening the Black Box. *Academy of Management Review*, **34**(4), 689–709.

Takala, T., & Pallab, P. (2000). Individual, Collective and Social Responsibility of the Firm. *Business Ethics: A European Review*, **9**(2), 109–118.

Tate, W. L., Ellram, L. M., & Kirchoff, J. F. (2010). Corporate Social Responsibility Reports: A Thematic Analysis Related to Supply Chain Management. *Journal of Supply Chain Management*, **46**(1), 19–44.

Teece, D. J. (2007). Explicating Dynamic Capabilities: The Nature and Microfoundations of (Sustainable) Enterprise Performance. *Strategic Management Journal*, 28(13), 1319–1350.

(2009). *Dynamic Capabilities and Strategic Management: Organizing for Innovation and Growth*. Oxford University Press.

Teece, D. J., Pisano, G., & Shuen, A. (1997). Dynamic Capabilities and Strategic Management. *Strategic Management Journal*, 18(7), 509–533.

Terchek, R. J., & Conte, T. C. (2001). *Theories of Democracy: A Reader*. Lanham: Rowman & Littlefield.

Thommen, J.-P. (1983). *Die Lehre der Unternehmungsführung: Eine wissenschaftshistorische Betrachtung im deutschsprachigen Raum*. Bern: Haupt.

Tidd, J., Bessant, J., & Pavitt, K. (2005). Case Studies: Learning to Look – Stakeholder Innovation in Novo Nordisk. 2010 (June 15). Retrieved from www.managing-innovation.com/case_studies/Novo%20Nordisk.pdf.

Tirole, J. (1988). *The Theory of Industrial Organization*. Cambridge, MA: MIT Press.

Trott, P., Maddocks, T., & Wheeler, C. (2009). Core Competencies for Diversifying: Case Study of a Small Business. *Strategic Change*, 18(1–2), 27–43.

Tsai, C.-A., & Wen, C.-T. (2009). The Effects of Relational Embeddedness on Entrepreneurship: Taiwanese Subsidiaries in China. *International Journal of Entrepreneurial Behaviour & Research*, 15(5), 453–472.

Tsai, S. D., Pan, C.-Y., & Chiang, H.-Q. (2004). Shifting the Mental Model and Emerging Innovative Behavior: Action Research of a Quality Management System. *E:CO*, 6(4), 28–39.

Tsang, E. W. K. (2006). Behavioral Assumptions and Theory Development: The Case of Transaction Cost Economics. *Strategic Management Journal*, 27(11), 999–1011.

Turcotte, M.-F. (1995). Conflict and Collaboration: The Interfaces Between Environmental Organizations and Business Firms. In D. Collins & M. Starik (Eds.), *Research in Corporate Social Performance and Policy, Supplement 1: Sustaining the Natural Environment: Empirical Studies on the Interface Between Nature and Organizations* (195–229). Greenwich, CT: JAI Press.

Tushman, M. L., Newman, W. H., & Romanelli, E. (1986). Convergence and Upheaval: Managing the Unsteady Pace of Organizational Evolution. *California Management Review*, 29(1), 29–44.

Tushman, M. L., O'Reilly, C. A., Fenollosa, A., Kleinbaum, A. M., & McGrath, D. (2007). Relevance and Rigor: Executive Education as a Lever in Shaping Practice and Research. *Academy of Management Learning & Education*, 6(3), 345–362.

Tushman, M. L., & Romanelli, E. (1985). Organizational Evolution: A Metamorphosis Model of Convergence and Reorientation. In L. L. Cummings & B. M. Staw (Eds.), *Research in Organizational Behavior* (Vol. 7, 171–222). Greenwich, CT: JAI Press.

Tversky, A., & Kahneman, D. (1986). Rational Choice and the Framing of Decisions. *Journal of Business*, 59(4), 251–278.

UBS (2010). Annual Report 2009. Retrieved from www.ubs.com/1/e/investors/annualreporting/2009.html.

Uzzi, B. (1996). The Sources and Consequences of Embeddedness for the Economic Performance of Organizations: The Network Effect. *American Sociological Review*, 61(4), 674–698.

(1997). Social Structure and Competition in Interfirm Networks: The Paradox of Embeddedness. *Administrative Science Quarterly*, 42(1), 35–67.

Uzzi, B., & Spiro, J. (2005). Collaboration and Creativity: The Small World Problem. *American Journal of Sociology*, 111(2), 447–504.

Vallentin, S. (2009). Private Management and Public Opinion: Corporate Social Responsiveness Revisited. *Business & Society*, 48(1), 60–87.

van Buren III., H. J. (2010). Taking (and Sharing Power): How Boards of Directors Can Bring About Greater Fairness for Dependent Stakeholders. *Business and Society Review*, 115(2), 205–230.

Van de Ven, A. H. (2007). *Engaged Scholarship. A Guide for Organizational and Social Research*. Oxford University Press.

van Oosterhout, J. H., & Heugens, P. P. M. A. R. (2006). Much Ado About Nothing: A Conceptual Critique of CSR. *ERIM Report Series Research in Management*. Retrieved from http://papers.ssrn.com/sol3/papers.cfm?abstract_id=924505.

Venkatraman, N., & Lee, C.-H. (2004). Preferential Linkage and Network Evolution: A Conceptual Model and Empirical Test in the U.S. Video Game Sector. *Academy of Management Journal*, 47(6), 876–892.

Veser, M. (2005). *The Influence of Culture on Stakeholder Management: Social Policy Implementation in Multinational Corporations*. Bern: Haupt.

Vidal, D. J. (2009). Post-Enlightenment Capitalism. *The Journal of Corporate Citizenship*, 34(Summer), 23–25.

Vining, A. R., Shapiro, D. M., & Borges, B. (2005). Building the Firm's Political (Lobbying) Strategy. *Journal of Public Affairs*, 5(2), 150–175.

Visser, W., Matten, D., Pohl, M., & Tolhurst, N. (2007). *The A to Z of Corporate Social Responsibility: A Complete Reference Guide to Concepts, Codes and Organisations*. Chichester: John Wiley.

von Krogh, G., Nonaka, I., & Aben, M. (2001). Making the Most of Your Company's Knowledge: A Strategic Framework. *Long Range Planning*, 34(4), 421–439.

Vrba, E. S. (1985). Environment and Evolution – Alternative Causes of the Temporal Distribution of Evolutionary Events. *South African Journal of Science*, **81**(5), 229–236.

Waddock, S. (2001). Integrity and Mindfulness: Foundations of Corporate Citizenship. In J. Andriof & M. McIntosh (Eds.), *Perspectives on Corporate Citizenship* (26–38). Sheffield: Greenleaf.

(2008). Building a New Institutional Infrastructure for Corporate Responsibility. *Academy of Management Perspectives*, **22**(3), 87–108.

(2009). Pragmatic Visionaries: Difference Makers as Social Entrepreneurs. *Organizational Dynamics*, **38**(4), 281–289.

Waddock, S., & Bodwell, C. (2007). *Total Responsibility Management: The Manual.* Sheffield: Greenleaf Publishing.

Waddock, S., Bodwell, C., & Graves, S. B. (2002). Responsibility: The New Business Imperative. *Academy of Management Executive*, **16**(2), 132–148.

Wallsten, S., & Kosec, K. (2008). The Effects of Ownership and Benchmark Competition: An Empirical Analysis of U.S. Water Systems. *International Journal of Industrial Organization*, **26**(1), 186–205.

Waltz, K. N. (1979). *Theory of International Politics.* New York: Random House.

Wang, H., He, J., & Mahoney, J. T. (2009). Firm-Specific Knowledge Resources and Competitive Advantage: The Roles of Economic- and Relationship-Based Employee Governance Mechanisms. *Strategic Management Journal*, **30**(12), 1265–1285.

Wang, H. C., & Barney, J. B. (2006). Employee Incentives to Make Firm-Specific Investments: Implications for Resource-Based Theories of Corporate Diversification. *Academy of Management Review*, **31**(2), 466–476.

Weidenbaum, M. (2009). Who will Guard the Guardians? The Social Responsibility of NGOs. *Journal of Business Ethics*, **87**(Supplement 1), 147–155.

Weiss, J. W. (2009). *Business Ethics: A Stakeholder and Issues Management Approach.* Florence, KY: South-Western College Publishing.

Werhane, P. H. (2002). Moral Imagination and Systems Thinking. *Journal of Business Ethics*, **38**(1–2), 33–42.

(2008). Mental Models, Moral Imagination and System Thinking in the Age of Globalization. *Journal of Business Ethics*, **78**(3), 463–474.

(2009). Book Reviews: Conscience and Corporate Culture. *Ethics*, **119**(2), 353–356.

Werhane, P. H., & Freeman, R. E. (1999). Business Ethics: The State of the Art. *International Journal of Management Research*, **1**(1), 1–16.

Wernerfelt, B. (1984). A Resource-Based View of the Firm. *Strategic Management Journal*, **5**(2), 171–180.

(1989). From Critical Resources to Corporate Strategy. *Journal of General Management*, **14**(3), 4–12.

(1995). The Resource-Based View of the Firm: Ten Years After. *Strategic Management Journal*, **16**(3), 171–174.

Wheeler, D., Fabig, H., & Boele, R. (2002). Paradoxes and Dilemmas for Stakeholder Responsive Firms in the Extractive Sector: Lessons from the Case of Shell and the Ogoni. *Journal of Business Ethics*, **39**(3), 297–318.

Wilcox King, A. (2007). Disentangling Interfirm and Intrafirm Causal Ambiguity: A Conceptual Model of Causal Ambiguity and Sustainable Competitive Advantage. *Academy of Management Review*, **32**(1), 156–178.

Williams, G. C. (1966). *Adaptation and Natural Selection*. Princeton University Press.

(1992). *Natural Selection – Domains, Levels, and Challenges*. New York: Oxford University Press.

Williamson, O. E. (1989). Transaction Cost Economics. In R. Schmalensee & R. Willig (Eds.), *Handbook of Industrial Organization* (Vol. 2, 135–182). Amsterdam: Elsevier Science.

Willke, H., & Willke, G. (2008). Corporate Moral Legitimacy and the Legitimacy of Morals: A Critique of Palazzo/Scherer's Communicative Framework. *Journal of Business Ethics*, **81**(1), 27–38.

Wilson, E. J., Bunn, M. D., & Savage, G. T. (2010). Anatomy of a Social Partnership: A Stakeholder Perspective. *Industrial Marketing Management*, **39**(1), 76–90.

Wilson, E. O. (1998). *Consilience: The Unity of Knowledge*. New York: Alfred A. Knopf.

Windsor, D. (2001). The Future of Corporate Social Responsibility. *International Journal of Organizational Analysis*, **9**(3), 225–256.

(2006). Corporate Social Responsibility: Three Key Approaches. *Journal of Management Studies*, **43**(1), 93–114.

(2008). *Stakeholder Dynamics*. Paper presented at the International Association for Business and Society (IABS) Annual Meeting, Tampere, Finland.

Winkler, A. (2004). Corporate Law or the Law of Business? Stakeholders and Corporate Governance at the End of History. *Journal of Law and Contemporary Problems*, **67**, 109–133.

Winn, M. I. (2001). Building Stakeholder Theory with a Decision Modeling Methodology. *Business & Society*, **40**(2), 133–166.

Winter, S. G., Cattani, G., & Dorsch, A. (2007). The Value of Moderate Obsession: Insights from a New Model of Organizational Search. *Organization Science*, **18**(3), 403–419.

Witt, M. A., & Redding, G. (2009). The Spirits of Capitalism: German, Japanese, and US Senior Executive Perceptions of Why Firms Exist. *INSEAD Faculty & Research Working Paper*. Retrieved from www.insead.edu/facultyresearch/research/doc.cfm?did=42956.

Wolf, K. D. (2000). The New Raison D'État: International Cooperation Against Societies? In M. Albert, L. Brock & K. D. Wolf (Eds.), *Civilizing World Politics: Society and Community Beyond the State* (119–132). Lanham: Rowman & Littlefield.

(2003). Normsetzung in internationalen Institutionen unter Mitwirkung privater Akteure? "International Environmental Governance" zwischen ILO, öffentlich-privaten Politiknetzwerken und Global Compact. In S. von Schorlemer (Ed.), *Praxishandbuch UNO: Die Vereinten Nationen im Lichte globaler Herausforderungen* (225–240). Berlin: Springer.

Wong, E. (2010). As China Aids Labor, Unrest is Still Rising, *New York Times* (June 20). Retrieved from www.nytimes.com/2010/06/21/world/asia/21chinalabor.html.

Wood, D., & Ross, D. G. (2006). Environmental Social Controls and Capital Investments: Australian Evidence. *Accounting & Finance*, 46(4), 677–695.

Wood, D. J. (2010). Measuring Corporate Social Performance: A Review. *International Journal of Management Reviews*, 12(1), 50–84.

Wood, D. J., & Jones, R. E. (1993). Stakeholder Mismatching: A Theoretical Problem in Empirical Research on Corporate Social Performance. *International Journal of Organizational Analysis*, 3(3), 229–267.

Wood, D. J., & Logsdon, J. M. (2001). Theorising Business Citizenship. In J. Andriof & M. McIntosh (Eds.), *Perspectives on Corporate Citizenship* (83–103). Sheffield: Greenleaf Publishing.

Wright, C. M., Smith, M. E., & Wright, B. G. (2007). Hidden Costs Associated with Stakeholders in Supply Management. *Academy of Management Perspectives*, 21(3), 64–82.

Yang, J., Shen, G. Q., Ho, M., Drew, D. S., & Xue, X. (in press). Stakeholder Management in Construction: An Empirical Study to Address Research Gaps in Previous Studies. *International Journal of Project Management*.

Yaziji, M., & Doh, J. (2009). *NGOs and Corporations: Conflict and Collaboration*. Cambridge University Press.

Yin, R. K. (2009). *Case Study Research: Design and Methods* (4th edn). Thousand Oaks: Sage Publications.

Zadek, S. (2001). Partnership Alchemy: Engagement, Innovation and Governance. In J. Andriof & M. McIntosh (Eds.), *Perspectives on Corporate Citizenship* (200–214). Sheffield: Greenleaf Publishing.

(2004). *Tomorrow's History*. Sheffield: Greenleaf Publishing.

ZKB (2009). *Geschäftsbericht*. Zurich: Zürcher Kantonalbank (ZKB) Retrieved from www.zkb.ch/etc/ml/repository/prospekte_und_bro-schueren/corporate/geschaeftsbericht/geschaeftsbericht_2009_pdf. File.pdf.

(2010). *Verantwortung für Umwelt und Gesellschaft*. Zurich: Zürcher Kantonalbank (ZKB). Retrieved from www.zkb.ch/etc/ml/repository/prospekte_und_broschueren/sparen_anlegen/213155_nachhaltigkeit_wwf_pdf.File.pdf.

Zollo, M., & Winter, S. G. (2002). Deliberate Learning and the Evolution of Dynamic Capabilities. *Organization Science*, **13**(3), 339–351.

Index

Page numbers with 't' are tables; 'g' are glossary terms. Page numbers in italics are figures and in bold shows extensive coverage of the topic.

Lightning Source UK Ltd.
Milton Keynes UK
UKOW06f0955241115

263424UK00009B/380/P